AWAKING
THE DEAD

AWAKING
THE DEAD

BRIAN J HEARD

JOHN BLAKE

Published by John Blake Publishing Ltd,
3, Bramber Court, 2 Bramber Road,
London W14 9PB, England

First published in hardback in 2003

ISBN 1 904034 62 4

British Library Cataloguing-in-Publication Data:

A catalogue record for this book is available from the British Library.

Design by ENVY

Printed in Great Britain by CPD (Wales)

1 3 5 7 9 10 8 6 4 2

Papers used by John Blake Publishing are natural, recyclable products made from wood
grown in sustainable forests. The manufacturing processes conform to the environmental
regulations of the country of origin.

Every attempt has been made to contact the relevant copyright-holders, but some were
unobtainable. We would be grateful if the appropriate people could contact us.

CONTENTS

PROLOGUE

I received a panic call to a post mortem, from the officer in charge of a murder case. A putrefying body had been found on a hillside with a hole in the front of his forehead. The problem was that someone, and I never found out who, had declared that the victim had been killed by being stabbed in the forehead with a length of sharpened reinforcing rod. It wasn't until he was placed on the post-mortem table that another area on the back of the skull was seen to be leaking.

Normally my clients are fresh, sometimes even warm, and the post-mortem examination is merely horribly smelly and something out of any sane person's worst nightmare. I don't have any problem with watching the post mortems of such bodies, but putrefying bodies I have difficulty with. They are usually black in colour, with skin peeling off, the body cavity and face are hugely distended with gas, and often they move of their own accord due to the thousands of maggots and insects inside. Personally I cannot deal with the smell once the body is cut into and have to stand well back, with a face mask covered in something strongly perfumed, chewing the strongest mints I can find.

This particular body was pretty bad: the eyes and lips had been eaten away and maggots were crawling out of the eye sockets, mouth, ears and every other orifice. To make matters worse, the body cavity was starting to split open with the gas pressure inside. Luckily, I merely had to examine the head, where the only visible wounds were, and I politely asked the pathologist if we could deal with that first so that I could escape outside to sanity and fresh air. As we turned the body on its side the brains, which had turned to liquid, poured out of the two holes in the head, accompanied by an appalling smell.

It was obvious that this was a gangland execution, with a gun held close to the base of the skull and his head bent forward. The angle also suggested that he was on his knees.

On stripping off the skin it could be seen that it was a fairly large, slow-moving bullet, probably about .45 calibre. An analysis of minute lead fragments from the edges of the entry hole showed a lead/tin/antimony composition, the ratios of which could only have come from homemade bullets. Gun-smoke residues recovered from the hair and skin round the entry hole showed that the ammunition was of modern type, probably originating in America. A particle of unburnt propellant also confirmed this hypothesis. No cartridge case was ever found, but that was probably due to the location – a hillside covered in very heavy undergrowth.

In the end I came to the conclusion that he had been shot with the muzzle of the gun in loose contact with the base of the skull and that the calibre of the weapon was .45. The ammunition used was probably hand loaded using a home-cast, solid lead bullet with an American propellant and primer. Subsequent investigations revealed that the man was a fence, selling stolen gold, and that he had been creaming off an extra 15 per cent of the proceeds for himself.

x

CHAPTER 1

SEX AND ALCOHOL

I have no doubt that if one were leaving school today at the age of 18 and with only one GCE A level in chemistry it would be difficult to find a job of any note. Not so in those heady days of the early Sixties in the heyday of the Stones and Beatles, when America and Russia were racing for the moon. Jobs were there for the asking.

I had little idea what I wanted to do, but with some assistance from my mother and a quick look through the telephone directory under the heading 'Analytical Chemists' I soon had a number of letters in the post. Before long, the interviews were lined up and I was off in my best, and only, suit; all washed and polished to a fine shine. One interview I remember was with a firm called Heard and Monday, a very small family outfit which was, for some unknown reason, extremely interested in having me on board. I have no idea why they should have been so keen, as the interview was a nightmare with me stumbling over the most innocuous of questions and making a complete fool of myself in the process.

In the end, however, I declined the offer from Heard and Monday and settled for the position of assistant chemist at Charrington Breweries in the East End of London. This momentous decision was taken for no reason other than they were offering an additional 2 shillings and 6 pence a week, a heady sum in those days.

The factory itself was a huge, Dickensian pile of rusting iron, reeking of stale beer, vinegar and fermenting ale. In one far-flung corner of the yard were the coopers, busily churning out wooden barrels. Next to them were stabled the huge dray horses, which were, even by then, something of an anachronism. It was an area I loved to visit, the smell of freshly cut wood and the craftsmanship of the coopers as they shaved, completely by eye, the segments of fine oak to a perfect fit. On those cold, grey December mornings, the wonderfully placid drays gently steamed in the rays of the sun after their delivery runs. Initially I found their sheer physical size intimidating, but a few slices of apple would have them nuzzling up to me and all my concerns would fade away.

'Chemist' was something of a misnomer at the brewery, since my job mainly comprised filtering the various liquid components of the beer during its transition from water and malt to finished product. The filters were plated on to sterile agar, incubated and then examined for yeast and bacteria populations. I think the small section that carried out this work was more for show than anything else. Whenever anything abnormal was found, the results seemed to be ignored. There were two labs at the Mile End plant: one a fairly new, bright and shiny affair where the testing for yeast and bacterial infection was carried out; the other in a dark and dingy corner of one of the oldest buildings. In the older lab the ceilings were low, the windows small and the lighting limited, making the whole lab a dingy and depressing place to work in. The only redeeming features of this lab were the benches, which were solid pewter, something I had never seen before and haven't since. If the place was dingy then the work carried out there was a thousand times worse. Basically the lab had two functions. The first was to mix the witch's brew of chemicals – some of them really evil-smelling – that were added to every batch of beer brewed. This mixture controlled, among other things, the amount of time for which the beer retained its head, the deposition of protein and the quantity of dissolved oxygen.

The second function of this lab was to determine the alcohol content of returned ullage (for the uninitiated, ullage is the liquid collected from the drip trays underneath counter-top beer pumps). This waste beer runs down from the collection trays into a barrel in the cellar which, when it is full, is returned to the brewery for a rebate. The rebate is calculated on the basis of the alcoholic content, quantity and quality of the ullage. Unfortunately, publicans considered this easy money, and everything they could think of was poured into the ullage barrel: dregs from the tables, half empty glasses, the contents of wet ashtrays and so on.

Monday morning was ullage day and it was a disgusting job. The barrels contained everything imaginable, from cigarette butts to vomit, and the whole lab used to reek for days after a particularly bad batch was sent in. What I found even more horrific was that, after filtration and pasteurisation, the ullage was poured into the brown and mild ale. Since discovering that fact I have never touched dark beer of any type!

After six months at the brewery I was transferred to the bottling plant in Tottenham: a newish facility, housed in an enormous single-storey factory shed. If I thought my job at the brewery was boring, I hadn't seen anything yet. At the brewery I had overseen every stage of the brewing process from sampling the water tanks, taking swabs from the cleaned fermentation vessels, checking the strength and purity of the malt extract, checking the efficiency of the various beer filters and finally the quality, purity and shelf-life of the final bottled, barrelled or kegged product. In the bottling plant I just tested the machines and the bottled product: a repetitive undertaking.

Factory life presented many unforeseen perils for a raw recruit straight out of school. My main problem, however, was with the factory girls, who made my life hell by ambushing me on my rounds. They would then take great delight in carrying me off to some remote corner of the factory where one of them would attempt to have their way with me. For the first month or so my life was a complete nightmare. Soon, however, I had turned the tables on them and my days settled into a routine of prodigious quantities of sex interspersed with taking the odd sample of the beer that was used for agar plating.

Despite having other distractions I did manage to compile huge quantities of statistics on possible bacterial and wild yeast contamination sources and made a number of suggestions on how the situation could be improved. Only once, however, can I ever remember my advice being taken seriously and that was during the pre-Christmas rush when the plant was working flat out, 24 hours a day, to meet the anticipated thirsts of the seasonal revellers. Samples were taken every three hours from each of the bottling units, the output from which was phenomenal. I was on late shift that particular night, and in the early hours of the morning I discovered that someone had inadvertently connected four of the bottling units to the wrong vat and the bottles coming off the machines labelled 'brown ale' in fact contained pale ale. By the time they got round to shutting down the machines, some 25,000 wrongly labelled bottles were in crates ready for distribution. Re-labelling the bottles was clearly out of the question; the only solution was to pour all the beer down the drain. It was enough to make a drinking man cry.

My boss, Victor, was only six years older than me, but to say that he was uninspiring would be an understatement. The love of his life was a Morris Minor 1000 with an Abarth exhaust system which made it sound like a Formula 1 car, but it had the gusto of a snail. If all I could look forward to, after another 35 years of yeast-colony counting, was becoming a clone of Victor, then changing jobs was a matter of urgency. Not only that, but I had got into the habit of waking up in the bus garage at 4 o'clock in the morning, having tasted more beer than I sampled. On reflection I suppose that it could also have had something to do with the machinations of the ladies on the factory floor. It was clearly time to go, but where to?

CHAPTER 2

STARTING OUT AT SCOTLAND YARD

In October, I think, of 1964, one of my really good friends Martyn Odam, then a chemist in the New Scotland Yard Forensic Science Laboratory, informed me that they were recruiting and suggested I apply. I did, and after a few weeks the offer of an interview came. I don't remember much of the interview: a few questions about my current position, a couple of more about the courses I was attending at night school, one of them on the crystalline shape of sugar (which I was well prepared for as Martin had already told me it would be a likely question) and then the killer: 'Tell me, Mr Heard, how would you separate a mixture of salt and sugar?'

'Preferential crystallisation, separation by specific gravity in an appropriate organic solvent, or a fine pin and a microscope?' I suggested.

I think the interview chairman was most impressed by the pin method: he was a well-known microscopist. I was offered the job on the spot.

New Scotland Yard was then down on the Thames Embankment, housed in a glorious old Victorian building with so much history it seemed to seep out of the grime-ridden walls. It was a fantastic place, with winding, oak-panelled corridors, numerous mezzanine floors, back staircases that few knew about and more canteens than you could count. It seemed that every week a new eatery, known and used by only a select few, was discovered lurking on some partially disused floor.

The labs themselves were straight out of Conan Doyle: row upon row of strangely labelled and coloured bottles; acid-stained teak benches; Bunsen burners with orange flames flickering in every corner; brass microscopes; and all around the walls photographs of legendary murderers and crime scenes. Every drawer you opened contained treasures beyond a forensic scientist's wildest dreams: gall stones from the acid-bath murders; the gas tubes from Crippin; broken false teeth; pieces of a hangman's rope; and a collection of the most gruesome photographs – luckily only in black and white – that you could ever imagine.

Being a raw recruit I was given the simplest of cases to work on: small breaking and entering jobs; simple road traffic accidents; and, the worst job of all, the testing of urine samples in drunk-in-charge cases. For some unknown reason the 'P Lab', as it was called, was located in a room far removed from the main laboratory in what appeared to be an old dungeon, deep in the bowels of the earth. You could smell the lab well before you arrived, and this smell not only clung to your clothes but hung around in your nostrils and throat for days after doing your turn on the rota. Everything you ate or drank tasted and smelt of stale urine, every stitch of clothing had to be washed and rewashed. I suppose that if there was one consolation of working in the 'P Lab' it was that you always got a double seat home on the bus. Nobody in their right mind would sit next to you.

The routine in the 'P Lab' was always the same: receive the samples first thing in the morning; describe the packaging; break the seal; describe the colour of the urine; and smell the contents. Why we had to smell it I never found out, but religiously smell every bottle we did. 'Yellow/green clear liquid with an alcoholic urine odour' was the norm. Next a small quantity of the urine was pipetted by mouth (a very unpleasant undertaking; it was easy to get a mouthful if you weren't very careful) into a petri dish, which was then suspended above an accurately measured quantity of potassium dichromate in sulphuric acid. This was then sealed in a small glass jar and placed in an incubator overnight for the alcohol to evaporate and react with the potassium dichromate. By determining how much potassium dichromate was left at the end of the incubation period (via a technique called 'back titration'), you could accurately determine the percentage of alcohol in the original urine sample. Classical wet chemistry and not at all like the techniques used today.

One danger in the 'P Lab' which I never got used to was that caused by the stored urine samples. These had to be kept for a minimum of two years in case there was ever an appeal. As they aged, various mould and bacterial growths appeared in the urine, which gave them the appearance of something out of a Quatermass experiment (a famous early science fiction series involving evil-looking masses of bubbling liquids with a life of their own). Every now and then one of these would start to ferment and build up pressure until the bottle burst with a huge explosion, spraying the whole lab, and anyone in the vicinity, with razor-sharp glass shards and decayed urine.

Fresh urine was pretty nasty, but the worst samples of all that we had to deal with were those from dead bodies, especially if they were not too fresh. Normally these consisted of putrefying, semi-congealed blood which, like the urine, had to be pipetted by mouth as the rubber bulbs we had were not man enough to deal with the lumpy blood. Pipetting such liquids by mouth was a disgusting technique and it is a wonder that none of us went down with anything really serious.

None of the cases I dealt with at that time was particularly impressive as I was still very much under training. It seemed to be a never-ending stream of gypsies' clothes, which had to be taped and swept clean. After that, the resulting debris was minutely searched for glass or paint particles. Any particles found were then compared against control samples from the burgled houses to determine whether the refractive index (RI) and density of the glass matched, or the layer structure of the paint was the same.

For anyone who has not had the pleasure of examining the clothes of gypsies, or as they were often known 'didicoys', it is something that I would recommend be avoided at all costs. The jeans usually have a black shiny appearance from the body grease they contain, and will stand up of their own accord. Underclothes, when worn, are a definite health hazard; socks and shoes stink beyond description; and shirts and jackets are seriously nasty. In addition, there is nearly always a fair amount of livestock present – in the form of fleas, lice, pubic crabs and maggots. In fact, it is one of the peculiarities of being a forensic scientist that it is much more important to wash one's hands before going to the toilet than after!

The examination process itself was quite simple, although a little long-winded. First the pockets were turned inside out and all the debris inside carefully removed. Obtaining every last fragment from the folded seam at the bottom of the pocket is quite an art and one that can only be learnt by long experience. At that time, turn-ups on men's trousers were still sometimes found and they were always a particularly useful source of debris. Another area often overlooked is the fly cover to the trousers zip.

As new recruits we had weekly lectures from the more senior forensic scientists. One lecture I vividly remember was on the recovery of debris from clothing. Miss Pierara, in the middle of this sleep-inducing lecture, came out with the classic line 'I often find quite interesting things in men's flies'. Of course, the lecture turned into uproar and had to be abandoned.

Shoes are also a valuable source of evidential material, not only from anything which might have become lodged in the various seams, but, more importantly, glass embedded in the rubber sole. Shoeprints can also be extremely significant if the culprit has trodden in soft earth, dust or even snow. Their importance relies on the fact that, as the sole of the shoe wears, it takes on characteristics not only from the peculiarities of the way the wearer walks, but also from accidental damage to the sole pattern. The longer a shoe is worn, the more individual it becomes, until it can take on the uniqueness of a fingerprint or toolmark. By applying a light coating of either carbon or aluminium dust, depending on the medium in which the shoeprint was left, and then 'walking' the shoe across a wide strip of transparent adhesive tape, a negative print of sole irregularities can be obtained. After laminating the print with a sheet of clear acrylic it can be directly compared with a photograph of the shoeprint left at the scene.

While most of the cases dealt with in those early days were fairly mundane, one springs to mind, which involved the burglary of a stately home in Kent. Antiques, silverware, Purdy shotguns and paintings were the main attractions for this obviously very well-organised gang who were stealing to order. After the burglary, I was sent down to the premises to collect the usual control samples of paint and glass, which, as there were no suspects at that stage, were placed into storage. Several months later, a gang was located and the long, drawn-out process of sweeping and vacuuming clothes, making shoeprints and digging glass out of the soles of shoes began.

Weeks of painstaking work revealed absolutely nothing of significance – the paint all had different layer structures to the controls, the refractive index and density of the glass didn't match nor did any of the shoeprints. During the process of examining the soles of the shoes I did, however, find one tiny chip of a deep-red-coloured, glass-like material, which had the most peculiar density and refractive index anyone had ever seen. I thought it might of been part of a stained-glass window but none had been broken in the burglary and control samples I managed to obtain from a local church which was being demolished were completely different from those of the red glass from the shoe.

It wasn't until I started to look idly through the photographs of the items recovered from the arrest that I noticed an antique dress sword that had a huge semi-precious red gem on the pommel. A microscopic examination of the gem showed that the chip could have come from a small area of damage to the gem. After an awful lot of persuasion I managed to obtain permission to take a small control sample from the gem, a worrying business, since the sword was worth an enormous amount of money. It was, however, worth all the sweaty palms and damp brows, because the control from the sword and the chip from the shoe matched up perfectly, both in RI and density. Forensic evidence alone is rarely enough to lead to a conviction (it is usually viewed as supportive), but in this case the red glass proved to be the strongest piece of evidence available and the suspect was convicted largely on that basis.

One other case I was involved in, but only peripherally, was the 'bodies in the boot' murders. At that time prostitutes were being found dead all over London. They had all had sex just before being strangled and, from the fairly primitive blood grouping available then, it seemed from the recovered semen that it had been the same man in each instance. Nothing, however, could be found to positively tie all the cases together: no particular district, no time frequency, no peculiarities in the way they were strangled, no particular method of dumping. After months of painstaking work, it was noticed that tapings taken from the bodies all contained microscopic spots of cellulose paint of various colours. It was also found that each body had exactly the same frequency of colour distribution – for example six reds to three blues to two whites.

Fibres found on the tapings could only have come from the boot mat of a car, strongly suggesting that the murderer was transporting the victims' bodies from the scene of the crime to the dumping spot in the boot of his car. The presence of the paint spots also suggested that the car had been kept in the vicinity of a garage that was involved in the spray-painting of cars. A truly massive random stop-and-search operation was then started with cars all over London having their boots taped for paint spot distribution. So large was this random stop-and-search that most of the scientists in the lab, including myself, were stopped at some time or other. The forensic side of the investigation was terribly manpower intensive, to say nothing of being exceedingly tiring work. Looking through hundreds and hundreds of tapings and counting the number of paint spots and their colours, resulted in severe eyestrain, splitting headaches and neck and back pain.

Apart from the small, dedicated team, everyone in the lab had to do a stint at the microscopes, searching the boot tapings for paint spots. I found it amazing that nearly every taping examined contained these microscopic paint spots, but it was finding the right colour distribution with the colours in the correct ratio that was so important. Several times we thought that we had the murderer and the boots were re-taped, but each time the ratios were just not quite correct.

The taping of the bodies was not pleasant. This was done with an adhesive tape, the glue of which had to be specially formulated so that it did not alter the colour of any paint or fibres that it picked up. It also had to be free of any contamination, enabling the paint to be qualitatively or quantitatively analysed. The tapings were taken by pressing the sticky side of the tape over the surface of the body being taped, after which it was stuck sticky side down on to a microscope slide for future examination. Normally it was quite an easy process, but one of the bodies had been thrown in the Thames and had got caught under a barge. Each time the tide went out the body was crushed under the barge and when it came to delivering it to the mortuary all that was required was a couple of buckets. Luckily, I didn't do the taping but it must have been an appalling job. The tapings were, however, excellent and showed that the girl had been in the same boot as all the others.

After months and months of really intensive work, not just by the lab but also the hundreds of police officers involved, the murders came to a sudden stop. The boot tapings continued to be taken for some time but nothing was ever found that matched the paint on the bodies and eventually the case was put on the unsolved list. As far as I know the culprit has never been apprehended.

Unfortunately, my time at the old Scotland Yard building was destined to be short, as the laboratory moved some 10 months after I arrived. The new premises were in a modern high-rise building situated at High Holborn, above the immigration office and High Holborn Police Station. The move was a shambles: boxes of old exhibits had to be sorted, old chemicals thrown out and dusty corners investigated.

At that time much research was going on into the individuality of new shoeprints and one of my jobs prior to the move was to sort out the collection of reference shoe patterns and styles. Most of these were simply shoe soles supplied by various manufacturers, but in one box I found a brand new pair of dark brown brogues and, as I had been instructed to dispose of those items that we had finished with, I thought that these might do me quite nicely. Bit odd, I thought as I picked up the box, as it was much heavier than expected. It wasn't until I attempted to put the shoes on that I found out why. The shoes were not, in fact, part of the reference collection but an exhibit from a road-traffic case: the victim's feet were still inside.

CHAPTER 3

GANGLAND MURDER, DRUGS AND POISONINGS AT HIGH HOLBORN

Holborn was a great place when we first moved in, with large, fresh, clean offices and plenty of new equipment. The cops in the station downstairs were also very friendly and most evenings found us in the Red Lion, together with all the senior staff of the lab. There was one PC, whom I shall call Clive, who was always getting himself into the most ludicrous situations and always had us in stitches with his stories.

On one particular occasion, Clive went missing for nearly a week and when he eventually turned up it emerged that he had been told to keep surveillance on a lorry park where there had been a number of loads stolen. It was a cold night, close to freezing, and with a fierce wind blowing which chilled to the bone. After a couple of hours of trying to keep out of the worst of the wind he decided that a better location would be under a lorry tarpaulin, where he would be snug and warm but still able to keep an eye on the park. Unfortunately, Clive fell asleep and the next thing he knew he was thundering through the Bordeaux countryside.

One evening, not long after the lorry incident, I was in the Red Lion and in walked Clive, clothes in tatters, covered in scratches and bite marks, and filthy dirty. It appeared that while on foot patrol he had come across a stray brown dog. Having nothing better to do, he decided to take it back to the station dog pound. Unfortunately the dog wasn't too keen on being manhandled and put up a fierce struggle. Clive, however, was not to be beaten and after some two hours of fighting managed to get the protesting mangy mutt back to the station. I thought it would be interesting to have a look at this giant of a dog that had caused Clive so much of a problem, so back to the pound we both went. There in the pound was this very unhappy, growling mutt, but no ordinary mutt: it was the largest male fox I had ever seen.

During the early days in Holborn I was working in the toxicology section, screening various body parts for drugs, poisons and heavy metals. Interesting work and, once again, real wet chemistry which I enjoyed immensely. Some of it was a bit smelly, though, as 50 per cent of the work involved found bodies that were usually well past their prime rather than those which had merely died under suspicious circumstances and were still relatively fresh. Whatever the situation, the pathologist would decide which bit to send along for toxicological analysis. Sometimes it would be the stomach; other times the lungs; often the brains. Once, a body had been found with a syringe sticking out of the leg, so the whole leg, complete with embedded syringe, was sent in. I was particularly wary of brain samples as they would, if left alone for any period of time, start to ferment in their sealed jar, gradually build up pressure and explode. If there is one smell that is really bad, it is putrefying brains. To come in first thing in the morning after a night out with the lads and find this mess plastered all over the insides of the fume cupboard is not the most pleasant way to start the day.

One case involved an old lady who had been found dead in her bed. Beside the bed were some prescription drugs, but as she was quite rich and supposedly in good health there was some question as to why she died. The drugs were found to be as labelled and the glass by the bed was found to contain only milk residues, so there was nothing suspicious there, but just to make sure they sent along a bag containing the bedclothes which had some body fluid stains on them. The lady had been dead for some time, so such things were to be expected, but what was not expected were the thousands of ravenous fleas and bed bugs which leapt out of the bag as soon as I opened it. Within minutes, despite almost drowning myself in DDT, I was covered in hundreds of bites and in no time at all I looked as if I had chicken pox. One of these bites happened to be situated right in the middle of my navel and like the rest of them it itched terribly. The only problem was that whenever I scratched it I ended up with a huge erection. My girlfriend thought it was hilarious – I didn't.

One spring morning, I had – for Southern Region Railways (now known as Network South East) – an unusually hassle-free journey in from home and was looking forward to an hour's read of the paper before starting work. Some hope, for there was an urgent call from one of the regional forces to say they had a strange man at the counter who claimed that he could no longer live with the guilt of having murdered his wife with thallium. Now thallium is quite an unusual metal and whilst it is highly toxic and has been used as a poison, it isn't exactly common. On further questioning this man claimed to have tried it out on his dog first just to make sure that it worked. The dog eventually died and he showed us the spot where he claimed to have buried it. So, spades were issued and digging began, but all that could be found in the garden was an old sack with some stones in it. Upon closer examination, it was obvious that the sack was in fact the dog's skin, all the hair having fallen out due, presumably, to the thallium poisoning. What we'd taken to be stones were, in fact, broken-up bits of the dog's skeleton.

Eventually the remains were sent in for a lengthy analysis, which started with the bones being digested in a mixture of boiling nitric and sulphuric acids. Once the skin and bones were in solution and the acid had been neutralized with ammonia solution, a strip of clean copper wire was inserted into the liquid on to which any heavy metals present in the solution would be deposited. The wire immediately went a dull, greyish black colour, which was to be expected if thallium were present. The deposit was then removed for a quantitative and qualitative analysis, which showed that there had been enough thallium present in the bones to kill an elephant, let alone a dog.

The next step was an exhumation of the wife's body, but there we were stumped, as she had been cremated and all that was left was a small urn of ashes under a rose tree. At this stage we all but gave up as it was assumed that the ashes distributed by the crematorium were not from a particular person, but whatever happened to be left over at the bottom of the furnace. Just to make sure we did an extraction and, lo and behold, thallium; not in any great quantity, but enough to say that the body of someone who had been cremated on the same day as the suspect's wife contained the substance. Unfortunately, cross-contamination with the ashes from other bodies could not be ruled out and there was insufficient evidence, despite his confession, for him to be charged with murder. Rumour had it that he committed suicide some time after.

Not long after the thallium case I had another heavy-metal poisoning, this time with mercury. The local GP had declared death by natural causes, which must have been a case of 'don't bother me with trifles, I'll just write out the death certificate' because mercury poisoning is not very nice at all, and should be spotted by any GP. Once again it was a case of the guilty conscience of the husband leading to a confession to a friend who duly reported it to the police. This time, however, things were a little easier as the body had been embalmed and buried and not cremated as before. Exhumation orders are not, however, that easy to obtain but eventually one was in our hands and we proceeded to the depths of Lincolnshire to retrieve the body.

For some unknown reason, exhumations have to be carried out at dawn (well at least that is what I am led to believe) and few more scary places exist than a graveyard at dawn on a cold, wet, misty morning. Straight out of a Hammer film: the mist was swirling, bats were flitting and owls were hooting. All present were aware of the atmosphere and said little until the time was thought right to start digging. The two gravediggers, hired at extortionate rates, were not at all impressed at digging up this year-old coffin, but eventually shovel struck wood and they clambered out of the hole refusing to do any more.

Being the most junior there, I was delegated to jump down into the hole with two PCs and hoist up the coffin. As the PCs got under the head end and started to push the coffin up, I pushed the foot end along the bottom of the grave until it was nearly in the upright position. At that moment, with a creak and a groan, the lid swung open and the corpse, or what was left of it, fell forward on top of me with its arms around my neck. The PCs both screamed, jumped out of the hole and ran off yelling, as did the gravediggers and the officer in charge. I was gibbering like an idiot, but there was little I could do about it, I was alone at the bottom of a six-foot grave being enveloped by a rotting corpse.

Apart from being covered in an evil smelling corpse, I was wet through from the disgusting black-coloured water which had cascaded out of the coffin with the corpse and was shaking like a leaf. Eventually the officer in charge ventured back and I persuaded him to get the body off me so that we could close the lid and get the coffin out of the grave.

Eventually we managed to get the coffin out of the hole, into the body van and back to the mortuary. The post mortem was interesting in that I had never seen an embalmed, year-old corpse before. Apart from the eyes, lips and ears, the body was in remarkably good shape. The bottom half of the body had a distinctly dark discolouration from the water that had seeped into the coffin but apart from that the skin was relatively normal, for a corpse. All orifices had been filled with 'Filling Sand' to prevent the escape of bodily fluids, and the body cavity had been stuffed with paper and old rags to give it, well, body, I suppose! There was also a distinct smell of formalin about the tissues, presumably from the embalming process. Samples were taken from various parts of the body as well as soil and coffin water to ensure that any heavy metals found in the body samples were not as a result of ground contamination. After a similar extraction to the thallium case, large quantities of mercury were located from the body samples resulting in the husband being given 15 years for murder.

Back doing general casework once again, the first case I dealt with was a road-traffic accident. It started off as a particularly nasty robbery case in which a young female bank teller was beaten to a pulp with a lead pipe just for looking at the robber. After snatching sufficient money to fill a sack the robber and his accomplice legged it to their car, which was waiting outside. Unfortunately for the robbers the car stalled and wouldn't start again, so off they went at a great rate to a close-by multi-storey car park where they had a second getaway car waiting. Police joined in and during the chase one robber was side-swiped by one car and severely run over by another. The car which hit the robber went out of control and just as the robber with the lead pipe reached the kerb the out-of-control car neatly guillotined off both his feet between its bumper and the kerb. Divine retribution, one could say.

The late Sixties saw two infamous gangs plying their trade: one in the south of London, the Richardsons; and the other in the East

End, the Krays or Twins as they were known. When we heard that there was a case involving a well-known south London gang we were all vying for the job, because we were sure that it was going to be one of the leaders and that the resulting court case would get someone's name in the papers. The gangs were, however, too fly to be caught out that easily and it was only a fairly minor member of the gang who had been arrested. The arrested person, whose name I cannot remember, was suspected of taking a nightclub owner out to sea in a speedboat, tying concrete blocks to his legs with bailing wire then, while he was still alive, throwing him overboard.

Eventually, when it was sufficiently full of decomposition gases to overcome the weight of the concrete blocks, the body bobbed up out of the sea and the murder came to light. All I had to do was determine whether it was possible to find a positive link between the suspect's boat and the body. 'Jack', as the deceased had been called, was undressed and his clothes, the wire, some tools found in the boat and some others from the suspect's garage were sent for examination. The interesting part about the wire was that, where the body had swollen up and covered it, it was in pristine condition due to the saponifying fat. Where the wire was exposed, despite being galvanised, it was completely rusted through. After examining a number of cutting tools it was possible to prove from the matching striation marks that one particular pair of pliers from the suspect's garage had been used to cut the wire.

The next step was to prove that the body had at some time been in the boat and that, as usual, meant removing all the debris from the clothes by brushing. On taking the wet clothes out of the bag, I noticed that the man's skin and three inches of underlying yellow subcutaneous fat (he was a rather large, rotund person) had separated from the body and was attached to the inside of the jacket and trousers. Lurking in the skin and fat were hundreds of shrimp and crabs that had been feeding off the rotting flesh. It was a pretty nasty job removing this putrefying mass from the inside of the jacket and trousers, but it had to be done so that they could be examined properly. In the end, however, it was worth all the retching. After drying and brushing out the clothes, paint flakes and manmade fibres were eventually located which matched exactly with those from the boat and its carpet and the case was proven beyond reasonable doubt. It was, however, years before I touched another shrimp or crab.

At that time it was also fashionable for the large crime gangs to incarcerate their victims in the support pillars of various motorway bridges that were under construction. I remember spending days hanging from a climbing rope, with densitometers, which were very crude in those days, looking for cavities in concrete bridges and pillars. The civil engineers and police were visibly relieved when we found nothing and they no longer had to contemplate the nightmare of dismantling part of an operational motorway. From the information we had at the time I have no doubt that there are a number of man-sized cavities which will prove a conundrum for the demolition experts when the bridges are finally dismantled many years from now.

Another case involved, once again, the disposal of unwanted rivals but this time by grinding them up and feeding them to pigs. I'm not quite sure how I became involved, since I was a chemist and that sort of thing would normally be dealt with by the biologists, but being presented with several buckets of very liquid pig faeces does stick in my mind and, for that matter, nostrils. I think I was looking for teeth or bone fragments which the pigs might not have been able to digest too well, or that was how the theory went. It could have been lack of motivation on my part, but nothing was found and the next thing I knew I was knee-deep in the real things at some farm in the wilds, way north of London. I remember being carefully lectured by a yokel on the pigs' eating habits to the effect: 'E, lad e be right careful o' 'em 'ere porkers, if 'ey 'ave a mind 'ey eat e ar e stand'. Not quite sure if he was telling the truth or not, but they looked mighty savage beasts from where I was standing, to say nothing of them smelling abominably, and I made doubly sure that at all times I was as far away from them as possible. Once again nothing found.

There was another case where rival gang members were cut up and disposed of, but this time in a very small furnace at a farm in Surrey. It was suspected by the police officer in charge that we might find some remains in the ashes, or body residues in the chimney. We were, to say the least, sceptical. As we didn't have anyone small enough to climb up the chimney, we decided to take it apart, brick by brick, and what a filthy job that was. Not, as one might have expected, very fine black soot, but buckets and buckets of white ash. Was this, we asked ourselves, ash from a cremated body or just the result of a high-temperature furnace? Unfortunately, there was no way of telling. The ashes underneath the furnace were once again white, but that was quite normal. After passing the ash from under the furnace through a series of sieves, and picking out all the unburnt pieces of coke, fractured stones, lumps of rusty metal, strands of wire etc., we did eventually find a few small spheroidal particles of silver alloyed with tin. These could have been part of the amalgam from teeth fillings, but as the mercury would have evaporated due to the heat of the furnace there was no knowing where they came from.

For some time I was attached to the drug analysis section, which I didn't find very entertaining. Once you have analysed your 500th case of Purple Hearts (methyl amphetamine) or the 1000th case containing cannabis, it all becomes a little boring. Most of the famous pop groups of that time appeared on my table for possession of one sort of drug or another as did some rather infamous members of the aristocracy.

At that time the person in charge of the drugs section was one of forensic science's true characters, John Jackson. A slip of a man, no more than 5 foot 2 inches tall, with huge glasses and a permanent smile, who was an absolute mine of information about every type of tablet and capsule that you could ever imagine. One day John gave me this case of 'drugs found' that contained dozens of different tablets including some very large unmarked yellow ones which I just could not identify. As I went through all the normal acid, alkali and neutral extractions I noticed that John seemed particularly interested in what I was doing. In the end I gave up, unable to dissolve these tablets in anything, and asked for his assistance. 'Eat one, you'll soon find out,' he said. Being a little sceptical about taking unidentified tablets I asked him if he knew what they were. 'Of course I do, now just go ahead and chew one,' he said. So chew one I did, expecting at any moment to either begin hallucinating or writhing in pain before dropping dead, but nothing. About an hour later there was this peculiar churning rumbling in my bowls before an enormous, abysmal-smelling fart exploded from my behind. 'Thought so,' said John. 'Two-gram sulphur tablets. Does the trick every time.'

One type of case I found particularly distressing was death by abortion, especially when it involved young girls. Tablets of every type imaginable were involved, some absolutely useless, others horribly dangerous, but what appalled me most of all were the implements used. They were always filthy dirty, rusty and covered in dried blood and included knitting needles, the spikes from umbrellas, pieces of sharpened wood, filthy iron rods, even wooden pencils. Medical instruments, when they were used, were almost invariably caked in blood and filthy dirty. I did absolutely all I could to extract every iota of available evidence from those cases, often working late into the night and all through the weekend. It always gave me a great sense of pride and satisfaction when my work resulted in a conviction and a lengthy custodial sentence.

After the drugs I was posted into the Emission Spectrograph section. In those days scanning electron microscopes were a long way off and, apart from carrying out a wet chemical qualitative analysis, the only convenient way of determining the elemental composition of an inorganic substance was by emission spectrographic analysis. In this type of analysis a very small portion of the substance is burnt in a carbon arc. The light emitted by burning the substance is passed through a prism where it is separated up into its various wavelengths. The light is then focused on to a highly sensitive photographic plate. As each element will, when burnt in this way, emit light at certain discrete frequencies it is a relatively simple matter to find out what elements are present in the sample.

Generally this technique is used to compare samples of glass or paint, to determine whether they contain the same elements and could thus have come from the same source. This was a really boring job, as it was simply providing an analytical service to all the other sections. Generally all you received were some brief details on a case file together with four or five samples for analysis. Most of your time was spent in a dark room either developing the plate or reading the results that simply consisted of hundreds of short black lines on a clear glass plate. It was a job I hated with a vengeance, but working there was necessary to build up the general background experience required to competently give expert forensic evidence in a court of law.

On one particularly hot spring day, as I was desperately trying to remain awake while plate reading, in rushed the section head clutching a small glass phial containing a few small filings of a dull reddish metallic substance. 'Drop everything you are doing, Brian, and analyse this for me,' he said. There were no case notes, no file jacket, not even a letter.

'No can do, boss, I need the papers,' I said.

'Impossible,' he replied. 'This is of the utmost urgency and secrecy.'

However, having recently received written instructions from the director that no emission spec work was to be carried out without the correct documentation, I was not to be budged and out he stormed. Ten minutes later the director was beside me whispering words such as MI5, Special Branch and CIA. 'Sorry, Brian, Top Secret. No files, nothing. Just do it now.'

Duly I loaded the plate and burnt the sample together with a control sample of RU (Rays Ultime) powder, which contained virtually every stable element known to man. With the boss looking over my shoulder, the developing and washing of the plate seemed to take forever and I was very glad to have the plate in the reader without having made some blunder or other. The plate, however, was really strange, covered in black lines in areas no one had ever seen before, and it took some time before I could sort out what it all meant. And then it dawned on me, pure 100 per cent uranium! The director snatched the plate from the holder, recovered the few remaining specks of sample and, before rushing out, whispered in my ear, 'National importance, Brian, not a word to anyone, do you understand? Official Secrets Act is very pertinent here, you must not say a word.' And that was it.

The subject was never mentioned again by anyone. The sample and plate disappeared off the face of the earth and I had all but forgotten the matter, until a few weeks ago when I read the headline in the *Mail on Sunday*, 'LOCK STOCK AND SMOKING ATOM BOMB'. It seemed from the article that in 1967 two East End petty villains cum scrap metal dealers had bought a 'mislaid' 11-kilo chunk of very dense metal. They, the Mafia, the Krays and several secret service organisations believed that it was U235: pure bomb-grade uranium worth millions of pounds on the black market and capable of making half-a-dozen Hiroshima-sized atomic bombs. Everybody had wanted to know whether it was Uranium, and at every turn the dealers were being asked to file off small quantities for analysis. Eventually the metal disappeared, presumably bought by someone in the Middle East, but I don't doubt that the sample I was asked to analyse was the uranium belonging to the two dealers. Whether it was U235 or just uranium ore I will never know as the emission spec isn't capable of distinguishing between isotopes. My only real concern is whether the vapour from such a radioactive source will have any long-term effect on my body.

It was around this time that my fiancée, Barbara, and I were in the process of saving up to get married. One stipulation I had always made was that we would not tie the knot until we had a house of our own to move into. Despite saving every penny we could it was not going to plan and I decided that we would have to put off the marriage for another year. Not exactly a popular decision. In a vain attempt to recoup some Brownie points, I suggested we have a camping holiday in Spain.

Four weeks of lazing in the sun forgetting the pressures of work was wonderful, but all too soon it was time to pack up for the long and tiring drive back. Just outside Limoges in southern France, while travelling along one of those suicidal three-lane roads, the cars in front of me started to skid all over the road to avoid an accident. The mini estate we were driving was loaded to the hilt with camping gear and was probably overweight for the brakes. After standing on the brake pedal for what seemed like an eternity, it soon became obvious that we were just not going to be able to stop before hitting a large Citroën that had come to a halt sideways in front of us. It was at that stage that everything went into slow motion and I apparently had all the time in the world to evaluate the various options: go straight on and hit a stationary car broadside on, not a good idea; swerve over to the right and try and get round the pile of cars by going over the grassy bank, also not a good idea as there were several families having a picnic there and it would mean going through the middle of them; swerve to the left into the path of the oncoming traffic, a quick look through the windows of the stationary Citroën – now only 20 yards in front of me – showed an apparently clear road, so that had to be it.

I was not going too fast as I pulled round the front of the stationary car, but at that moment, seemingly out of nowhere, came a Dyane 6 doing about 50mph, not even attempting to slow down.

Corner to corner we hit with a huge crash of tortured metal and smashing glass. There were no seat belts in those days and Barbara disappeared through the windscreen followed by a fusillade of large peaches that were in the back of the estate. Both cars were completely wrecked, Barbara had a broken wrist and thumb and something like 200 stitches were required in her face, shoulders and legs. I was relatively unscathed, but we both spent two weeks in a local hospital. The hospital itself was a disgrace; like a nineteenth-century Bedlam. Injured people were strapped naked to the bed with leather belts and covered in Gentian blue; the toilet was a 50-gallon, plastic bin in the middle of the ward with no curtains; twentieth-century medicine was non-existent, and cleanliness and disinfectants were almost unheard of. Those 2 weeks are worthy of a book in themselves.

The adventure did not, however, end there. We had a Mercedes ambulance take us the 500 miles to Calais and it was a white-knuckle 130mph drive all the way, with three very close accidents to add to the excitement.

With our car a write-off, all of our possessions stolen from the wreck and a large sum of our hard-earned savings wasted in France, even the rescheduled date for the wedding was not looking too hopeful. We were determined not to put the wedding off again but we just couldn't save any more from our meagre salaries.

Some time before, John Moore (a colleague from the Met Lab) and I had set up a small printing business to supplement the paltry salary we were receiving from New Scotland Yard. With a bit of advertising I managed to increase the orders quite considerably and in no time I was working night after night way into the small hours to make up the money lost in France. I couldn't keep that up for too long, though, as I was going to night school three times a week trying to get my degree, as well as working all day Saturday at another job. Soon, however, we were back on track for the March 1969 wedding and I could return to my studies.

CHAPTER 4

SAFE BREAKINGS AND GUN SIGNATURES

One of the forensic sections which I really enjoyed working in was Physical Science. This dealt mainly with toolmarks. In this type of case one is looking for similarities in scratch marks, called stria, which are left when a tool is used to scratch or cut another surface. Minute irregularities, which are placed on to the cutting surface of the tool during its manufacture, are transcribed on to the cut or marked surface when the tool is used. These irregularities are totally random and are unique to that tool. Statistics show that stria are several orders of magnitude more specific than fingerprints, and as such the evidence obtainable from a good stria match can be beyond reasonable doubt. The type of examination can range from the simple scratch caused by a screwdriver being used to force open a door, bolt cutters to cut the hasp

of a padlock, a knife used to slash a car's tyres or a huge crowbar used to jemmy open a safe.

One case I was asked to attend involved the attempted forcing open of a safe on the tenth floor of a factory building in Wapping, east London. It was a really old building, allegedly built by prisoners in the Napoleonic wars. There being no lifts, I, with all my equipment, laboriously climbed the old creaking wooden stairs up to the tenth floor. It was a huge building with hundreds of small offices on each floor. I looked everywhere for this safe, but there was nothing to be seen. Eventually I located a police officer and asked him where I might find the burgled safe. He pointed to a large safe-sized hole in the floor that continued on down all ten floors and through two basements to the concrete foundations. It appeared that, after unsuccessfully trying to drill and jemmy open the safe, the would-be safe crackers had placed three sticks of dynamite on the top of the safe and detonated them. The huge explosion and the weight of the safe were too much for the old wooden floors and it was sent plummeting down through wooden floor after wooden floor until it hit the concrete basement. Remarkably, the safe was still in one piece, although it was a little bent and twisted. Unfortunately there was nothing for me: the toolmarks were of no use.

Another safe breaking, or attempted breaking, occurred in a new town in Essex. I was told that an unsuccessful attempt had been made to drill the lock and that they had a suspect. Drills are the same as any other cutting tool in that they leave stria from irregularities on the cutting edges of the drill bit. They are, however, only of use if the hole has not been completely drilled through and the marks caused by the cutting edge are still present. Eventually I found the rusty safe sitting in a dingy, filthy little office in what was obviously a very downmarket strip joint. From my first look it was obvious that this was not an attempt to drill the lock as the holes were in completely the wrong place. There were a couple of semi-drilled holes towards the top of the door which were perfect for taking silicone casts, so I started to mix the various components I required on a nearby desk. It was then that I noticed this peculiar, acrid smell in the back of my throat. It took me some time to identify it as nitrogen dioxide. Nitrogen dioxide is a slightly brown-coloured gas that is often given off by very concentrated nitric acid. I hunted round for the source and eventually it became obvious that it was emanating from the bottom of the safe door, from where it was leaking after being poured in via one of the drilled-through holes. But what was someone doing pouring concentrated nitric acid into a safe? That was never going to destroy the combination lock mechanism. The liquid slowly leaking out was a really oily fluid which didn't look at all like nitric acid was supposed to, the latter being quite fluid.

Then it hit me. The oily liquid was not acid but nitro-glycerine, which was slowly decomposing, giving off nitrogen dioxide in the process. The burglars had obviously thought that filling the hollow cavity of the safe door with this exceedingly high, and now terribly unstable, explosive, then exploding it via a detonator pushed into the drilled hole was the way to open this rather poorly-built safe. We made a rapid exit to say the least: we were half a mile away within seconds. When the bomb disposal guys arrived they confirmed it was one of the most dangerous jobs they had ever dealt with and that there were nearly two pints of nitro-glycerine in the door, enough to take out every building on the block.

Working as a general forensic chemist was great for its variety, but I soon became disillusioned with the sheer drudgery of most of the casework. However, I did discover that I had a particular flare for dealing with toolmarks and possessed almost a sixth sense about whether a particular set of toolmarks on the microscope were going to be a positive match. Even so, after dealing with hundreds of telephone coin boxes which had been jemmied open and an equal number of cut padlock hasps, even something you enjoy becomes a little tedious. But where to next? Where could I best put this 'talent' with toolmarks to use?

At that time firearms cases were on the rise, and the workload of the two firearms examiners in the Met Lab was more than they could handle. A vacancy was there for a suitable candidate, but what could I offer as I knew nothing at all about firearms?

One thing I did know about, however, was toolmarks. Regular toolmarks are made when a hardened tool leaves scratch marks (striations), which are unique to that tool, on a softer material such as a brass lock. In firearms it is exactly the same principle, with the rifled barrel of the gun being the tool and the bullet being the object on which the scratch marks or stria are left. The rifling in a barrel has its own class characteristics, i.e. the direction of twist, the number, width and depth of the grooves, which are unique to a particular make and sometimes model of weapon. For example, most Colt revolvers will have six left-hand twist grooves, Smith and Wesson have five right-hand twist grooves and Webley revolvers seven right-hand twist grooves. The individuality of a particular barrel comes, however, from random irregularities that are introduced at the time the barrel was manufactured. Each barrel has its own individual signature and even consecutively manufactured barrels from the same manufacturing machine will have completely different signatures.

So, I thought, why not try for the job of trainee firearms examiner in what was called 'the Gun Room'?

Other matters had, however, to be attended to before I transferred to the Gun Room. I was getting married. New Wife – New House – New Job: sounded like a good combination. Cars, flowers, church service, wedding bells, bridesmaids, in fact everything was arranged for the wedding. All I had to do now was fit in my stag night. Despite howls of protest from my bride-to-be, it had to be as tradition dictates, on the night before the wedding. And so began a night which, even now, is extremely patchy as far as my memory goes.

Nothing really spectacular, just a crawl from one pub to another ending up somewhere near my mother's house where we were all due to stay that night. The memory, however, begins to get rather vague around about 11.00pm when a vile mixture of spirits was given to the groom-to-be, by the manager of a bar we were barely standing upright in. From there it is all a bit of a blur until I woke up in my mother's front room feeling like death, but then I looked into the mirror and felt even worse. My left eye was completely black, almost closed and the size of a tennis ball, and my face looked like a piece of raw steak. One arm was bereft of skin and hurt so much I thought I had broken it. My best man and two of my other friends were also quite severely damaged and together we all looked, and felt, in a very sorry state. According to some reports I fell off the top of a gravestone face first on to the granite grave, but what I was doing on top of the gravestone, or even in a graveyard for that matter, is anyone's guess.

Damage limitation was definitely the order of the day, but I only had a few hours in which to work a miracle. Luckily, there was a rather upmarket ladies' make-up establishment nearby and they thought it was a great hoot me getting married with a face that looked as if it had been run over by a horse and cart. Within minutes, I had four make-up specialists fussing over me, and some time after that I was semi-presentable, with half an inch of make-up smeared over my very damaged face. The top hat pulled down at a jaunty angle also hid quite a lot until, that is, it was taken off inside the church and Barbara, my bride-to-be, had her first glimpse of me. Half the congregation couldn't contain themselves and the other half were tutting away like a battery of hens. Barbara was struck dumb and her sister, the maid of honour, had a face like thunder. However, that was nothing compared with the vicar who was a bit of a fire-and-brimstone preacher and started on a full-volume tirade, with his face inches from mine, about how holy wedlock was an institution that one should not take lightly. I had 1,001 road drills hammering away in my brain, was on the point of throwing up and really didn't need a sermon at that particular moment. All I wanted was for the ground to open up and swallow me whole.

All in all a very painful lesson and one that still lurks like a skeleton in some dusty corner of my mind.

CHAPTER 5

POST MORTEMS, PIG SHOOTINGS AND POLICE HUMOUR

The head of the firearms section at that time was a retired superintendent named John McCafferty. Mr Mac, as he was known, was a first-class firearms examiner, one of the best comparison microscopists I have ever known, and a tremendous person to boot. The second in command was Brian Arnold, a laconic sort of person but possessing many of Mr Mac's attributes. Brian and Mr Mac made the training really easy, pushing me just enough to keep me on my feet, but not so much that I became lost in a jungle of new terminology, techniques and knowledge. Having never fired a real weapon in my life, I was not allowed access to guns and ammunition until I had attended a very intensive course at D11, the marksman unit of the Metropolitan Police Force. A bit of a harrowing experience that, but after two days of firing hundreds

and hundreds of rounds of ammunition they declared me 'fit for limited firing', whatever that meant.

During my early days in the Gun Room Mr Mac was clearing up the last few items that had been seized from those two well-known gangs, the Richardsons and the Krays. Both had only recently been sentenced to very lengthy spells in prison.

One of the exhibits being examined by Mr Mac was a briefcase containing a spring-loaded hypodermic syringe, operated from a trigger built into the handle. The case was intended to be swung gently into the back of someone's leg with just enough force for the protruding needle to penetrate. On pulling the trigger the spring-loaded plunger was released injecting the contents of the syringe into the leg. Rumour had it that the case, with the syringe full of cyanide, was intended for use by Paul Elvey, a Scots fellow, on Jimmy Evans. Evans was giving evidence in the Old Bailey against, amongst others, Freddie Foreman over the death of Ginger Marks. The Twins were arrested and charged with conspiracy to murder over this case but it never got past the committal proceedings. The briefcase was also supposed to have been used on a member of Parliament who was investigating the gang's activities but, once again, nothing could be proved.

To test the case we took it to police training school, filled the syringe with water and tried it out on an unsuspecting recruit during a training exercise. So preoccupied was the recruit with what he was doing that he hardly noticed 0.1cl of pure water being injected into his leg.

The Krays also had an extremely powerful crossbow with a lethal hunting bolt. It was, I understand, intended to kill George Caruana, who had upset the Twins over the spoils of a robbery. We were, however, unsure whether it was capable of firing over any great distance with such a heavy bolt. To test this, Mr Mac and I took it to the outdoors firing range at the Met Police recreational club just outside London. At the end of this range was a 25-foot-high wall, behind which was the club's car park. To test the accuracy of the crossbow we set up a wooden target at 75 feet, which was halfway down the range. Aiming straight at the target had the bolt hitting the floor about 10 feet in front of where we were standing. Elevating it by about 15° got it another 40 feet and by this time we were both despairing about whether we'd ever reach the target. With a last effort, as it was really difficult to cock the thing, I raised the bow to about 25° and pulled the trigger, only to see the bolt soaring up into the air, way over the end wall and descend into the car park with a very loud metallic 'Thunk'! On peering gingerly round the end of the wall, there was the arrow embedded right up to the flights in the bonnet of the Deputy Commissioner's car. Not a happy man.

One item which lurked in the corner of the office like a black cloud was a very large, metal-jawed vice. Allegedly, this item had been used by the Richardsons to crush a victim's testicles, one at a time, until they popped. It wasn't clear why we had the vice in the Gun Room, but no one would go anywhere near it. Just looking at this evil instrument of torture made one wince and go weak at the knees.

Although I used to drink in the Blind Beggar, the pub where Ronnie Kray shot George Cornell, and was aware of their activities, I did not realise how feared the Kray brothers (Ronnie, Reggie and Charlie) were. That was until some years later when I was part of the team investigating the Barns murder in Essex. My recollection of the exact details are a little hazy now, but as far as I remember there was, in the early hours of 5th November 1972, a botched burglary attempt at the Barn Restaurant, Braintree, Essex. Two gunmen broke into the restaurant and tried to force the owner, Bob Patience, to hand over the keys to the safe. When he refused, they shot him, his wife Muriel and their daughter Beverley, in quick succession. Muriel Patience later died of her wounds whilst Bob and his daughter Beverley survived. George Ince, who had already been charged with a major silver bullion robbery, was – falsely as it turned out – identified as one of the gunmen and charged with the robbery.

The trial was at Chelmsford Crown Court and was presided over by Justice Stevenson who had previously tried the Kray twins in their first trial for the murders of Cornell and McVitie, and who was not known for his leniency.

Ince did not do himself any favours during the trial, continually clashing with the judge and his own defence team whom he eventually sacked. Beverley Patience gave her evidence against Ince and positively identified him as being one of the gunmen, something he strongly denied throughout the trial. One thing which was a little surprising, and which went completely against him, was that Ince refused to give an alibi for the night in question. Nevertheless, most of the evidence against Ince was somewhat dubious and even Beverley Patience made a poor showing in the witness box.

Eventually, the trial ended and the jury went into retirement for over six hours eventually returning with the verdict that they could not agree on a result.

Within a week he was on trial again, this time with a different judge, Justice Eveleigh. Now Ince had an alibi in the form of a Mrs Grey, who turned out to be Charlie Kray's wife Dorothy. Ince had, on the night in question, been sleeping with Dorothy Kray and although Charlie Kray was in jail for ten years, the Krays' influence was so strong that George Ince would rather have gone to jail for murder than admit to having an affair with Charlie's wife.

Ince was found not guilty at the second trial and, when he was finally released from jail for the silver bullion robbery, he continued to see Dorothy and eventually they had a daughter, Nancy. In the end Charlie did divorce Dorothy but, for some unknown reason, never took revenge on George Ince.

Some time later a petty part-time crook called John Brook was arrested for waving a gun around in a pub in the Lake District. He was arrested and when the gun was sent in for analysis it was found to be the murder weapon. Brook was eventually convicted of murder and given a life sentence. For those with further interest in this case, which brought about a substantial change in the way in which eyewitnesses' accounts are treated, there is a book entitled *Can You Positively Identify This Man?*.

It was during the first few weeks in the Gun Room that I attended my first gun-related post-mortem (PM) examination; a grisly part of the job but one that can be vitally important in determining the exact sequence of events which occur during a shooting incident. It is not the job of the firearms examiner to actually cut up the body, of course, that is the responsibility of the forensic pathologist. The firearms examiner is present to examine the body clothed and unclothed and then witness the dissection to determine the bullet-wound track. From these examinations he can determine the range of firing, whether there was a struggle for the gun when it was fired and, most importantly of all, what the deceased was doing at the moment he was shot. These will answer such crucial questions as, was there a struggle for the gun? Did he have his hands in the air in a gesture of submission? Was he attempting to stab, shoot or punch the shooter? Was he crouching in a defensive posture or was he even running away at the time he was shot?

This post-mortem examination was a particularly messy one involving a shotgun murder. It transpired that the man was shot by one of his wife's old boyfriends. It appeared that the boyfriend was completely devastated when the relationship broke up, driving him to a mental breakdown. In the intervening years he spent more time in mental institutions than out, but on those occasions he was out he was obviously astute enough to track down the love of his life and her new husband.

On the fateful morning the husband, as usual, drove his daughter to primary school dropping her off in the playground. On walking back to his car he was confronted by the ex-boyfriend holding a self-loading, 12-bore shotgun. The first round he fired went through the left side of the husband's ribcage, tearing out several ribs and a large chunk of his lung. The second shot was through the upper right arm severing it all but for a small area of skin. It was then that the gun jammed and despite several attempts he could not get it to work again. The scene at this stage must have been absolute hell, with children and mothers screaming and running for cover while this poor innocent man lay writhing in agony as blood poured out of his wounds on to the pavement and down a nearby drain.

Being unable to free the gun's mechanism the man calmly walked back to his car and recovered a double-barrelled, side-by-side, 12-bore shotgun and some additional rounds of ammunition. He then proceeded to put a round through the centre of the man's chest, which must have killed him almost instantly, followed up by a contact shot to the right temple. Just to make sure, he reloaded the gun and shot him again in the chest.

It was a bit of a baptism of fire that PM examination, what with the arm dangling by a thread, the complete left rear of the skull plus brains missing and three huge holes in the chest. I must admit that I only stood at the foot of the examination table and I did go out halfway through for a breath of fresh air.

I am not a particularly religious man, but having seen and carried out examinations on hundreds and hundreds of bodies over the years it is obvious to me that there is something missing from a dead body which made it a human being when it was alive. Police officers I have been working with one day have been killed the next and have arrived on the slab for my examination, but what I see lying before me is not the person I knew before. Now it is just an empty shell. Whatever that missing thing may be, whether it is a soul or some other spark, it disappears with death. The only way that I have been able to rationalise some of the truly horrible sights that I have seen over the years is to consider the body as no more than an inert exhibit upon which I am working and not the remains of a human being. Without that rationale I do not think I could have coped.

I was still under training and was desperate to see as much of the cases and how they were dealt with as possible. As a result I tried to get on as many raids as I could, something which was not very common in those days.

We had been told by an informer that a particular suspect was as mad as a hatter and had amassed a large collection of arms and ammunition and that he was hiring them out to robbery gangs. With the prospect of a possible armed confrontation, a full armed-response team was the order of the day for this one.

I am afraid that the location of the premises escapes me after so long but I think it was south of the river. A 6 a.m. knock was arranged and, with everyone in bullet-proof vests, we waited until the signal came. It was a raw November morning, freezing cold and blowing a gale. Nobody wanted to hang about for long, but the call to action never seemed to come. You could feel the tenseness in the air and hear the distinct heavy breathing as the adrenaline-fuelled 'flight or fight' syndrome kicked in. We were all closely bunched together with the armed team in front, the detectives behind them and me at the very back. Guns were all cocked and held at shoulder level ready for action and, with everyone being so close together, each person had the gun barrel of the person behind only inches from his ear. There was not a sound to be heard: the traffic had been stopped well away from the flats, everyone had been evacuated from the surrounding apartments, and even the birds semed to have stopped singing. Suddenly, with a sound which seemed in the silence like a hammer hitting an anvil, someone pulled the trigger of his gun. We waited for the crash of the round going off but there was nothing: whoever it was had forgotten to load his gun. All we could hear was the sound of urine escaping from someone's trousers.

Then it came through the radios, 'Go, Go, Go'. With one swing the steel battering ram did its work on the lock and D11, the Metropolitan Police SWAT team, went in first with the detectives close behind. But there was no drama, no firing of guns. Nothing. Eventually I was called in and there, in the kitchen with apron round his waist, was the suspect calmly stirring the contents of a pot simmering on the stove.

The kitchen was really steamy with water running down the cold walls, and whatever was in the pot had a smell not unlike a lamb stew. 'Nothin' like a good trotter for breakfast,' said the suspect. 'Plenty to go round if you would like some'. And with that he fished out from the pot a human foot! Even I was close to throwing up, especially as the toenails were thick, yellow and still dirty.

The flat was searched and, neatly cut into joints and stored in the small freezer, was the best part of a whole human body. In the rubbish bin we found the remains of last night's meal which had obviously consisted of human chops, chips and peas. But no guns, and so nothing at all for me to deal with, thank goodness. I just couldn't wait to get out of that place and back to a world of relative sanity.

Even to this day I am not quite happy with the thought of eating lamb, as the smell always conjures up images of that foot coming out of the pot!

After eight months of training I was eventually, and prematurely to my mind, let loose on very simple possession of arms and ammunition cases. It was then that I felt I had really begun to earn my salary. I vividly remember my first appearance in court; it is etched upon my mind as if with a branding iron. The defendant was charged with possession of 10 rounds of military issue 9mm Parabellum calibre pistol ammunition. A very simple case, the ammunition was live and, to cover all eventualities, I fired a couple of rounds just to make sure. The headstamp markings identified it as military ammunition and gave the place and year of manufacture. What more could be asked?

The case was set for 9.30am but, as with all Magistrates' Courts, pleas were heard first, which pushed it back to about 11.00am. As time went on I became more and more nervous until I could wait no more and fled to the toilet where I became incarcerated, not daring to move off the pan for fear of there being a very nasty, and messy, accident. Eventually the court usher found me and called me from my throne. Carefully I eased myself out of the cubicle and, with very tight cheeks, waddled into court to give my 'expert' opinion. The only question of any significance was 'And how much would one expect to pay for a round of this ammunition, Mr Heard?' Panic. I had no idea. It was the last thing I thought they would ask me. Velocity, kinetic energy, maximum pressure, maximum range, history, designed for use in what weapons, I could answer them all plus many more; everything, that was, except its value. I made a guess and was informed by the defence counsel that I was out by 50 per cent, but nobody was really interested and the next thing I knew it was all over. I was out of the door and rushing back to the toilet.

That first appearance taught me two invaluable lessons: never underestimate the defence counsel and always expect the unexpected. Also, be extremely wary when they start with 'Now tell me, Mr Heard, I know absolutely nothing about firearms and ammunition' for it is at that stage you know the opposite is true. The counsel has had weeks to study every book available and think up stupid, irrelevant questions just to try and make you look foolish and discredit your evidence in front of the magistrate or jury. If he does it well enough, then that is the end of your career and you will never be allowed to give evidence in a court of law as an expert again. It doesn't matter how good a forensic firearms examiner you are, if you are discredited just once then it's time to look around for a new career because your current one is finished.

Another of my early cases involved the shooting of a large pig. It appeared that one farmer had a herd of really well-kept and well-fed pigs which always fetched the highest prices on market day. The next-door neighbour was not quite so lucky, but that was down to his own lackadaisical farming practices and the fact that he kept his pigs in small, filthy pens rather than letting them have free rein as the neighbour did. Consequently, his pigs were not in such good condition and sold for considerably less than the neighbour's. This irked him no end and with each passing market day he became more and more jealous and more and more angry. To vent this anger he decided to make his neighbour's pigs suffer by taking pot shots at them with his air rifle. The air rifle was a particularly powerful Webley Mk.3 which was .22 calibre and capable of discharging pellets at about 500 feet per second. At close range the pellets would undoubtedly have had the penetrative power to reach deep-seated organs and be capable of killing the animals. The pigs were, however, over 90 yards away and at that range the pellets would normally not be capable of penetrating the thick skin of a pig. When shot at this range the pigs would squeal and jump about, delighting the farmer no end. After a few weeks of this the pigs started to become very nervous, wouldn't eat and lost weight, which delighted him even more. After some time he started to tire of this and decided to move in to less than 60 yards, and it was at this stage that one of the pigs dropped stone dead.

A veterinary surgeon was called in and I attended the post mortem, which, surprisingly, wasn't so different from that of a human being. After taking lots of X-rays, the pellet was found embedded right in the centre of the brain, but the question was, how could it have got there? There were no obvious wounds on the head and no holes in the major part of the skull. Eventually the bullet track was traced through the thin bony membranes of the sinuses and into the cranial cavity. The pellet had in fact gone straight up the pig's nose which is why no pellet entry hole was visible.

There was, however, still some doubt about whether a pellet at that range could have caused the damage it did, and the only way that could be tested was to obtain a pig and shoot it with the same rifle, pellets and range. Getting a 200lb pig was not easy, since they usually go straight to the slaughterhouse where they are killed and butchered all in one go. Another problem is that very soon after death the skin and muscle toughen up and become much more difficult to penetrate. The only option was to obtain a live porker and shoot it while it was sedated. What a job that was: the pig wouldn't stand still so that we could tranquillise it and, when we did manage to get the drugs in it, it involuntarily emptied its bowels all over us as soon as we attempted to move it. On top of all that, manhandling 200lbs of sleeping pig is all but impossible: it behaves like a 200lb sack of jelly.

After several near hernias the long-suffering pig was in place at the end of the police sports club range with its head tilted up so that I could see down its nose. Not a pretty sight. Then came the difficult part: getting the pellet in just the right place. The trouble was that the slightest breeze would send the lightweight pellet way off its mark, either completely missing the pig or just grazing its shoulder. After one particular grazing shot the pig awoke with a great snort and a squeal, taking off like a bat out of hell. Up and down the range it ran, round and round in circles, squealing, snorting, grunting and making so much noise we soon had a huge crowd of spectators. It was also making an awful mess of the range by relieving itself everywhere, which made us even less popular, if that was possible, with the club manager.

After what seemed like hours we managed to re-tranquillise the pig, but this time the vet used enough of the drug to ensure that it was in a coma. After only the second shot I hit the spot and the pig just stopped breathing altogether and was dead. The PM showed that I had managed to exactly duplicate the shot which killed the original pig and the case was solved.

In those early days legislation did not exist which required that air guns over a certain power limit required licensing. As a result, each case, and the question of whether the weapon was an arm for the purposes of the charge, was decided on its own merits. One such case involved a particularly nasty youth who fired an air pistol at a police officer who was trying to arrest him. The whole case hinged on whether the air pistol could cause a lethal injury and thus satisfy the definition of a firearm, i.e. 'a lethal, barrelled weapon'. The gun was .177 calibre and the penetration limit for human skin for that particular calibre pellet is about 300 feet per second. The argument was: if a missile was capable of penetrating skin, then it could cause an injury from which death could result. As this particular gun was capable of discharging a pellet at 350 feet per second, then it would satisfy the definition and the charge of discharging a firearm with intent would stand.

In court, the arguments went back and forth with the likelihood of death resulting from mere skin penetration being the most contentious subject. Pathologists and doctors were called by both sides, each having a different opinion depending on who was doing the calling or paying the bill. In the end, the defence counsel said to Mr Mac, whose case it was: 'I would have absolutely no hesitation in allowing this air gun to be fired at my new-born baby's fontanelle [the space between the bones in the skull of a baby].' This was obviously a nonsensical statement and a dangerous one under the circumstances. It did, however, catch the ear of the judge, who instructed Mr Mac to find out more about this possibility. Mr Mac obtained, totally legitimately, an aborted foetus from the mortuary and a test firing showed that a pellet travelling at 350 feet per second would penetrate to the centre of the brain when fired through the fontanelle. The next day he duly reported his findings to the court and the case was closed, with the jury finding the defendant guilty of discharging a firearm with intent to resist arrest. The court reporters, of course, had a field day accusing Mr Mac of shooting live babies, carrying out unethical testing etc all of which was, of course, absolute rubbish. It did, however, cause Mr Mac an awful amount of grief for a very long time.

Reading all the papers on the penetrative capabilities of various missiles, especially low-velocity ones, is all well and good, but there is no substitute for reproducing the tests yourself and gaining first-hand knowledge. To this end I carried out hundreds of test firings using air rifles of different calibres and velocities to build up my own database. Samples of fresh human skin were obtained from cadavers donated for medical research to compare the difference in resistance between human skin and pig skin, both fresh and old. I also carried out numerous experiments on pigs' and bulls' eyes to determine what damage would be caused by pellets at various velocities. It took me a long time to sort out how to do that properly as an eye is extremely resistant to penetration. Not only that, but pellets tend to skid off round the side due to its wet, elastic and very smooth surface. The other problem is that if you just put one on the bench and shoot it, the eye ends up bouncing round the room like a rubber ball. In the end I had to construct an eye socket from a large block of Plasticine, then securely embed the eye into this socket so that it wouldn't move or rotate when hit. I am not squeamish at all, but I really didn't like dissecting the eyes as I always had the impression they were looking at me.

Interestingly enough it takes a velocity of about 450 feet per second for a .177 calibre pellet to actually penetrate an eye, but when it does the eye is totally destroyed, bursting like a balloon. At velocities below that, the pellet merely knocks off a bit of the white of the eye, leaving what appears to be another pupil. Casework has shown that when an eye is hit by low-velocity, non-penetrating missiles they tend to skid round to the back of the socket where they become lodged. While there is normally no lasting damage to the eye, it has to be removed from its socket before the pellet can be recovered. It must be damned painful for the owner of the eye. Everything to do with eyes has shivers running up and down my spine and I am really glad that I don't have to shoot them any more.

As a follow-on from the pig-shooting case I wondered what would happen with a human head. To gather first-hand knowledge I contacted Professor Taffy Cameron, a good friend and one of the best forensic pathologists I have ever had the pleasure of working with. Taffy dissected a head for me, then cut it up into thin strips with a band saw so that I could see the bone density of the various sinal regions. What I then needed was a skull on which to carry out penetrative tests. Obtaining a skull was not all that easy, as there aren't all that many left for medical research and those that there are generally end up in the hands of the trainee surgeons and trainee forensic pathologists. Taffy said that he would see what he could do for me, but I did stress that all I wanted was a skull, no tissue or brain matter.

A couple of weeks went by and nothing so I gave Taffy a call. 'Yes, yes, don't worry, one is on its way to you.' So I waited a while longer but still no skull. Another call resulted in exactly the same response. After a couple of months I was beginning to think he had forgotten me altogether so I made one last call with a big 'please' added on the end. 'OK, OK, OK, it's on its way.' By this time I had given up, until one morning I came in to find the cleaning lady in a dead faint by my office desk with a plastic bag clutched in her hands. Taffy had delivered all right, but he had merely sawn a head off from the neck and it was completely intact with skin, eyes, hair etc. The cleaning lady had obviously wondered what was on my desk and being nosey had taken a quick peep inside to see this head with eyes open wide staring up at her. That was definitely the last time she ever did that, in fact it was the last time we ever saw her as she handed in her notice the next day.

I hadn't been taking my own cases and call-outs all that long and it must have showed, especially to a long-serving desk sergeant whom I came across one evening after a call to the scene of a domestic dispute. I was about to go home when the old desk sergeant put his arm round my shoulders and said: 'Before you go home, son, why not have a beer with us? It's been a long night and we are just about to go off duty and we would like to say thanks for helping us out.' As they had arranged a squad car to take me home and I didn't have to drive, I thought, Why not? Unfortunately, the station didn't have a mess so we took over the interview room and, like magic, a dozen beers and some sandwiches arrived. It was a really good atmosphere, with jokes and banter going back and forth, and time just slipped by. I hadn't drunk a lot, four bottles of beer at the most, when the desk sergeant said: 'No more beers up here, I am afraid, someone has to go and get them up from the fridge downstairs.' I didn't know it at the time, but I was being well and truly set up. Suddenly everybody was in animated conversation with someone else and I had no option but to offer to go.

Unbeknown to me, under the station was the mortuary and in the mortuary was the fridge which supposedly contained the beer I was to collect. 'Don't worry, son,' he said, 'they are all dead down there, they can't harm you.' So out of the back of the station and down the stairs to the cellar below I went. Very gingerly, I opened the door which creaked like something out of a third-rate horror movie. It was only a small mortuary with eight slabs in two rows of four, with a space in between down which I had to walk to get to the fridge. Every slab had a body on it, each of which was completely unclothed and nude but for a small identity tag tied to the right big toe. Hanging in the centre of the room was a single bare lightbulb dimly glowing and casting eerie black shadows everywhere. As the room doubled up as the mortuary cold room body store it was also absolutely freezing cold.

Immediately I entered the morgue I started to shiver, more through the cold than anything else, or at least that was what I tried to convince myself. Can't back out now, I thought, and carefully I made my way down the row of slabs being careful not to touch any of the bodies on my way. I was about to open the door when I heard this very quiet moan. I must be imagining things, I thought, but as I turned round the body next to me sat up with a really load groan and put its hands out towards me. I screamed, shouted, gibbered, waved my arms in the air, jumped up and down and fled for the door. And there, standing in the doorway, was the desk sergeant and everyone else from the station absolutely curled and completely beside themselves with laughter. The 'dead body' said: 'Fucking cold in here, ain't it?', got himself a beer out of the fridge and started to pull on a tracksuit.

Talk about set up. I was suspicious, but was convinced nobody in their right mind would lay naked and completely still on a mortuary slab in that cold alongside seven real bodies. It took me about two days to stop shaking, but the half bottle of whisky they poured down my throat helped a bit. It was also a valuable lesson I never forgot: never, ever, trust an old desk sergeant.

Soon after, it was back to the police recreation club range again, this time to test some 12-bore bird-scarer cartridges that someone was trying to sell to farmers without a licence. In those days shotgun cartridges containing more than nine pellets didn't require a licence, but these bird-scaring cartridges only contained one single pellet of some pyrotechnical chemical mixture in a cardboard container. Having only one pellet it was, therefore, technically ammunition. We had not seen this particular type of cartridge before so off to the range we went for some test firings.

Quite impressive, really, the contents of the cartridge screaming off before making a huge bang which scared the birds for miles around. Unfortunately, the third or fourth round must have dislodged the plywood we were using as a target allowing it to slip down at an angle. The contents of the next round, instead of penetrating the wood and being captured by the sand behind, soared off up into the air screaming and wailing to a height of about 100 feet. Eventually it reached the top of its trajectory and started to fall, still burning but not yet exploding, into the car park where it went off with an earth-shattering explosion. We didn't dare look. Could we sneak off without being seen? Not a chance, the club manager was out like a shot to see what had happened, and whose car should have several windows shattered and a huge dent with a large area of paint alight on the roof? Yes, you guessed it, the club manager. And that was it. We were banned forever.

CHAPTER 6

MORE GANG WARFARE AND FREAK FIREARMS INCIDENTS

Cases came and went, air gun after air gun, weapons found in the street to be checked against the unsolved crime index, possession of tear-gas guns, in fact anything which wasn't going to involve too much scene of crime investigation or the possibility of a drubbing in court. Then, after about three years, I was given my first big gang shooting.

One gang was being paid protection money by a drinking club in Soho, a notorious area of London famous for its clubs and Chinese restaurants. At that time there were a number of different gangs vying for exclusive control of Soho, and street fights, usually with knives and broken bottles, were the normal way to sort them out. The gang being paid protection money obviously had some warning that another gang was up for a fight and that they were going to use guns. For several nights the gang took up strategic positions and were well prepared for their rivals, but when nothing happened they became lax and began drinking to pass the time. The other gang hadn't timed their entry quite right, as the resident gang was still fairly sober and as they burst through the door all hell broke loose with bottles, glasses, lead pipes, motorcycle chains, pistols and several sawn-off shotguns all being used in the ensuing fight. In the end, nearly everybody had to go to hospital to have something sewn up or set in plaster. Luckily, however, nobody was killed.

My job was a nightmare, with bullet holes and shotgun patterns everywhere. In the end I concluded that two .38 calibre revolvers, one 9mm pistol, a sawn-off .410 calibre shotgun and two sawn-off 12-bore shotguns had been used. But trying to determine who was where when the shots were fired was virtually impossible. Eventually I went along to the hospital to have a look at the wounded villains to see if I could determine what they had been shot with.

On arrival at the ward I was first shown a really hard-looking villain who was lying on his stomach. It wasn't until they pulled the bedclothes back I could see why: there on his backside was a perfect pellet pattern from a .410 shotgun! It was obvious that it would be weeks before he sat down again. At the other end of the ward was one of the opposition, with a really sorry look on his face. With great glee the nurse whipped back the bedclothes, which were supported on a wire frame over his middle, to reveal this rather large penis with a shotgun pellet hole straight through one side and emerging out of the other just back from the tip. Talk about making you wince. It was obviously going to be some time before he was fit enough to entertain the ladies again.

These two wounds were so classic that I made an application to the director to have them on the Gun Room's Christmas cards, but he didn't think it appropriate – no sense of adventure, that was his trouble.

Another club shooting involved a huge bouncer who must have weighed 320lbs, very little of it fat. A couple of Chinese Triads had tried to put the strong arm on the manager to pay the local gang protection money but the manager was having none of it and employed this Neanderthal to act as his first line of defence. On cue, the two local Triads turned up and a fight began which was initially very one-sided. After a few minutes, reinforcements arrived and Mr Apeman started to lose ground in a big way. It was at this stage he pulled out a self-loading pistol and started shooting.

At the scene were two bodies, and cartridge cases and bullets everywhere. The, now, ex-bouncer was arrested and in his possession was a .380 calibre Model 1934 Beretta which, when I got it back to the lab, matched up with the fired bullets and cartridge cases. I tested the pressure required on the trigger to fire the gun and found it to be 6lbs, which was about average for a pistol of this type. I then tried to make the gun go off by striking it with a soft hammer in various strategic places and dropping it on the ground. The mechanism was, however, in perfect order and short of destroying the mechanism it was incapable of discharging accidentally.

In court the only thing our thick bouncer had to say, in a very pugilistic East End of London accent, was: 'Well, I'm a real big boy and I must have squeezed the trigger too hard and it wouldn't stop firing.' When it was my turn I was asked the usual questions about the trigger pressure required and whether it was prone to accidental discharge or whether it could go fully automatic (i.e. fire continuously until the finger is taken off the trigger). The clincher came, however, when I revealed that there were twelve rounds fired at the scene and the maximum capacity of the magazine was only seven rounds, meaning that he must have changed magazines when one became empty. He was, of course, found guilty of murder and sentenced to life imprisonment.

One lovely sunny spring Monday morning, I had booked a day off and was looking forward to a walk in the woods with my family. We were just walking out of the door when the phone rang. Should I ignore it or not? I really didn't want to miss a day out with Barbara, but it was obviously work (you can always tell by the ring!) and I had to answer it. At the other end was a very perplexed officer from the

Surrey constabulary explaining that this man had been up a ladder painting his house when he suddenly fell off and before he hit the ground he was dead. Everyone had thought it was a heart attack, but there was what looked like a bullet hole right on the crease where the neck meets the shoulder. A bullet fired from an aeroplane, perhaps? No, impossible. There was no sense in going to the scene, so I told the officer that I would meet him at the mortuary.

Although it was a sunny day, the temperature was close to freezing and the mortuary was absolutely Arctic. 'No problems,' said the mortuary attendant, 'I'll soon sort that out.' In a jiffy all the windows were closed and ten three-bar electric heaters were rapidly changing the temperature from sub-Arctic to tropical. Hotter and hotter it got, until I thought I would soon be in my underpants, but that wasn't the real problem. The real problem was that the mortuary attendant had opened up a dozen bodies ready for the pathologist to inspect and the stench was appalling. The intestines, which were neatly piled up beside each body, were slowly filling up with decomposition gases; the brains which had been removed from the skulls were slowly crumbling and the stomach contents which had been removed for identification were putrefying in a dish. Just to make matters worse the attendant had a really morbid sense of humour; at least, I think it was humour. He kept asking us which bit we would like cut out and put in newspaper for our breakfast. 'How about a nice kidney or two? Really fresh, just came in this morning. Or what about a slice of nice juicy liver, go lovely with some scrambled eggs?' I was really glad when the pathologist turned up.

All that could be seen on the body was this small, almost closed-up hole at the base of the neck, which bore none of the characteristics of a typical bullet hole. On opening him up the wound track showed that if he had been hit whilst standing upright the bullet must have come straight down from above. Eventually, the bullet was located still embedded in the muscle of the heart having got there without hitting anything other than soft tissue.

The biggest shock of all was that the bullet was a 7.62x51mm calibre military bullet.

The 7.62x51mm calibre ammunition is a highly powerful round of ammunition for use in military rifles such as the FN, and medium machine guns such as the GMPG. With a velocity of 840 metres per second (2,750 feet per second) it has tremendous penetrative capability and unless it was fired from extreme range should have been easily capable of penetrating the body lengthwise, especially if it did not encounter anything other than soft tissue.

A microscopic examination of the bullet showed the presence of spiral scratch marks on the nose portion of the bullet, indicating that it had struck something hard before hitting the deceased. A quick look at the Ordnance Survey map of the area showed a military range some two miles from where the deceased was found. Enquiries showed that, at the time the deceased fell off his ladder, an army squad were using GPMGs (General Purpose Machine Guns) on a range directly in line with the scene. All the guns were brought in for test firing and it was eventually discovered that it was the gun being used by the squad leader that had fired the fatal shot.

On questioning he admitted that during full automatic fire the gun had 'got away from him' meaning that he had lost control of it. It was obvious from the damage to the nose of the bullet that one round had struck the top of the butts and had ricocheted up at a very steep angle eventually coming down nearly two miles away with just enough terminal velocity to penetrate all the way to the deceased's heart. If it had hit even a rib it would not have had sufficient energy to penetrate and the man would have lived.

At around this time, in 1970, there seemed to be a plane hijacking every week, and occasionally they would generate work for my department. George Habash's Popular Front for the Liberation of Palestine was particularly active with no less than four airliners being hijacked in the month of September. Two of these were

American, one Swiss and the fourth was Israeli. The Israeli plane was hijacked by a rather attractive young Palestinian woman named Leila Khaled, assisted by an American whose name seems to be lost to history and which I have forgotten.

Leila Khaled had managed to get through the Israeli security system carrying a homemade .22 calibre self-loading pistol with her accomplice carrying a dummy grenade. The plane took off as scheduled and the hijack went smoothly, with no shots being fired until the plane was forced to land at Heathrow Airport, London, through, if my memory serves me correctly, a lack of fuel. After a 24-hour stand-off, the plane was stormed by the anti-terrorist SAS unit during which the American was killed and Khaled arrested.

Knowing what good security the Israelis had at their airport, nobody could understand how Khaled managed to get past the metal detectors with a gun. Eventually the gun came to the lab and all became clear: the gun was a homemade self-loading pistol, not one piece of which was made out of a ferrous metal. The barrel was brass, the frame aluminium, and all the springs were made from phosphor bronze. With the ammunition being made from a brass cartridge case and a lead bullet there was nothing to trigger the metal detectors.

The problem, at that time, was that nobody realised a weapon could be made entirely from non-ferrous metals and the metal detector gates were only tuned to pick up iron and stainless steel objects. The airport authority went into panic mode and we spent weeks with the various manufacturers of these security gates, testing them against every type of ammunition and metal you could imagine. Nowadays the gates are so sensitive that they will even detect epoxy resins which have been strengthened with aluminium dust.

Eventually Khaled was released after the PFLP hijacked a British plane and threatened to blow it up with all 300 passengers on board, but that was the last time any terrorist organisation held the British

Government to ransom. As for Khaled, she received numerous offers of marriage from rich and not-so-rich Japanese, but as far as I can remember she declined. Recently she resurfaced with another terrorist Nayef Hawatmeh over their being allowed to enter the autonomous Palestinian areas in the Gaza to attend meetings of the Palestine National Council. Whether this means she is back in business or not I do not know.

At this stage I think that the scene at the Gun Room in the Holborn building should be set. Far from being a purpose-built laboratory building with all the necessary sinks and fume cupboards that are required in a modern well-organised laboratory, it was merely a poorly built office block which had been converted, at the lowest cost possible, into a working laboratory.

If the general laboratories were unsuitable, then the Gun Room was a real danger to everyone concerned. The main office was a room about 35 feet long by 18 feet wide. The windows were glass down to about three feet from the floor, where they became hardboard. Mr Mac had a small office down the corridor, but apart from that everything was done in that small space.

In the centre of the room was a large wooden bench on which sat an old tea chest filled with telephone directories. This was used to test fire guns for operability and range of firing where it was not necessary to recover the fired bullets. Everything was fired into this box, from air guns to sawn-off 12-bore shotguns. Next to the shooting box was a six foot by one foot by one foot wooden box filled with the softest grade of cotton wool available. This box was used if we wanted to collect undamaged bullets for comparison purposes. Behind the shooting boxes was the comparison microscope, which wasn't exactly convenient, since every time someone wanted to test fire a weapon all work had to stop. The room contained no soundproofing or anti-ricochet tiles on the walls and worse of all there was no extraction system. On an average day,

30 or more rounds of ammunition would be fired from 12-bore sawn-off shotguns and the noise and lead pollution were absolutely terrible. The only piece of safety equipment available to us at that time consisted of rather poor quality ear protectors.

One of the most worrying things about the office was that the windows faced across a narrow street directly on to another office building. The potential for an accidental discharge is always present with any type of gun recovered from a criminal, no matter how many safety precautions are taken. Even to this day I am amazed that nobody across the street was injured or killed.

The accidents were sometimes alarming. Once, a double-barrelled shotgun went off as the action was closed and, although the barrels were pointed down at the bench, the shot ricocheted off the wooden surface and bounced all round the room, breaking several glass cabinets in the process. Another time a self-loading pistol, which had been tested and re-tested without ammunition to make sure it worked properly, went fully automatic when the firing pin snapped off and jammed in the firing-pin hole on the first shot. That, luckily, only resulted in a bullet hole in the back wall and two in the ceiling. On another occasion a sub-machine gun decided to start firing as the magazine was inserted. Now that was seriously dangerous; the first two bullets which ricocheted from the floor were only prevented from going through the thin hardboard below the window by a fortuitous rifle butt blocking the way. The rest of the rounds bounced around the walls and ceiling, causing all sorts of damage but, luckily, injuring not a soul.

Another accident involved an old .320 calibre revolver firing black powder loaded ammunition. On firing there was, as usual with black powder ammunition, a huge quantity of white acrid smoke and sparks. Brian, who was carrying out the test, decided to wait until the smoke had dissipated before recovering the bullet from the cotton wool. With coffee cups in hand, we sat down and started to discuss a difficult case we were both involved in. After about 10 minutes we were both starting to feel decidedly hot and it just continued to get hotter and hotter. It wasn't until Brian decided to recover the bullet that we noticed the entire box of cotton wool was on fire. The wool was so finely divided that it burnt with a completely colourless flame. The automatic fire alarms went off, firemen with axes and rolls of hosepipe came running up the stairs and, all in all, it was a very embarrassing experience. After that we had a hinged lid made for the recovery box and always kept it closed, no matter what ammunition was being fired.

Black powder ammunition had been used when I was called to a house in Hackney where an old man had decided to commit suicide with an ancient .320 calibre revolver he had owned since the 1920s. The ammunition was definitely on its last legs and it took three attempts before a round actually fired. He held the gun in tight contact with his right temple which, if you are really intent on a sincere display of self-criticism, is a pretty sure way of doing it.

When I got to the scene the body was lying on the floor with a bullet entry hole at the right temple. Severe blackening and some splitting of the skin was typical of that caused by the muzzle of a gun being either very close to or in contact with the skin. On the left temple was a bullet exit hole which, due to the relatively low power of .320 black powder ammunition was, I thought, a little unexpected. With such ammunition the bullet should only have had enough power to penetrate one side of the skull.

I got out a small magnifying lens to have a closer look at this exit hole and as I was there, down on my hands and knees with my head no more than inches away from the deceased, he let out this loud groan and sat up! I nearly died, one of the PCs fainted on the spot and another ran out of the room screaming. When I finally got my heartbeat down below astronomical levels and regained the ability to talk I had quite a normal conversation with the man. Eventually he was carted off to hospital for treatment and observation. X-rays of his skull showed no damage to the skull at all. On re-examining the ring of blackening and tattooing round the entry hole, I saw that there was a slight elongation of the ring towards the top of the head which indicated that the gun must have been held at a slight angle to the skull allowing the low velocity bullet to glance off the bone without penetrating. The bullet then carried on under the skin, travelling right over the top of the skull until it reached a change in angle between the skin and bone, when it exited at the left temple area.

About a week after the incident I thought that I would pay a hospital visit to the old guy who had nearly caused my heart to stop. Quite a pleasant old chap really, who was full of stories about the First World War. The really surprising thing about him was, however, the completely bald half-inch-wide stripe going from the bullet entry hole right over the top of his head and down to the exit hole. The passage of the bullet just under the skin had obviously destroyed all the hair follicles leaving this bald strip in its wake.

Generally speaking, dead bodies do not really upset me, other than when it is of a child. In my whole career I think that there were only three cases involving the death of a child with a firearm, but in each instance the experience always stayed with me long after the event.

One particularly disturbing case involved the death of a small girl of five. She, together with her seven-year-old brother, lived with their parents in a very nice five-bedroom property in Surrey.

As I remember, it was a pleasantly warm Summer day. Dad was at work and Mum was in the garden dealing with the washing. The children had become bored with playing in the garden and were seeking entertainment in the house. In Daddy's study, which was normally out of bounds, was a large cabinet containing his hunting guns – obviously a magnet for any seven-year-old boy. With his sister's help, he dragged a chair over to the cabinet and, by climbing up on a chair, he managed to open the cupboard and extract what must have been for him a very large and heavy rifle.

For a while they played cowboys and Indians until eventually he had his sister hemmed in a corner of the room. 'Bang! Bang! You're dead,' he said as he pulled the trigger. With what must have been an enormous sound, the rifle exploded into life nearly cutting the small girl in half.

The father had committed the cardinal sins of leaving the gun loaded, leaving the cupboard unlocked and not chaining the guns to the inside of the cupboard.

The rifle was a beautiful hand-finished Winchester in 25-3000 calibre and had been successfully used on many occasions by the father for deer shooting. The 25-3000 cartridge it fired is a very potent round being of .25-calibre and reaching that magical speed of 3000 feet per second. At that speed the whole characteristics of a bullet's wounding capabilities – its 'terminal ballistics' – change dramatically when compared to slower-moving missiles. Once a bullet reaches this sort of speed it is capable of transferring huge amounts of energy to the surrounding tissue, which appears almost to explode away from the bullet as it passes. This is often referred to as 'tissue quake'. Bones five or six inches away from the bullet's path will be shattered, and blood vessels completely destroyed.

The bullet, which had a soft point and is sometimes wrongly referred to as being a 'Dum Dum', entered the little girl's body at the bottom of the rib cage just to the left of the centre line and virtually exploded. In doing so it completely destroyed the bottom half of the left side of the rib cage, tearing out most of her intestines in the process. The tremendous 'tissue quake' effect also destroyed the bottom half of her liver and one lung together with both kidneys. Part of the spine was also shattered.

How she ever survived the initial blast is a miracle, but how she didn't die of blood loss or shock is even more astounding.

The doctors put back what intestines had not been completely minced and reconstructed as much of the rib cage as possible. She continued to live, but only with the assistance of huge banks of equipment which continued performing the vital functions that her tiny body was now unable to manage. Sadly, despite all the technology available, she died within thirty-six hours.

There was precious little that could be done at the post mortem other than try to estimate the range of firing, which was found to be no more than two foot six inches, but it was all a little academic.

As to the bullet, we never did find most of it as it had almost completely disintegrated, leaving only a few fragments of lead and thin jacket material. One of the pieces, no more than .08 inch by .1 inch, was sufficient to determine that the gun in question had in fact fired the round but that was about all that could be done.

The sight of that tiny frail body with such huge amounts of damage is an image I still see in my mind's eye to this day. It convinces me more each time I think about it that there is no excuse, other than being a farmer, for keeping weapons at home.

Sometimes I got praise from the most unexpected quarters. The Mad Axe Man was a seriously nasty piece of work and a psychopath to boot. As the name would suggest, he always carried, in a specially made shoulder holster, a stainless steel hand axe sharpened and honed to a razor-like edge. The weapon came out at the slightest provocation, with arms, hands and large pieces of flesh being carved off his victims often for no more than looking in his general direction. As time went on he progressed to sawn-off shotguns and occasionally self-loading pistols, which he used with equal abandon. Eventually all these evil deeds came home to roost and in the late Sixties he was locked up for life in Dartmoor's highest security wing, for killing a man with his axe in a pub fight. As far as I know the man did nothing more than take a sideways glance at the Axe Man's girlfriend, for which his head was cleaved in two.

Like many of the seriously nasty criminals I have dealt with he had, despite being a psychopath, a brilliant mind and it wasn't long before he was out of his 'inescapable' compound and on the run.

Nothing was heard of the Mad Axe Man for some while, although a number of armed robberies had his stamp on them. Ruthless robberies, committed with absolutely no consideration for human life, involving shots being fired, without provocation, at anything that moved. In one, a payroll robbery, a guard was shot in both legs for doing no more than standing there. His accomplices were nasty too. On the way out of the premises another of the masked men said: 'Thought you had got away lightly then?' and shot him again, first in the chest and then in the face, killing him instantly with the second shot.

Eventually I was told that they had information about where the Axe Man was hiding out and, because I had done so much work on the case, I was taken along on the raid. As usual, the address was kept secret to avoid leaks and it wasn't until I jumped out of the van along with the assault team that I discovered we were no more than a quarter of a mile from where I formerly lived. His room was on the first floor of this small Victorian terrace house in Elthorn Road, Holloway. The front door was quickly jemmied open and as we quietly edged up the stairs the adrenaline started to flow through my veins in torrents. Very quietly we lined up on each side of the door to his room, with me very much in the vanguard. Then, shouting at the top of their voices and blowing whistles, the team suddenly kicked in the door and the four of them, armed with revolvers and shotguns, burst in.

They needn't have worried. There he was, with his girlfriend, having sex. And she was astride him, preventing him from reaching the cache of loaded sawn-off shotguns lying beside the bed. There was a bit of a struggle but he and his girlfriend were soon in handcuffs, face down on the floor.

My job was quite simple. All I had to do was make sure the guns were safe without leaving any of my fingerprints or rubbing off any of his. As I was doing this he was read his rights and then asked if he had anything to say. To this he replied: 'Any robberies that Mr

Heard can prove I did with these guns I'll cough to, the rest you can go and fuck yourself for.' Admittedly a glow came to my face at the thought that he should rate my abilities so highly. In the end I tied his guns up to five robberies and two murders and he was soon back inside once again for another life sentence, or at least until he made another escape.

I had for some time been working on a very big case involving a London-based gang who were carrying out armed robberies all over the country. This was long before the days of such wonders of modern computer technology as the Integrated Ballistics Identification System (IBIS). With such a system, digitised photographs of cartridge case and bullet striation can be sent all over the world via a modem for checking against other unsolved crime indexes. In those days, to preserve exhibit continuity, the exhibits had to be taken by a police officer from one lab to the other with all the paperwork and wasted time that it entailed. It was, therefore, a huge undertaking, but in the end I managed to link the guns belonging to this gang with numerous armed robberies from Devon through Somerset, the Home Counties and all the way up to Scotland. The gang was charged and, since many of the robberies were in the Midlands, it was decided to hold the court case in Manchester Crown Court.

My evidence was quite lengthy and very complicated, so I was booked in for a four-day stay at a small hotel on the outskirts of Manchester. Travelling to give evidence was almost unheard of in those days so it was a very big occasion. I arrived mid-afternoon and immediately went into a long conference with the case officer and the prosecution counsel. I was scheduled to give evidence the next day so it was a quick bite to eat and straight to bed.

The next day I was led through the main part of my evidence by the prosecution counsel and, although it took some two-and-a-half hours, it all went very smoothly. The judge decided to adjourn for lunch at midday and as I was still under oath I had to sit by myself and could not talk to anyone connected to the case. Being made to sit alone like that always makes me feel very uncomfortable, almost as if I have done something wrong myself.

In the afternoon the defence counsel tried hard, but my evidence was rock solid and after nearly four hours they gave up and I was out of the box and could relax once more.

That evening we all celebrated. I was the last witness to give evidence and the gang were all clearly going to go down for a very long time. The Manchester CID really did me proud that evening wining and dining me as if it was going out of style. We ended up in a working men's club where there was quite a bit of on- and offstage entertainment as well as very cheap beer. The entertainment wasn't too bad: a half-decent comedian; a couple of leggy dancers; a scantily dressed singer; and then, the star turn of the evening, Big Bertha. On she came to rapturous applause, this mighty mountain of a woman sporting the largest chest I have ever seen, wearing a bowler hat and a sparkly morning jacket and 'G' string. She was definitely a sight to behold.

Big Bertha tried first to sing, but it was awful, then to dance, but that was even worse, and just as she was about to be booed off stage she started stripping and that had everyone fighting for breath. When she finally set free these Hindenburg-sized breasts, everyone in the audience let out a huge gasp, for they were truly gigantic. It did not stop there; the things she did with these breasts had everyone cheering for more and more, but the best was yet to come. As a finale, and how I will never know, she stuffed her breasts into a bowler hat and then, by throwing her shoulders back, she sent the hat rocketing across the club with a very loud pop. The place was in uproar. In the end I had laughed so much I couldn't stand. All that remained was for me to be poured into bed.

CHAPTER 7

TERRORISTS AND A TRIGGER-HAPPY TEACHER

It was October of 1973 and a time of major change for the Gun Room. After 25 years of working for the Metropolitan Police, many of them as the liaison officer between the forensic scientists and the police, and seven years as head of the Gun Room, Mr Mac had to retire. He was adamant that he didn't want to go, but Civil Service regulations are there to be obeyed no matter what.

Before Mr Mac arrived in the Gun Room the few gun cases which were submitted to the lab had been shared out among the available, more senior, forensic scientists. With nobody really specialising in such cases there was no specific area or equipment set aside for the examinations and the evidence was very simple in nature. Mr Mac changed all that. He set up the Gun Room, equipped it as best he could on a limited budget, placed it on a formal basis and, in the process, gained tremendous respect from all the police forces with which he dealt.

Apart from having lost one of the most experienced forensic firearms examiners in the country, one of the most worrying aspects of Mr Mac's departure for us was that he was now in a position to work for the defence. It was not that we had anything to hide, it was just that with his knowledge and experience he was in a position, if he chose to, to make our lives very difficult indeed. He assured us that he had no interest in such work; if he did take any on, he said, it would be insurance work or civil cases, definitely not crime. How that was to change.

Now with the dizzying title of Deputy Head of the Laboratory, my work took on another dimension, and I was given the job of training new recruits, something which I enjoyed immensely. At about that time a new member of the staff arrived: Jack Bewsey. Jack was retired from the Colonial Service and had been everywhere and done everything. He had been deputy commissioner of this colonial police force; commissioner of that; in charge of bomb disposal at another force; in charge of forensic ballistics somewhere else. He also knew more about pistols, revolvers, rifles, sub-machine guns and ammunition than anyone I had met before or have since. Being so equipped with this encyclopaedic knowledge and tremendous breadth of experience, the Civil Service made him – a clerk. He was, however a tremendous asset and helped shape the Gun Room into what it is today.

At around the same time the IRA and its splinter groups were beginning to make an impact on the mainland with bombings and shootings. For one reason or another I seemed to end up dealing with most of these cases. Often they went unsolved, as the culprits inevitably fled back to Northern Ireland after the crime.

One case involved the shooting of the In and Out Club, a prestigious gentleman's club not far from Marble Arch. It seemed fairly pointless; all they did was spray the front of the building with bullets and then run away. The perpetrators had positioned themselves across a dual carriageway and behind some railings in a park. It was obvious that they had used the cross bar of the railings as a support for the guns but, there was no obvious human target, merely random shots fired at the outside of the building. What was even more unusual was that there were five different calibres of weapon used, with no more than two rounds being fired from each. They must have come armed to the teeth but with almost no ammunition. Despite roadblocks and searches everywhere nobody was ever convicted for the shooting.

Next came a particularly bad shooting involving a taxi driver. The cab was hailed by three men with Irish accents and told to drive to several locations. No one got out at any of them. The last location was in Hampstead, down a dark, partially tarmacked road leading to the ponds on Hampstead Heath. The houses down this road are very expensive and all owned by multi-millionaires. While the taxi driver waited for further instructions, one of the men pulled out a .30 calibre M1 carbine with a cut-down barrel and shot him through the glass security screen. The bullet hit the taxi driver in the back of the neck, passing out through the left side of his throat. The bullet had obviously started to break up and tumble after breaking the glass, which caused it to tear out the side of his throat, including most of his jugular vein. The men calmly got out of the cab and disappeared into the night.

Realising he was dying, the cab driver lurched out of his cab with blood pumping out of his neck at an unbelievable rate and started to stagger down the road. After about 100 yards, judging by the huge quantity of blood on the ground, he staggered up to one of the large houses and, by now almost unconscious, rang the bell. The owner answered and, with tremendous presence of mind, picked up a pillow and stuffed it into the wound. Then, while kneeling on the pillow, he phoned for an ambulance. The doctors said it was a miracle that he survived; never before had they seen anyone with such blood loss still alive. If it hadn't have been for the house owner's swift action he would be dead. He survived, but the people who caused the damage are still at large.

Another case I was called to was the bombing of another very exclusive gentlemen's club, once again in Mayfair. When I arrived at the scene it was absolute chaos: ambulances, dozens of police cars, police everywhere, trampling all over the evidence; and hordes of press. There seemed no reason for the attack other than it was a vicious and cowardly strike at the 'old school' establishment. It seems that the pillion passenger on a motorbike threw a bomb through the first-floor window of the club and then sped off. There was no warning at all. The bomb itself was particularly nasty, consisting of about 1lb of high explosive surrounded by 1lb of six-inch nails.

It had landed on the floor of the club's main bar and had gone off with a huge explosion blowing a one-foot-diameter hole straight through the foot-thick reinforced concrete floor. Down below were the toilets and the – thankfully unoccupied – one directly underneath the bomb was completely destroyed. The toilets either side were occupied and, apart from a severe ringing in the ears, both occupants were unharmed.

I couldn't believe the damage caused by such a small amount of explosive. The walls had all been pushed out by six inches and the ceiling lifted up by about the same. The 20-foot oak bar had been turned upside down, and the whole room was scarred with six-inch nails, some of which were embedded for half their length in the concrete walls. But the most amazing thing of all? Of the 23 occupants, all of whom were covered in white plaster dust, there was not a single scratch on any of them.

The dust was still settling when I got there and one ex-military type was stoically operating a one-armed bandit while sipping a pink gin. Several other characters were waiting for the barman to replenish their, obviously spilt, drinks. The fortitude of the true English gentleman has never been more poignantly demonstrated for me. I was only called to the scene as the gentleman with the pink gin thought he had heard a pistol shot just before the bomb went off but, despite carrying out an exhaustive search of the scene, I could find nothing at all to suggest a weapon had been fired.

In the November of that year I received a call from Taffy Cameron to say that an armoured van had been robbed and the driver shot dead. He also said that, since there wasn't that much of interest on the body as far as forensic firearms was concerned, it might be best to remove the relevant parts for later examination. He suggested that I examine them the next day in his lab and afterwards we could have lunch together. As I was rather busy, and try to avoid unnecessary PM examinations where possible, it seemed a sensible suggestion to me. After some discussion on the case we arranged to meet at his office in the London Teaching Hospital at 10.30am the next day.

The case itself was a particularly nasty one. The gang had forced the van off a motorway and down on to a slip road where they ran it into a ditch. With a gun held at the driver's head they told the guards in the back to open up or they would kill him. The guards didn't have much option and the gang got away with £250,000. As a parting gesture, one of the gang, who was armed with a large Second World War-vintage Webley revolver, calmly shot the driver in the mouth. He lived for several hours before succumbing to his wounds.

I thought that it would be a simple job, since the .455 calibre bullet would have passed straight through the driver's neck and out the back, possibly severing his spine on the way. But 'never expect the expected' is one of the tenets of forensic science.

At the due time I arrived at the hospital, but wasn't quite sure where Taffy's office was located. After a lot of searching around I found the right floor but, as I was walking down the long corridor, what should be there, right before my eyes? An enormous rabbit, hopping from door to door. It was brown and white with ears that dragged along the floor. It must have weighed 30lbs. After pausing to take a long thoughtful look in my direction, it hopped off.

Eventually I found Taffy and felt a little reluctant to ask him about the rabbit. When I did, he said: 'Oh, so you've met Toby, have you?' He went on to explain how that part of the teaching hospital kept a number of animals for testing drugs etc. It seemed that Toby had been a resident for years and, while various experiments had killed off several intakes of rabbits, Toby was immune to them all. He was such a friendly rabbit that they decided to keep him as the lab pet and he had free run of the floor. I caught up with Toby later that day and he was exceedingly friendly, but he was so large it was almost impossible to pick him up and give him a proper hug.

Eventually I managed to start my work on the 'relevant bits' of the deceased, which were spread out on a large stainless steel tray on a white bench next to Taffy's desk. The 'relevant bits' consisted of the tongue, oesophagus and trachea, which were all lacerated to shreds. After carefully dissecting the tongue and part of the oesophagus it became clear that he had not been shot with a .455 bullet but a .410 shotgun cartridge containing shot pellets. The curious thing was, however, that there were not enough pellets to constitute even a short two-inch .410 cartridge. There was also a curious lack of the thick felt buffer wads which would normally be found between the propellant and shot in a shotgun cartridge of this type. All I could find was a thin wad, which would normally sit on top of the propellant, and another thin one, which would normally sit on top of the shot.

Some quick measurements, and it soon became obvious that he was not shot with a gun loaded with bullets, nor with a normal .410 calibre shotgun. What he had been shot with was a revolver loaded with .410 shotgun cartridges, which had been reduced in length to fit the revolver's chamber. The thick cushion wads had been removed so that more shot could be used and some traces showed that it had all been held in place by pouring wax over the top.

While I was finishing up, Taffy poured a couple of very large whiskies and informed me that he had ordered some sandwiches for lunch. His secretary bought in this large platter piled high with sandwiches and covered with a white damask cloth. It all looked wonderful until I took off the cover: they were tongue sandwiches. Quite suddenly I lost my appetite and requested another whisky instead.

Never having heard of a similar case (the cut-down shotgun cartridges, not the tongue sandwiches) I decided to do some more work and write it up as a technical paper for the Association of Firearms and Toolmark Examiners' journal. Subsequent experimentation taught me how quickly the pressures involved can escalate to extremely dangerous levels, if one is not aware of what is going on. I had duplicated the load used in the murder and was just experimenting with the best method of keeping the top wad in with molten candle wax when suddenly the gun I was using blew up scattering parts all over the range. It appeared that the wax had formed a plug in the rear end (forcing cone) of the barrel which had just enough resistance for the pressures to rise exponentially until the weakest parts of the gun, the chamber wall and top strap, dramatically gave way. I took a few of these cartridges down to the London Proof House where they have pressure-testing equipment and it wasn't long before they refused to test any more as the pressures were too great even for their equipment.

Eventually some arrests were made and a .455 calibre Webley revolver was recovered, loaded with cut-down .410 shotgun cartridges. I obviously couldn't match the pellets from the victim's tongue with the gun, but the thin wads from the body did show that they had been fired through a weapon with seven-groove rifling which was of the same type as the recovered Webley. It also showed that the cartridges in the gun contained the same components as those recovered from the victim's mouth. Not conclusive but good supporting evidence, as forensic science often is.

I was not the only one learning just how unpredictable shotguns could be. A sports master at a very prestigious boys' private school had decided that his pupils were a slovenly lot and decided to whip them into shape with early-morning runs round the football field. In the depths of winter, however, nobody in his right mind wants to put on a pair of shorts and T-shirt and run round a muddy field, no matter how character building it might be. The boys were consequently not too keen and, as soon as they got round the opposite side of the field to the master, they slowed almost to a stop and huddled together for warmth. The master was furious, so the next morning he came armed with a 9mm calibre shotgun which he started to loose off in the direction of the boys every time they stopped. This really did the trick and the master was mightily pleased with this new motivational method. Unfortunately for the master, after the third morning of this 'encouragement' one of the boys dropped down with a large ragged hole in his chest. Luckily a major hospital was nearby and after some intensive surgery he survived.

Now, the 9mm calibre shotgun really is quite a pipsqueak of a weapon and is only really of use for the elimination of vermin in confined spaces where a larger-calibre weapon might do some damage, perhaps for shooting rats in a barn where the use of a 16- or 12-bore might result in large holes in the wall. At a range of a few feet a 9mm calibre shotgun could probably cause death, but under normal circumstances the pellets would have been lucky to reach the other side of a football field. However, on this occasion the ammunition the master was using was quite old, and on very rare occasions the shot in such cartridges can 'ball' together coming out of the barrel as a solid lump. When this happens, instead of 50 or 60 very small pellets with little carrying power, what emerges is, in effect, a rifle bullet with all the power and range that this entails. Here the 'balled' shot had penetrated the boy's sternum, and this was probably what saved his life. On striking the sternum the shot had separated once again and although most of the pellets had penetrated the heart and nearby major veins and arteries, the holes were very small.

The boy's troubles were not over yet, though. His heart now pumped these tiny pieces of shot all over his body. Finally they ended up where the arteries and veins narrowed to such an extent that the pellets became lodged. He had these blockages all over his body, which had to be freed by surgery to prevent gangrene setting in. Apart from major surgery to his heart and the large veins and arteries (which contained dozens of small holes in need of stitching up), operations had to be carried out on his wrists, ankles, the backs of his knees, his lungs and the vessels leading to his brain. Shot pellets kept appearing for years afterwards, leading to further surgery, but he survived.

CHAPTER 8

HARD TIMES AND REVENGE CASES

I left school with just one A level. At the time I had felt this to be a great achievement, but I have always known that, had I worked harder, I could have gone to university. In those days I was preoccupied with rock climbing and going to dancing clubs and parties; school work was way down my list of priorities. At the brewery I had been looked upon as a mental genius, having one A level while those around me, including Victor, had nothing. But I knew that was not enough and at the first opportunity I enrolled for night school.

I had to start from the beginning and it was a long, hard slog: one full day and three nights a week, with the other free nights being taken up with homework. On top of that I was living in Sittingbourne, Kent, which was nearly two hours away from college. On those evenings I was at college I often didn't get home until one in the morning, which was really hard on the marriage. Five years it took to obtain my degree, only to be told at the end that as all my earlier qualifications were science-based I would have to obtain an arts or commercial-based O level (the equivalent of a GCSE) before I would be given the degree certificate. So I returned to night school for another year, alongside people very much younger than myself, to sit for an O level in Economics. The final examination couldn't come quickly enough, so that I could get my degree certificate.

The stress of all those years of examinations, coupled with the extremely high caseload and a terrible salary, was taking its toll and I had severe ulcers. Once the examinations were over, the pressure eased off somewhat, but the pitiful salary made it difficult to survive. It was all brought home to me one day when I was examining a body found in St James's Park and the PC keeping back the crowds was, even without overtime, earning twice my salary. Our last pay rise had been £2 per month at a time when my monthly train fare had escalated by £40. I started to do a bit of overtime, but as I was travelling nearly four hours a day it meant that I was spending less and less time with my young son Edward, who had been born two years previously. As well as the printing business, I started up another small business from home, selling winemaking supplies, a very popular hobby at that time. The business thrived and I was soon making enough money to survive, but for how long?

The police were in the process of upgrading their weapons and ammunition, not that there were many on general issue in those days, and the Gun Room was asked for some input. I had gone down to the City Road police indoor range to witness some of the training and trial some of the ammunition. While waiting for one of the targets to become free, I was idly watching the instructor giving one of the trainees some tips. At the time the force was using old Second World War .380 service revolvers firing .38 S&W commercial ammunition. The .38 S&W ammunition was a little oversized for the .380 revolver and the ammunition itself was a bit suspect, with misfires not uncommon. In one instance I remember being sent a revolver with five bullets jammed in the barrel. The first round was obviously a misfire with insufficient force to drive the bullet out of the barrel. The officer had not realised what had happened and kept on firing until the bullet from the fifth round became stuck between the chamber and barrel resulting in the whole action becoming jammed solid.

As I was watching the training, I became aware of the different sounds the ammunition was making: some going off with a large explosion and some with a gentle pop. The particular officer I was watching at that time had the trainer standing right behind him looking over his shoulder so that he could see exactly what the officer was doing. The first and second round fired as they should, with both hitting the target. The third, however, was considerably quieter with the bullet going so slowly that you could actually see it travelling through the air. Much to my surprise it actually hit the top of the target, but then even more surprisingly it came straight back towards the firer. The officer saw the bullet coming and at the last moment ducked, but the trainer did not and it hit him straight between the eyes. More out of surprise than anything else the officer fell as if poleaxed, with this bullet still neatly sticking out of the skin. The officer soon recovered, and two small stitches repaired him, but what had caused the bullet to come straight back? On examination of the target it soon became clear that the bullet had struck a large flat-headed nail which had been used to fix the target to the supporting post. The bullet didn't have enough energy to push the nail through the target so it bounced straight back.

The fact that bullets will often come straight back was illustrated most clearly to me as a result of some testing I was doing on a material called Linotex. This is a rubber material which was originally designed to cover the fuel tanks of fighter aircraft. As the material is almost completely self-sealing when penetrated by a bullet, it is ideal for this application. At the time I was, however, determining whether it was suitable for use in front of the backstop in ranges to prevent back splash of bullet fragments towards the firer.

I was firing a really old Webley .455 self-loading pistol with ammunition which must have been the best part of 50 years old. The ammunition was really unreliable, with misfires or hang fires occurring virtually every other round, and even when a round did fire the bullet often came out at such a low velocity that it was possible to see it go down the range. To see how the Linotex coped with such low-velocity large-calibre bullets I decided to hang a sheet of the material in front of the range backstop. Not knowing whether the bullet would penetrate or come bouncing straight back as the bullet did at City Road, I stood well to one side.

The first couple of rounds penetrated the Linotex as expected, but the third one was a particularly bad hang fire which, when it finally discharged, could be seen all the way to the target. There was a loud 'thwack' as it hit the Linotex then, instead of ricocheting as expected, it came straight back along the line of sight hitting me fair and square in the testicles! The pain was excruciating and my wedding tackle was black and blue for weeks. I must have been the only person for 30 or 40 years to have been shot with a .455 calibre Webley self-loading pistol and I will probably be the last. It also taught me a valuable lesson about dealing with elastic materials.

I was called to the exhibits reception desk one day to receive a case involving the shooting of a very wealthy widow. She had been shot five times in the back with a type of ammunition we had never seen before in the Metropolitan Police Laboratory. It was .22 calibre, but what was odd about it was that it was fully jacketed, i.e. rather than being made of plain lead, it had a copper/zinc alloy jacket covering the whole of the bullet. A bit of searching through the ammunition catalogues showed that it was a round which was almost unknown in the UK at that time, called .22 Magnum rimfire calibre. With the submitted bullets were five cartridge cases, which would normally have suggested that a self-loading pistol or rifle had been used.

Once I had the exhibits on the comparison microscope it soon became clear that there was something very odd about this case, as the stria on three of the bullets matched with each other very well and the other two also matched very well. While there were some similarities between the two sets I could not conclusively match them with each other. It was the same situation with the cartridge cases – three and two matching. Another odd thing was that, while all the cartridge cases bore extractor marks, none had an ejector mark. While this is not unknown in self-loading mechanisms it is rather unusual.

A quick look at the post-mortem photographs revealed what appeared to be three distinct sets of shots, two groups of two and one single one, all of which had been fired at very close range. This looked very similar to the effects produced by 'double tapping', whereby two shots are fired in rapid succession at exactly the same spot. This is a method used by highly-trained police tactical units and specialist anti-terrorist units such as the SAS, but I had never heard of it being used at such close range and against such a target

As a result of these findings it was concluded that either two self-loading .22 magnum rimfire calibre rifles or self-loading pistols had been used in the shooting. That was, until a man walked into the office one day and calmly said, with a very British accent: 'I am James, her ladyship's butler. I shot her ladyship, I just couldn't stand her rudeness any more.' After a bit of questioning he admitted that on a recent trip to the USA with her ladyship he had bought a two-shot .22 Magnum calibre derringer. One evening when she had been particularly awful he calmly shot her in the back twice, reloaded, shot her twice more, reloaded again and shot her just once. He ejected the fired cartridge case then went to the Serpentine, a lake in Hyde Park, and threw the gun into the water.

The very next day we had the police divers out dragging the area with large magnets for the gun. In all I think we found something like 15 bicycles, six old prams, dozens of wire baskets, several car wheels and seven guns before we found the derringer. Unfortunately, the gun was far too rusted for a comparison to be carried out as by then it had been in the water for several months, but it was loaded with a single unfired round. We purchased a new gun of the same make and model and the rifling specifications were found to be the same type as those on the bullets recovered from the body. The firing pin impressions and the extractor marks on the fired cartridge cases were also similar in design to those on the cartridges from the scene. The suspect was eventually convicted of murder; the butler did it.

The cases involving revenge were many. One such was that of Paddy, his wife Colleen and her brother. Paddy was an Irish navvy on a building site and 'thick in the arm and thick in the head' pretty much summed up his mental prowess. His life consisted of hard manual labour all day followed by eight pints of Guinness in the pub. He would then go home and knock the wife, Colleen, around until he fell into a stupor. Occasionally, if Colleen was really unlucky, he would be sober enough to sexually abuse her as well.

Colleen took this all in her stride: black eyes, broken ribs and all, accepting it as part of her lot as a dutiful wife. Her younger brother, who lived with her, was not so accepting and hated seeing his sister being beaten to a pulp most evenings. After a particularly bad bout of abuse, when Paddy broke Colleen's nose, the brother swore that he would sort out his no-good brother-in-law once and for all. Having a few friends from dubious backgrounds, it didn't take him long to get his hands on an old First World War .455 calibre Webley revolver and some ammunition, which he hid in his bedroom until the time was right.

Now the .455 calibre round of ammunition is hardly what any self-respecting target shooter would choose, as it has a huge, slow bullet with a trajectory like a trench mortar. For really short-range shooting against a human target it is, however, a deadly round, ploughing its way through bone and tissue leaving a large gaping wound in its wake.

Predictably, the right time wasn't long in coming: Paddy had lost most of his money fighting in the pub and came home in a foul mood. Colleen lost several teeth, gained two black eyes and yet another broken rib before he decided to viciously sexually assault her as well. Eventually he fell into a semi-coma of a sleep, snoring heavily like the pig he was. The brother-in-law could stand it no more. He got out his gun, loaded one round into the cylinder and, putting the muzzle to Paddy's temple, fired. The bullet went straight through Paddy's head and out the other side, depositing half a pound of his frontal lobe on the pillow in the process.

When I arrived at the scene I expected a corpse, but no, he was still breathing and obviously still very much alive. Whatever Paddy had lost on the pillow he obviously didn't have all that much use for. While waiting for the ambulance I thought I would take the opportunity to have a closer look at the entry and exit holes to estimate the angle of penetration and the range. What was peculiar was that the bullet had obviously taken out his optic nerves because he no longer had any control over his eyes; they were moving independently of each other. It was really spooky to see these eyes roll round in circles, disappear into the sockets then come back out again. 'Poor Paddy, he never did have very good eyesight,' said Colleen, in a really thick Irish accent, as she came up behind me.

Paddy survived for about 10 days before they switched off all the life-support systems. The brother-in-law was found guilty of murder but only received a relatively light term in jail due to the extenuating circumstances of the case.

If you really want to damage a man, though, aim for his manhood. My first experience of this eye-watering brand of revenge was a long time ago, but it occured in Wood Green, north London.

There had obviously been a violent argument between a couple over his infidelity with his wife's sisters. Yes, he was doing it with all four of them! There was some kicking and scratching, he broke her nose and she kicked him in the crotch, which he didn't enjoy at all. She tried to kick him again at which point he poured a can of lighter fuel over her and tried to set her alight with a box of matches. He did, in fact, strike and light several matches, but, when he threw them at her they went out without igniting the petrol. As he was fumbling with the box trying to light another match she picked up his .410 calibre shotgun and shot him in the testicles, shredding them and his penis beyond repair. Makes me wince just to think about it.

One case, if any, deserves a limerick. This concerned the daughter of an Italian fishmonger named Rosa. She was known by the local youths as being something of an 'easy lay'. Daddy, however, thought his 'Little Pink Bambino' was the most innocent of girls and the apple of his eye and he wouldn't have a wrong word said against her. One day, however, she went missing and didn't turn up that night or the next day and Franco the fishmonger was beside himself with worry. She was, of course, sleeping rough with her latest love, a real lowlife if ever there was one, in some squat not far from where she lived.

It was at this stage that the local flasher became interested and thought that he would make life for Franco the fishmonger even more of a living hell than it already was. Duly he appeared at the fishmonger's shop and in a loud voice, so that all the customers could hear, informed Franco that 'I know where your daughter is, I've got her locked up somewhere private and I've been fucking her non-stop for the past 10 hours.' There was more, but it deteriorated and isn't worth repeating.

This, as one can no doubt imagine under the circumstances, did nothing at all for the state of poor old Franco's mind, and the next thing Fred the flasher knew was that Franco had pulled out a First World War .455 calibre revolver from under the counter. 'Youa feelthy littla pervert. I'lla techa youa not to toucha mya littla Rosa, you filty piga.' With that, he shot Fred the flasher right in the crotch, neatly severing his pride and joy in two and removing one of his testicles in the process.

When I got to the scene, there was Fred being attended to by the medics with, understandably, tears rolling down his cheeks. The inspector in charge of the case had the gun in one poly bag and the remnants of Fred's wedding tackle in another. 'Aren't you going to take them out and examine them?' he asked with a gleeful grin on his face, proffering poor Fred's remains. I didn't take the bait, or open the bag for that matter.

One thing that always puzzled me about Fred the Flasher was whether his opening line had to be altered to 'What do you think of my stump then darling?'

CHAPTER 9

POLICE BLUNDERS AND UNFORSEEABLE ACCIDENTS

The mindless questions asked by senior police officers never cease to amaze me. They often give the impression that a frontal lobotomy is a prerequisite for advancement to the senior ranks. Of course, not all officers act in this way but some instances are worth repeating.

One classic comment involved the shooting of a general construction worker on a large building site. Among the first things to be dug on a construction site was a deep pit, for the latrines. This pit could be 15 feet or more deep and was provided with a toilet bowl on one side and a large open area on the other for urinating. They were not nice places at all and stank abominably, especially towards the end of a large construction project.

Our worker in this case had been carrying out some fencing of stolen goods on the side and had really upset a particularly vicious gang by not paying them the full proceeds. So, one morning, while he was urinating in the shed, one of the gang shot him twenty times in the chest with a fully automatic 7.63x25mm calibre Mauser Model 1932 pistol.

The Mauser M.32 is one of those very rare pistols which is a true fully automatic handgun. Pistols are often referred to as 'automatics', but this is a misnomer as the trigger has to be released between each shot. The correct term for this type of weapon is, therefore, a self-loading pistol. The Mauser M.1932 is one of the very few exceptions in that it will continue to fire as long as the trigger is depressed. Fully automatic pistols are, however, totally impractical (probably the reason not many have been made) as the recoil between each shot results in the muzzle climbing uncontrollably. If the range from gun to target is anything over ten feet or so, only the first two shots will hit the target with the rest ending up in the ceiling. The Mauser M.1932 is particularly bad in this respect as it has one of the highest rates of fire of any fully automatic pistol. If the trigger remains depressed the whole magazine of twenty rounds will be discharged in less than a second! If, however, one is at very close range, say a couple of feet, the complete contents of the magazine can be discharged into a body with devastating effects, as happened in this case.

With a velocity of over 1400 feet per second this is an extremely penetrating round and our poor Mr Worker caught all twenty rounds in the chest, virtually cutting him in two. After being shot he toppled forward into this nearly full pit of stinking faeces, partially sinking below the surface.

When I arrived at the scene he had been lying there, face down, for two or three hours with his body nearly cut in two and his blood mixing with the putrid faeces. Eventually the senior officer in charge arrived and the first thing he asked me, with a very serious voice, was, 'Do you think he is dead then?'

'I hope so,' I replied. 'Otherwise he's going to have an awful case of halitosis.'

Similarly, one morning, after a particularly heavy rainstorm, I was called to a hillside to examine some remains that they thought might have been the result of a gangland shooting. The body had obviously been on the hillside for a long time and all that was left was a pile of bleached bones. The heavy rain had scattered the bones all over the slope and the wild dogs had also had a go, taking some away and scattering many more in the thick undergrowth. There was a noose hanging from a nearby tree, which showed that it was almost certainly suicide.

As with any suspected murder scene, the area was cordoned off and the position and condition of each and every bone carefully noted. The pathologist thought that the remains were those of a male, about 65 years old. From the neck bones he concluded that the man had probably died as a result of hanging, which fitted nicely with the noose hanging from the tree. It was then, however, that the senior officer in charge turned up, asked, 'Is there any sign of a struggle?'

Occasionally, the police are not just silly in word, but in deed, too. One Sunday morning I was called to the scene of a 'domestic' where a man had shot his wife in the chest with a 12-bore shotgun. The wife had bled to death, but had managed to walk downstairs and begin telephoning for assistance first. The shot had been fired at really close range and had hit the woman right in the centre of the chest, making a huge hole and completely severing her aorta in the process. On the way down the stairs her heart had pumped virtually every last drop of her blood out of the hole in her chest and the scene was a real mess.

The location was a small terraced house with three rooms downstairs and two bedrooms and a toilet upstairs with wooden flooring. On arriving at the scene I took a quick look at the body just to confirm the range of firing and the direction before it was taken away to the mortuary. My only other job at the scene was to check the gun and make it safe, but where was the gun? Eventually I was shown to the kitchen where an officer was dusting it for fingerprints.

He was doing this by resting the butt on the table while gently holding the barrel between forefinger and thumb. The problem was that he was trying to dust the trigger for prints and before I could open my mouth to shout a warning there was a huge explosion. The gun had fired and the shot had gone through the ceiling and the floorboards and into the bedroom above, bringing down a huge slab of ceiling plaster in the process. There was a stunned silence. There were four officers in the bedroom above checking out the scene of the shooting. We rushed upstairs to find an officer holding a clipboard with a shotgun blast straight through the middle. That it had missed his feet and face was a miracle. He did, however, have an ashen face and a very wet pair of trousers.

Another 'accident' occurred during a training session. This was, however, no normal training session for cops on the beat, but for the VIP protection unit. At that time they were all issued with Walther PPK pistols, which are very reliable and compact weapons. If my memory serves me right the ones on issue were, however, only in 7.65mm (.32) ACP calibre, which is really inadequate despite being the gun with which Ian Fleming armed 007.

Watching true professionals at work is quite an experience: practising quick draws; shooting on the run; doing forward rolls; hiding behind barricades; and shooting with both left and right hands. But there is always someone who gets it wrong, and there, sitting very forlornly in a corner with a heavily bandaged foot and leg, waiting for the ambulance to arrive, was one of the royal bodyguards. He had obviously been practising quick draws but had pulled the trigger before drawing the gun out of its holster. Not the brightest of things to do. The bullet had gone through his thigh, skidded down the bone and exited out the side of his ankle. He was, I understand, transferred to other duties after that.

Genuine accidents happen too, of course. 'Safety is not an accident', the manuals are always telling us. Nowhere is this more true than in a forensic firearms examination laboratory. However, as long as the basic rules are adhered to, even these incidents can be minimised. Sometimes, however, there are problems that no one could have foreseen.

During the height of the troubles in Northern Ireland there had been a big seizure of weapons and ammunition. The seizure was so big that the examination had to be spread out between several of the examiners, one of whom was a good friend of mine. Among the huge pile of weapons he had to examine was an old Second World War Enfield .303 calibre rifle. Being a very experienced examiner he did all the correct safety checks: running a patch through the barrel to make sure it was clear; checking the bolt and firing pin to ensure the lugs and receiver were not cracked; checking that the firing pin was not protruding; ensuring that the action was not prone to accidental discharge by jarring; and checking that the inside of the barrel did not contain excessive corrosion.

After all that, he was sure that everything was in good order and proceeded to the range to test fire it with several rounds of military .303 calibre ammunition. For some unknown reason he had this premonition that everything was not as it should be, and decided to completely disassemble the gun for further checks. It wasn't until he took off the stock that he discovered that the gun had been booby-trapped. The stock had been hollowed out and filled with 1lb of high-powered military explosive, designed to go off when the recoil from firing drove the butt stock back into the firer's shoulder. There was absolutely no doubt that if he had pulled the trigger he would have been killed instantly and taken most of the laboratory and its staff with him.

In the days when the Met Lab was in Holborn, there was a general forensic chemist called Mike who was an avid clay-pigeon shooter. I have always found 12-bore shotguns a bit hard on the shoulder, but Mike, despite being only about 5 foot 4 inches tall and very slightly built, was quite happy to fire off a couple of hundred rounds every weekend. One Monday morning he came into the lab proudly clutching his latest purchase, a beautiful 'over and under' handmade Italian 12-bore shotgun. He said that he hadn't fired it yet, but would we like to test fire it and, if it was OK, could he have a go as well? It wasn't okay to let outsiders fire guns in the lab's range, but we knew him very well and we all wanted to try out his gun.

One after the other we fired six or eight rounds into the bullet trap whilst Mike stood there drooling with anticipation. The gun worked like a dream: beautiful crisp trigger pull, nicely balanced and, although it was set up specifically for Mike, it didn't 'bite' the shoulder at all. Eventually this wonderful piece of equipment was handed over to its rightful owner and lovingly he put a round into each chamber, closed the action, took aim and pulled the trigger. There was a huge explosion, and there was Mike sitting on his backside with a severely broken middle finger and a huge bruise on his shoulder. For some unknown reason both barrels had fired together, resulting in tremendous recoil which drove the trigger guard back into his fingers and the stock violently into his shoulder, completely knocking him over.

We just all stood there with mouths agape. What could have gone wrong? We had fired perhaps 30 rounds through the gun and it had worked flawlessly; that was, until Mike picked it up. After getting Mike's hand put into plaster, we meticulously took the gun apart and checked every part, but could find nothing amiss. It was then, very gingerly, taken back to the range for further test firing. Once again nothing, it worked perfectly every time for everyone who tried it.

Mike was not satisfied so back to the factory it went. About two months later it came back with a letter telling him that there was absolutely nothing wrong with it and that they could not understand what had happened. Just to reassure ourselves we took the gun apart again and examined each piece under a microscope but it was, as the factory had said, in perfect condition.

Eventually Mike had his hand taken out of plaster and was ready to, very carefully, try the gun once again. Result: two broken fingers and a broken shoulder blade this time. Two months later the same thing happened again but by this time Mike had had enough and the gun had to go. The new owner had absolutely no problem with the gun and it is still in regular use today. After examining and re-examining the problem the only possible explanation I could come up with was that Mike's 90-pound frame was insufficiently robust for the type of weapon he had purchased, a double-barrelled weapon with a single selective trigger. Normally, double-barrelled weapons would have two triggers, one for each barrel, but in this type of weapon there is only one trigger for both barrels. The gun does have two mechanisms in the normal way but at any one time only one is connected to the trigger, with the other cocked and waiting for the first barrel to be fired. After firing the first barrel, the sharp impact of the recoil engages the second mechanism so that it can also be fired. This does, however, require a sharp impact on the butt to fully engage the second mechanism, something which Mike's light weight was unable to provide. As a result the second mechanism was unable to engage fully with the trigger which allowed the firing pin to strike the primer of the second round firing it almost immediately. Something which Mike found rather disconcerting to say the least!

I experienced something very similar with an old .455 calibre Webley Fosberry revolver which I wanted to test fire for the experience. The Webley Fosberry is an unusual weapon, being one of only a very few self-loading revolvers. In this type of revolver the barrel, cylinder and top half of the frame form a unit, which slides back and forth on the bottom half of the frame. The cylinder has a zig-zag groove around its outside surface which mates with a stud on the frame. On firing, the recoil drives the upper part of the weapon back against a recoil spring, re-cocking the hammer. In so doing the cylinder is turned by the stud riding in its cut-out groove, thus presenting a fresh cartridge to be fired. To prevent the weapon from firing continuously, i.e. fully automatic fire, the weapon is fitted with a disconnector, which stops the weapon from firing again until the trigger is released.

With any self-loading weapon the policy is always to fire it with a single cartridge just in case anything does go wrong. After firing two or three single rounds with absolutely no problem I fully loaded the cylinder, took careful aim and pulled the trigger. There was a huge roar and, the next thing I knew, the gun was pointing at the ceiling with all six rounds having gone off like a sub-machine gun. I checked the man-sized target and there was just one hole where I had been aiming, another was about a foot above the target and the rest formed a line across the ceiling to directly above my head.

I couldn't figure out what had happened as the gun had been working perfectly with only one round loaded. I tried it once again with single rounds and it worked perfectly, but each time I put more than one in, it went fully auto on me. Three other examiners tried it and for two it worked perfectly and for the other it likewise went fully auto. Like the shotgun it must have been something to do with the unconscious resistance of the body to the recoil and I can only assume that I had been holding the gun with an insufficiently rigid arm for the disconnector to work.

An Italian 10.4mm Vetterli Model 1881 rifle had been seized from a would-be firearms collector who, unfortunately, didn't possess a licence. As the seizure had been made outside the Home Counties area, the case was being handled by one of the regional labs and not, I am very pleased to say, the Met Police Lab.

During the examination the bolt was found to be well and truly stuck closed and despite using half a can of 'WD 40' it just wouldn't budge. In desperation, the examiner clamped the rifle in a vice and started to attack the bolt handle with a large mallet, which was probably not the best idea under the circumstances. Crash, crash went the mallet; huge bang and cloud of black powder smoke went the gun; and scream went the section head.

From the carnage it was obvious that the bolt was seized in the closed position due to a round of live ammunition being stuck in the rusty barrel. All the hammering had eventually jarred the firing pin free, which had struck and fired the round of ammunition. The bullet went straight through a wall into the boss's office through the boss's kneecap and out the other side of his office to finally embed itself in a concrete wall on the other side of the building. The boss never walked quite right again. His cycling days were well and truly over and the promotional prospects for a certain young examiner were somewhat thin on the ground.

Whilst giving a series of lectures in the States I was asked if I would like to comment on a tragic – but avoidable – accident which had occurred in one of the local labs where a fully automatic sub-machine gun was being tested in the lab's range. Two major safety rules were ignored: a magazine with 30 rounds was inserted into the gun without prior testing with single rounds; and the firer was the only person in the range.

Holding the gun in one hand the examiner used the other to pull back the bolt and release it, thus cocking the action and loading a live round into the chamber. Immediately the bolt closed, the first round fired, then another, and another without the trigger even being touched. As the firer was only holding the gun with one hand it was completely out of control, and the muzzle started to climb until he shot himself through the bottom of the chin and out through the front of his face. He fell forward on to the gun, which continued to fire until all 30 rounds had been exhausted. The examiner died almost immediately.

What he had not done was check the condition of the firing pin. If he had done so, he would have seen that it had broken off and was lodged in the firing-pin hole. As the bolt was released on to a live round, the firing pin struck the cartridge, firing it without touching the trigger. The gun continued to fire, completely out of control and unstoppable, until the magazine was empty. The problem was obvious: basic rules of safety had not been followed, and it was tragic that someone had to die to make people realise that such rules are there for a reason.

In a case involving a converted brass flare pistol and a hen-pecked husband, the problem with the gun occurred after the crime. This man had been nagged and nagged for years, whatever he did, however hard he tried, nothing was ever right. He had long since stopped going for a beer with his mates down the local pub and his wife was such a dragon that he no longer had any friends of his own. While she became fatter and more slovenly by the day, the house became filthier and filthier as she was too busy watching soaps on the television. With each passing insult the husband became more deranged, until eventually he cracked.

In the attic he found an old First World War one-inch calibre flare pistol which had been brought back from Germany by his father. With care, patience and precision he crafted a bronze barrel that would take a .410 shotgun cartridge and exchanged it for the old one-inch calibre barrel on the flare pistol. Now armed with a .410 calibre single-shot pistol he bided his time and waited for his moment. One Saturday morning this disgusting apparition of a woman was at the top of the stairs berating him for making too much noise with the vacuum cleaner and not being timely enough with her breakfast. He could stand no more, the end of his tether had been well and truly reached and he let her have it with the .410 shot pistol, straight in the centre of her chest. When she came to a rest at the bottom of the stairs he put another round in the same place just to make sure, not that it was necessary, since she had broken her neck on the way down.

There was nothing of significance at the scene as far as I was concerned and the post mortem merely showed us she had a bad case of BO as well as the two shots through her disgustingly large and pendulous breasts. Although post-mortem examinations in general don't have much effect on me, I am not very keen on those carried out on excessively fat people as they have three or four inches of yellow/orange bubbly fat below the skin which is really disgusting. It is a sight which has made me keep slim ever since I first saw a post mortem on a fat person. I just couldn't stand the thought that if I became fat I would be walking round with this revolting material under my skin.

Eventually the gun was delivered to me and I had to test fire it at various distances to check the spread of shot so that I could estimate the range of firing. First, I tested the gun for accidental discharge then measured the pressure required on the trigger to fire it. Being of military origin the action was really well made and it was impossible to make it discharge by jarring. The trigger pressure was found to be 14lbs which was really heavy. Using the same make and type of .410 cartridges as he had been using, I found that the first shot had been at about 15 foot and the second at about one foot which was what we had expected, given the statement by the husband.

The husband had used cartridges which were two inches in length for the shooting, but to cover all stupid questions which might be asked by the defence, I decided to find out what other length .410 cartridges it would fire. The two-inch-long cartridges were fired with no problem as were the two-and-a-half inch. That only left three-inch cartridges. Circumspection is called for with three-inch .410 cartridges, because they generate a terribly high pressure. The barrel was, however, made from thick phosphor bronze so I thought there wouldn't be any problems. How wrong could I have been? On firing the gun there was a huge explosion, the recoil sent my arm way above my head and in the range there was an enormous amount of metallic clattering. When the smoke had cleared, all I was left with in my hand was the gun's grip, the rest of the frame being embedded in the walls and ceiling. The barrel had opened out like a flat sheet of metal and was lying at my feet.

The huge pressure generated by the three-inch cartridge had obviously been far too great and the gun had disintegrated. I was really lucky to get away without losing my life to say nothing of some fingers or my eyesight.

Obviously I had a bit of explaining to do at the trial, but the judge was very understanding, as they generally are. The husband was, obviously, found to be guilty but due to the extenuating circumstances only received four years and was out in under two.

Another experience I had with a First World War gun was when I was sent a .455 Webley revolver which had been found in the possession of an old man who had died of natural causes. There had been nothing suspicious about the case or even the possession of the weapon; returning soldiers were allowed to keep souvenirs of their part in the war. In the Gun Room we did, however, keep all the fired ammunition from unsolved crimes and these had to be compared against all weapons that came into police hands to determine whether there was any connection. This involved firing a couple of rounds into the bullet recovery box and, by using the comparison microscope, comparing them with those fired bullets in the outstanding crime index.

Using ammunition from the Gun Room's supply I fired a couple of rounds into the recovery box and the gun functioned perfectly. Just for the sake of completion, I decided to fire three of the rounds which came with the revolver. I must have had some sort of hunch that something was going to go wrong, for in addition to the normal safety glasses I also put on a full-face shield, something which I very rarely did. I only loaded the gun with three rounds and on the first shot there was an ear-piercing explosion. There was no recoil or smoke, but I was left holding nothing except the grip. My face shield had shattered and my safety glasses were all but destroyed, but once again I did not have a scratch on me.

I had no idea what could have happened, I had carefully checked the cartridges beforehand to make sure they hadn't been tampered with and there was no obstruction in the barrel. There was absolutely no reason for the gun to blow up in the way that it did, especially as I had already fired it several times with ammunition from the laboratory. There just had to be something wrong with the ammunition which came with the gun.

Very carefully I took several rounds apart and found that instead of containing the normal tubular grains of yellowish cordite there was just this black tar-like material inside. It then became obvious what had happened. Cordite is made from a mixture of nitrocellulose into which has been dissolved nitro-glycerine. Nitrocellulose itself is a very stable explosive material which, when set alight, burns with a very hot flame and produces very large volumes of gas. Nitrocellulose is, therefore, an ideal propellant for use in ammunition. Nitro-glycerine, on the other hand, is a highly powerful, highly unstable and very sensitive explosive, and by itself is totally unsuitable for use in ammunition. However, when the nitro-glycerine is dissolved in nitrocellulose it becomes very stable and greatly increases the efficiency of the nitrocellulose as a propellant.

Long storage in the deceased's attic had obviously caused the nitro-glycerine to separate from the mixture and instead of merely igniting on being fired, the nitro-glycerine had detonated, causing the nitrocellulose to detonate as well. The first round had caused the second and third rounds to sympathetically detonate, completely destroying the gun in the process. Once again I was lucky to get away without being severely maimed.

CHAPTER 10

THE
TAXIDERMIST'S
GIRLFRIEND
AND THE OLD
GOLFER

The vast majority of cases I was dealing with in the Met Lab involved shotguns of one sort or another. I suppose one of the main reasons for this was the fact that at that time shotgun ownership was, unless you had a serious criminal record or had been declared legally insane, virtually a right. Once you had a shotgun certificate you could own as many guns as you wanted and keep as much ammunition as you could store without records being kept. This ease of access led to their use in virtually every major robbery in the UK. With a shortened barrel for portability, the 12-bore shotgun is probably the most formidable short-range weapon one can carry.

Contrary to popular belief, shortening the barrel does not lead to a huge spread of shot; in fact, there is not a lot of difference in the shot spread at any given range between an unchoked full-length barrel and one that has been shortened. The only difference is the reduced velocity of the shot from a shorter barrel and a vast increase in the noise, muzzle flash and recoil felt by the firer.

In many of the crime scenes I visited it was obvious that the criminals had removed the shot from the first cartridge to be fired and replaced it with rock salt or sometimes rice. At ranges of two or three feet this can still be lethal, but the intention was obviously for the first shot to be a warning shot and the second, which contained the full complement of lead shot, to be for real.

On several occasions I dealt with cases where people had, however, been shot and killed with these cartridges loaded with rock salt. All the fatal shots were, of course, very close range, as salt is much less dense than lead and consequently has almost no 'carrying power'. The wounds at that range were indistinguishable from those caused by a normal 12-bore shotgun at close range, being almost perfectly circular and about 0.8 in diameter. The wads were likewise always located in the wound, but never with a penetration of more than three or four inches. Generally that was where any similarity ended. Because the salt was very low in density, it was easily deflected by the tissue and bone, and because it was highly soluble it soon dissolved in the huge amount of blood which rushed out of the hole. On the first occasion that I saw such a wound I was baffled, but they soon became easily identifiable. However, despite having examined literally thousands of bullet and pellet wounds I have never had a case involving the mythical ice bullet of many movies and crime novels. I am sure that if you kept the gun in the freezer and were very quick to load and fire the weapon it would be possible, but it is stretching credibility a little far.

One case I dealt with involved the suicide of a police officer who was found dead on his bed holding a single-barrelled 9mm calibre shotgun. On examining the body I could not find any evidence of a wound but nonetheless he was, very clearly, dead. There was also a recently fired shotgun cartridge case in the gun's chamber. It wasn't until we had him X-rayed that we found the shot pellets in his brain cavity, but how did they get there? After some searching and poking around the corpse, it became clear that he had pushed the barrel up his nose and fired the shot. The shot had gone through the sinal cavity and into the brain, very much like the pig. Apart from a very slight reddening of one nostril there was nothing to indicate that this had been the site of the discharge.

Another police suicide, also using a shotgun, occurred in the Camden Town section house for single officers. The gun was a single-barrelled .410 calibre bolt-action weapon without a magazine. The officer had placed the gun in his mouth and pulled the trigger, assuming that it was all going to be over very quickly. The pellets shredded his tongue, took out the back of his throat and merely passed out of the back of his neck missing his spine and anything really vital.

I have no doubt that he would have eventually died from his wounds, but he was still alive and obviously in terrible pain and now wanted it to end as quickly as possible. But, to proceed further he had to open the bolt action, take out the empty cartridge, retrieve another round from his chest of drawers and reload the gun. This time, just to make completely sure, he pointed the muzzle of the gun up to the roof of his mouth and killed himself instantly.

It was a lovely Sunday afternoon, the birds were singing, there was not a cloud in a brilliant blue sky and the garden was pleading for my presence. I drew a pint of homemade beer which had spent the past month maturing in a pressurised barrel, up from my cellar, got out the papers and readied myself for an afternoon's dozing in the sun. Just as I was about to sink into the sun lounger the telephone rang with that shrill note that says 'you are wanted at a murder scene'.

The officer in charge of the case explained to me that there had been a domestic argument at the house of a rather well-off builder and he had shot his wife in the chest with a 12-bore shotgun. With a quick request to make sure that the body was not moved until I had a chance to examine the scene, I was off to a rather nice part of Essex which, being on the other side of London to me, was the best part of an hour-and-a-half's drive away.

There was nothing particularly startling about the house, other than it had about seven bedrooms, a couple of acres of lawn and an indoor swimming pool. The pool itself intrigued me; it was designed with a variable lengthways flow system. If you set the flow rate correctly you could swim for hours without moving an inch.

Inside the house it was clear that the wife had been shot while in the main first floor bedroom and had staggered downstairs, managing to reach the telephone in the hall before she died. There were huge quantities of blood on the bedroom floor, up the walls, out on to the landing and down the stairs to the front door where the base of the telephone was on a small table. She still had hold of the handset; she had obviously been trying to call for help.

The body had an entry hole in the upper centre of the chest caused by a close-range shot from a 12-bore shotgun. The pellets and wads had passed through the sternum, then on to completely destroy the aorta, which had caused the massive bleeding. The shotgun, which was on the floor in the bedroom, was an extremely high-quality handmade Italian double-barrelled side-lock weapon worth thousands of pounds. I opened the action and found one live and one fired round inside. During interview the husband had said he only got the weapon a few weeks before and had not yet tried it out. What had happened was a complete accident; he didn't know it was loaded.

Eventually the exhibits were submitted to the office and most of the examination was fairly straightforward. Range estimations showed that she was about four feet away from the muzzle when the shot was fired. At that range there could, therefore, be no possibility of a struggle for the weapon. An examination of the internal surfaces of the barrels showed that the right barrel had been recently fired and that the left barrel was clean. Next were the tests to determine the pressure required on the triggers to fire the weapon. Five-and-a-half pounds right, three and a half pounds left. Just about right. I usually take two or three readings and then take an average, so I tried again, four and half pounds right, two and a half pounds left; bit of a difference there and on the borders of acceptability, so better just try once more. Three pounds right and one pound left. Now this wasn't correct at all. I quickly took the locks off and the problem was immediately obvious. The bents had not been hardened during manufacture and the soft metal was simply wearing away with each shot. I had to fire the gun for comparison purposes, so I carefully refitted the locks and, even more carefully, fired the gun, loading each barrel individually. After that last firing the bents had worn away completely and the gun couldn't even be cocked.

The defence, naturally, played on the fact that the gun's mechanism was faulty and stated that it would be inappropriate to continue with the case when there was no way of proving conclusively that the gun could not have gone off accidentally. My argument was that the gun's mechanism was operational when I received it and that the trigger pulls were acceptable. It was undeniable that the mechanism deteriorated during my testing, but everything suggested that there was no fault which could have made it discharge accidentally at the relevant time. The judge decided that there was an element of doubt and that it would be unwise to proceed further. The husband was, therefore, acquitted on the charge of murder.

The next time I was called to a murder scene in Essex, I wanted nothing other than to be at home because rain was lashing down, it was blowing a gale and, with the temperature just above freezing, it was one of those days fit for nothing apart from staying in, in front of the fire. But, it was a Thursday and like almost every other Thursday in the year I was at work.

Everything about the case was strange, starting with the cottage where the shooting occurred. The whole place appeared to lean to one side with not a straight line or 90° angle anywhere. Located deep in an ancient wood, with bare branches howling in the wind it was like something straight out of a Grimm fairytale, and very spooky. The owner, the aggrieved party, was an amateur taxidermist and the whole bungalow was full of his creations. Owls, herons, crows and even hens were on every step of the stairs; badgers, foxes, weasels, stoats and otters languished on every flat surface; and fish of every type imaginable were in frames all around the walls. On the kitchen table was another creation in the making, its innards slowly drying in the centrally heated room, while glass eyes, bottles of various preservatives and packing materials stood by ready for use.

It appeared that there had been some type of domestic dispute between the taxidermist and the lodger over his live-in girlfriend. It seemed that the two were sharing her favours, but both wanted them permanently, although heaven knows why as she was one of the most disgusting women I have ever laid eyes on. Perhaps she had hidden talents, but she must have kept them well secreted for they were not at all obvious to me. The taxidermist had come home the previous night, somewhat the worse for alcoholic wear and found the lodger in bed with 'his' girlfriend. At this he flew into a rage, picked up his shotgun and threatened to kill them both. The lodger fled down the stairs, hotly pursued by the taxidermist who loosed off a couple of shots on the way. The lodger was on his knees begging for mercy as the taxidermist put a round through the TV set about two inches from his ear, which must have been exciting. For some unknown reason, the taxidermist then decided that the lodger should defecate in a corner of the living room. After what had happened up to that point I shouldn't think he required any persuasion and, although I must add at this point that I am not any sort of expert on the subject, he deposited in the appointed place the most enormous turd one could ever imagine.

At this point it would seem that the lodger ran out of patience and, after pulling up his trousers, wrested the gun away from the taxidermist. The tables were now well and truly turned, with the lodger chasing the taxidermist round the house winging shots past his ear. At one point the fridge was considered to be some sort of threat and it duly received a fatal shot through the door. As the taxidermist attempted to enter the kitchen through a waist-high swing door to tend to his fatally wounded fridge, the lodger fired through the door hitting the taxidermist in the leg. With all the splinters of wood from the door having entered his leg the wound was quite massive and he was slowly bleeding to death. Realising what he had done, the lodger dropped the gun and fled the scene only pausing to call an ambulance on his way out. The taxidermist obviously thought that his end was near and, rather than attempt to stop the bleeding, decided to shoot each of his stuffed animals in turn.

The ambulance men luckily arrived in the nick of time and managed to save his life despite the quantity of blood he had lost. After the insertion of drips he was unceremoniously carted off to hospital for some major repair work on what remained of his leg.

I arrived at the scene soon after they had left to find bird feathers and pieces of stuffed animal everywhere, shotgun patterns on virtually everything and a severely dead fridge. The taxidermist had lost a terrible amount of blood, but most of it had congealed into a huge lump of what looked like liver which was lying by the half-door to the kitchen. There was not really that much for me to do apart from count the number of shots, and try to determine from where and at what range they had been fired. The most important shot was, naturally, the one through the door, which had been fired at a muzzle-to-door range of no more than six inches.

The detective in charge asked whether I wanted to see the wound, which I thought might have been quite interesting if it hadn't been repaired by surgery. I did, however, go along just to see how they had stitched up such a big hole. After a bit of a drive we duly arrived at the hospital and I was shown into an operating theatre. Bit strange, I thought, as he had supposedly already been put back together and was in the recovery ward. The detective insisted otherwise and said that we should wait. After about 10 minutes a doctor brought in a parcel about three feet long, wrapped in white sheeting. Even more strange, I thought, until I undid the sheeting to find a very warm and newly amputated leg. Believe me that was really, really gross and something I never want to experience again.

The way the leg was lying with the outside uppermost I couldn't understand why it had been amputated. There was only a one-inch-diameter hole visible and little other obvious damage other than where some wood had been driven into the skin. It wasn't until I turned the leg over (the thought of it being warm still makes me shudder) that I could see why. The whole inside surface of the upper thigh was missing, including a two-inch section of bone. There was no way in this world that the surgeons were going to be able to repair that sort of damage. My job ended with a short report on the number of shots which had been fired and the range of firing between the shotgun and door. As for the lodger, he disappeared and was never seen again.

Arms Licensing Department sent in a request for the examination of a gun that a retired major had 'invented'. The gun in question was an old Second World War flare pistol, which he had converted to fire golf balls with the aid of the large blank cartridges used for driving hardened steel nails into concrete. The major was of the opinion that this was a sporting device and hence did not require a licence.

The conversion was quite good, with the barrel containing a steel sleeve of the correct diameter for the golf ball and with the breech end tapered down to accept the .38 calibre industrial nail-driving cartridges. The invention was intended for use by those with a passion for golf who were too old and infirm to swing a club. The elderly golfer simply inserted the correct-strength nail-gun cartridge (they generally come in four strengths depending upon the material the nail is being driven into) behind the golf ball, selected the correct elevation and fired. The golf cart would then be driven to where the ball lay, at which point the process was repeated until the pin was reached. I never did find out exactly what was supposed to happen once the ball was on the green, but I assume that the 'golfer' would have the ability to swing a putter at that stage of the game.

We tested the device at a golf range and it was really good fun propelling these balls with a huge bang and cloud of smoke way up into the air and down the fairway. The balls suffered quite a bit, being blackened and burnt in the process and the other golfers on the course were not at all amused, complaining of being put off their stroke. I think we spent a couple of days playing with this device and with a bit of practice we were getting very respectable scores without, I might add, the added complexity of having to putt for the hole.

In the end we had to refuse the major his request for exempting these from the necessity of licensing, as they were truly lethal. Anything which can propel a golf ball 300 yards has got to have the capability of being a lethal weapon and could not under any circumstances be freely available to all and sundry.

Early one Sunday morning I received a call to say that there had been a 'domestic' with a 12-bore shotgun and they required my assistance to find out what had actually happened and to unload the gun. As it was only about an hour's drive from where I lived I was soon at the scene and receiving an update from the officer in charge of the case.

According to the officer, the husband had been a bit of a wife-beater and had already been to Magistrates' Court on one charge of injuring his wife. The case was eventually dropped as the wife, who just happened to have a black eye from 'falling down the stairs', had refused to give evidence against him. It seemed that she had been having an affair with another man which, when the husband found out, sent him into a frenzy. This time he was beside himself with fury and started to punch her into a pulp. She then retaliated by attacking his manhood, telling him he was very small and that her lover did it much better. Naturally, this did absolutely nothing for his frame of mind and he picked up the first thing that came to hand, his loaded shotgun, and shot her in the face. The son, who was somewhat retarded and hugely strong, wrested the gun from his father and nearly battered him to death with it.

My examination of the scene showed that she had been frying eggs in the kitchen at the time she was shot and that the blast had obviously caught her in the jaw. There were bits of cheek, teeth and jawbone either embedded in or stuck to the wall, and blood was splattered everywhere. The really gruesome bit about the scene was that there in the frying pan, neatly being done to a crisp, lay most of her tongue and a piece of gum with a couple of teeth still attached.

Some of the shot pattern had obviously missed her face and the range from muzzle to wall was only about three feet which, when taking into account the width of the cooker, meant that she must have been no more than a foot away from the muzzle of the gun when the shot was fired.

As I was examining the bits and pieces embedded in the wall, this man in a grey suit started to pick up the pieces of bone and put them into a polythene bag. I was concerned to preserve the scene and asked him what the hell he was doing removing evidence. He replied that he was the county orthodontic specialist and was collecting as many bone and skin fragments as he could, to reconstruct the woman's face. I was convinced from the damage that she must be dead, but he assured me not and said that as every minute was vital he had to get on with his work.

Before I left the scene I was asked to ensure that the gun was safe, as only one shot had been fired and it was a double-barrelled shotgun. The son had, however, done a serious bit of damage to his father, as the stock had been shattered to matchwood, the action was completely mangled and the barrels were bent like a banana. In the end I discovered that the second barrel was still loaded, and very gingerly transported the gun back to the lab where I had to cut the gun in two to get the live round out.

A couple of weeks later I was asked by the officer in charge of the case if I would like to go along and see for myself the damage to the wife's face. She was still in a lot of pain and her face was swollen up like a balloon and surrounded by a framework of iron rods, bars, nut, bolts and screws. She couldn't speak, she could only nod her head, and I thought that was all she was ever going to do. Six months later, however, I went to see her again, this time in her new house, and I was truly amazed at what this doctor had achieved. Her face was still badly scarred, but her jaw was back in one piece, many of her own teeth had been put back in place and, although she was a bit difficult to understand, she could talk.

Eventually when the husband got out of hospital and was taken to court, he was charged with attempted murder, found guilty and sentenced to 15 years.

CHAPTER 11

THE MYSTERY MISSILE, SPIKE MILLIGAN AND KING ARTHUR

It was one of those typically English winter mornings: a few degrees above freezing, grey leaden skies, a stiff wind which chills to the bone, and although it was not raining there was a constant drizzle which defeated any rain protection ever invented. I had just walked from the tube station along the Embankment to work and was wet through, freezing cold and truly miserable. All I wanted to do was sit at my desk and read the paper until I warmed up. But no chance: as soon as I sat down, the phone rang with an urgent request for my assistance at a safe breaking, where some sort of military cannon might have been used. 'What?' I said. 'You must be joking.' The officer was adamant that it must have been a tank or something equally huge and that I should come as soon as possible.

The scene was located in a depressing office block in a run-down light industrial estate on the outskirts of a new town in Essex. It took me ages to find, as it formed part of a really seedy council estate, the inmates of which were, if not openly hostile, then far less than communicative. The industrial estate itself was separated from the residential area by a double razor-wire fence, which looked like something out of a concentration camp. All it really needed to complete the scene was a few uniformed men in jackboots holding snarling dogs on chain leashes.

Eventually I found the officer in charge, who was a detective constable (DPC) who led me to the scene, located in the general office on one side of the building. Despite the urgency and supposed importance of the case, the DPC had just a single PC as his back-up man. Apart from these two there was no one else in the whole building; all the staff had been denied access and were told to go home for the day. The safe itself was quite substantial for such a location and I was curious to find out what was felt to be so precious that it required such security. The safe itself was bolted to a brick wall, forming the partition between the general office and the typing pool.

Normally, safes are broken into either by drilling, using explosives or being squeezed open with steel cables and hydraulic jacks. The (unsuccessful) attempt in this case had been made by firing a huge missile at it, something I had never seen before nor have I since. The front panel of the safe's door was a quarter-of-an-inch thick and there was a hole in this which was over an inch-and-a-half in diameter. The sides of the hole were very smooth and there was some back flow of metal out of the hole, indicating a very high-velocity projectile. The amount of energy required to cause such a hole must have been truly enormous, but it wasn't until I shone a torch inside the hole that I began to appreciate its full power. The missile had not only gone through the front panel of the door, but through the back panel as well, and from there through the inside rear of the safe then out through the back of the safe. This amounted to a total of nearly an inch of high-quality safe steel. The missile hadn't, however, stopped there. It had smashed a two-inch-diameter hole in the brick wall behind the safe, demolished four wooden and two steel desks, passed through the brick wall at the other end of the room and through two stud walls. It was finally stopped by a reinforced concrete wall on the other side of the building but not before making a crater five inches in diameter and three inches deep.

The missile was not quite like any bullet from a cannon shell that I had ever seen before and was manufactured from a solid piece of extremely hard tungsten steel. It was over four-and-a-half inches in length, of a truncated cone design and with two strips of copper near the base to take up the rifling. Despite all the damage it had caused, the missile only had a few scratches on one side of the nose.

I searched the room where the missile must have been fired from but there was nothing: no signs of a heavy weapon having been fired either on the floor or on a desk. There were no obvious scorch marks from a muzzle break or any signs of discharge residue or gun smoke. The weapon itself must have made a huge noise when fired, but enquiries with the local residents turned up not one report of an unusual sound over the whole of the weekend. The whole case was a complete mystery. Nobody had heard even the slightest noise nor seen anything suspicious. The missile could not be identified despite being shown to some of the most knowledgeable armaments people in the UK and to this day there has never been an arrest.

Another surreal case that will forever stick in my mind concerned Spike Milligan, the famous member of the Goons. *The Goon Show* was at its peak in the early 70s, and even then the press hounded personalities, sitting outside their houses, climbing trees and drilling holes in their fences in the hope of catching them in some compromising position. Spike came in for particularly harsh treatment, with the press actually making a tented camp in a tree overlooking his garden.

He tried every legal method possible, but the Press Commission didn't exist and the police and courts were powerless to place any injunction on their activities. Eventually he snapped, as anyone would, and started to take pot shots at these reporters with a .22 calibre BSA air rifle. He was quite a good shot and each pellet was aimed to just miss. That did the trick for a while and they left him alone, but not for long. Within a week they were back again, camping out in the trees, but this time he'd had enough. As one reporter was sitting astride his fence trying to get photographs of the bedroom through a crack in the curtains, he crept to the other end of the garden, took careful aim and shot the reporter right in the centre of his left buttock.

That definitely did the trick, and although they never came back again, the comedian was charged with 'wounding with intent to endanger life'. The pellet had penetrated a good two inches into this man's backside and had to be taken out under a general anaesthetic. By all accounts he was unable to sit down for nearly two months.

My job was fairly simple: test the air rifle to make sure it was in good working order; test the pressure required on the trigger to ensure that it wasn't so light that it could have gone off inadvertently; make sure that it wasn't prone to accidental discharge by jarring; and measure the velocity and kinetic energy of the pellets fired from it. I then had to carry out a microscopic comparison between pellets fired from the gun and the one recovered from the reporter just to make sure that it had been fired from that gun. Everything tied up nicely: acceptable trigger pressure, not prone to accidental discharge, powerful enough to cause the injury at the range stated and the pellet had been fired from that gun. All that was needed now was a simple visit to the court to explain my findings.

My evidence was simple, with no awkward questions, but I thought I'd stay and see what the defendant had to say. I'd always thought he was a brilliant comedian but within minutes the court was in uproar. Absolutely everyone was howling with laughter: the magistrate, prosecution and defence counsel, the court reporters, even the reporter who had been shot. Everyone was in stitches, with tears running down their faces. Eventually, although he was beside himself, the magistrate had to try and restore some semblance of order to the proceedings. Spike was, of course, found guilty, but everyone had so much sympathy with him for what he had been putting up with, it was no surprise when the magistrate let him off with a warning and had the gun confiscated. In fact, the magistrate saved his biggest dressing down for the injured reporter and told him that, if he was ever brought to his court for a similar harassment charge, he would be sent down for a custodial sentence. The whole court applauded him.

There was another unusual case involving a celebrity, this time from history. Normally, the director of the laboratory tended to leave members of the firearms laboratory alone, but one morning I received a most unusual call from him concerning a table at Winchester Castle in Hampshire. It seemed that the table top in question had been hanging on the wall at one end of the Great Hall for longer than anyone could remember and, when they took it down for restoration, what should they find but a couple of dozen bullet holes? The table was not just any old table but a circular one reported to be that belonging to none other than King Arthur. Could I go down and find out who had been taking pot shots at it? I didn't need asking twice.

I had never seen this table top before and was amazed at its size: it must have been nearly 20 foot in diameter and at least 18 inches thick. It was also a couple of tons in weight and getting it down from the wall was a major undertaking in itself, involving a special mobile crane with a jib thin enough to fit through a tiny window above the table. After lifting it from its holding brackets on the wall, the crane had set the table in an upright position on a large gantry made from scaffolding. This enabled every piece of the table to be examined in comfort. It was discovered that despite being made from oak, the top of the table was in quite bad shape: the result of years and years of bird droppings and rain blowing through the small window above where it had hung for so long.

When I arrived, there were people all over the table taking small borings, removing flakes of paint and carefully drawing the supporting structure, which, I was told, was unique. The front of the table had obviously been repainted since it had been shot, because the front, despite being extremely grubby, contained no visible bullet holes. The back was, however, a different story: I located at least a dozen bullet exit holes. Some of these were still open; others had been plugged with corks, which, I was later told, were sack bottle corks. By using low-angle, oblique lighting I was able to find the entry holes on the front of the table to correspond with the exit holes on the back, together with another eight entry holes. That being so, I concluded, eight bullets must still be somewhere inside the table.

Having the table X-rayed was a little difficult, but eventually I had a series of negatives showing me not only the location of the missiles, but their shape and size, together with the trajectory through the table. All the bullets still in the table had struck heavy supporting beams on the underside of the table and had lodged there. I tried to obtain permission to remove at least one bullet, but they said that the table could not, under any circumstance, be damaged. How was I to identify the age of the missiles without removing one?

It was known that Henry VIII had the table repainted sometime in 1530, but it was obvious from the slight difference in coloration of the paint that the sack corks had been put in at a later date and painted over. Sack, a form of sherry, was quite popular in England by the accession of Queen Elizabeth I in 1558, but the design of the corks suggested some time after that. The shape and size of the missiles were quite telling, however, as they were obviously not cast, but were very rough and irregular and about three-quarters to one inch in diameter. That would suggest a very early type of military weapon dating from around 1600. A look through the history of the castle showed that it was first captured from the Royalists by Cromwellian forces in 1646 and held by them until England returned to the Royalists in 1660. This period would have fitted in very well with the type of weapon used to fire at the table.

As to the trajectory, measurements showed that the majority of the shots had been fired from approximately the same angle, indicating just one person, or several people standing in the same spot, doing the firing. Could it have been that the head of the occupying forces, possibly even Cromwell himself, enjoyed some after-dinner entertainment with a little target practise from the head of the dining table?

As far as the age of the table went, the first mention of it was in Robert Wace's *Roman de Brut* (1155), which stated that Arthur seated his knights at a round table. Historically, though, it was not mentioned until the fifteenth century, but it was apparently not new then. Tempting though it was to conclude that the table was the legendary Arthur's, the science of determining the age of wood by its rings, dendrochronology, showed that it could not have been made before the fourteenth century. An interesting bit of detective work and a very welcome change from all the blood and gore of normal casework.

Professor Martin Biddle, who organised the scientific investigation of the table, wrote a fascinating book on the subject called *King Arthur's Round Table*. My work on the table was included as a chapter.

CHAPTER 12

BANK JOBS
AND BANDIT-PROOF
GLASS

Over the years I have had much to do with the testing and development of security and counter systems for banks and building societies. Usually it amounted to no more than testing their 'bandit-proof' glass or door locks for their ability to stand up to close-range shotgun and pistol fire, but at one stage I was also involved in the design and installation of video surveillance cameras.

The cameras being used in those days were huge great things with low resolution and little in the way of reliability. Trying to identify a person or the gun he was holding from the out-of-focus, grainy picture was next to impossible and in most institutions the cameras were either permanently switched off or just dummy camera casings.

In an attempt to obtain a little more information from those actually being used, many of them were fitted with directional microphones in the hope that an accent or even a voice print could be obtained. They were next to useless: the microphone was usually pointing in the wrong direction or the background noise was so great it was impossible to hear anything at all. There was, however, one notable exception which I came across while reviewing a tape recording of a bank robbery in Brixton, south London. The officer in charge of the case wanted me to identify the gun being used to see if the MO could be linked up with any other recent cases in the area.

For once the picture was in focus and not too grainy, and the voice recording was clear enough to hear the voices of the individual customers talking to the tellers. In walked the lone perpetrator, shotgun in hand and with a stocking pulled over his head, completely obscuring his features. Identifying the gun was no problem: it was a 12-bore side-by-side shotgun, the barrels of which had been sawn off to a length of about 14 inches. There was nothing terribly significant about that, as virtually every robbery at that time involved a sawn-off shotgun.

Looking closely at the recording it was obvious that this was not a very experienced robber: the gun was visibly shaking in his hands. Taking a deep breath to try and calm his nerves he strode up to the nearest teller and in a loud and very West African accent said: 'Hey, man, hold up your stick, this is a fuck-up!' Despite the seriousness of the situation the teller burst out laughing as did the rest of the staff and all the customers, completely and utterly destroying any sense of purpose that the would-be robber retained. With a cry of despair he turned on his heel and fled from the bank empty-handed.

As far as I know the would-be robber was never caught, but the bank manager had a plaque made for the teller with the immortal words 'Hand up your stick, this is a fuck-up!'

The last major case I did for the Metropolitan Police Laboratory, although at the time I didn't know it would be the last, involved an armed bank robbery and murder in Ealing.

Late one afternoon, just before closing time, a man walked into the bank carrying a small paper sack and sat down at one of the tables, ostensibly filling in some forms. When the bank was free of customers he went to the door put up the 'Bank Closed' sign and pulled out of the sack a sawn-off 12-bore shotgun.

Very coolly he told the staff not to panic or push the silent alarm, and said that if they all did as they were instructed nobody would get hurt. Handing the sack to one of the tellers, he instructed her to fill it up with notes from all the tellers' tills. When that was done he said thank you to each of the tellers and then, as he left, turned and shot the first girl he'd spoken to through the 'bandit-proof' counter glass. He then walked out into the street and disappeared.

I went to the mortuary to examine the girl and she was in an awful mess. While most of the pellets from the cartridge had been stopped by the glass, the tremendous impact of the shot had caused the glass to spall off the rear face with such force that most of it had been driven deep into her body. Her face and upper body were cut to ribbons and the larger shards had done tremendous damage to her vital organs, killing her within a very short time.

My examination of the glass showed that it was of a type common at that time: a glass/plastic/glass laminate. While this would stop most attacks with hammers and axes, and was not prone to scratching in everyday use, a high-velocity impact would cause such a transfer of energy through the laminate that glass shards would be thrown off the back face with tremendous force. Today, with the advent of scratchproof plastics, this would not happen as there is always a plastic layer on the teller side of the glass to prevent such spalling.

The BBC produced a documentary on the case and a huge amount of high-speed film was taken of me shooting pieces of glass similar to that in the bank with a sawn-off 12-bore shotgun. As far as I am aware nobody was ever arrested for the case and it remains unsolved to this day.

Another case involved a teller and the shooting of 'bandit-proof' glass at a bank. That one, however, had a happier ending. This bank teller was an avid .22 calibre target shooter who used to practise his sport every evening at the local club. While not a brilliant shot, he was in the local county team and had won a lot of medals in his time. He also owned a very expensive target weapon with lots of fancy attachments.

The UK legislation on the possession of such recreational weapons was, even in those days, quite strict. Transport between the shooting venue and the owner's home was allowed but the weapon was not to be kept loaded during transportation or while stored. Our bank teller, however, believed that one day someone would try to rob 'his' bank and he would be ready for them. To this end he carried his loaded weapon to and from work in a shoulder holster, 'just in case', and while he was at work it lived in his teller's drawer alongside the £20 and £10 notes.

And then, one day, his day came. In walked a robber with a stocking mask over his face and a cheap Spanish .32 calibre revolver in his hand. Up he walked to our target-shooting teller's window and proceeded to tell him that if he didn't keep quiet and fill up the proffered bag with money he would shoot him. Nirvana. All his Christmases had come at once. Out from the drawer came the gun and with a 'make my day' he proceeded to empty his gun at the robber. Shocked at first, the robber soon responded and started to fire back: bang, crash, gun smoke everywhere and empty cartridge cases ricocheting around the room. The teller's gun was soon empty and in went a fresh magazine as quick as a flash, and firing continued. Then the robber's gun ran out of bullets, but he had another, equally cheap, .32 revolver which he pulled from his waistband and continued to fire in the general direction of the teller.

Suddenly it was all over, and when the smoke cleared Mr Teller and the robber were the only two left standing; everyone else had dived for cover. Neither of them had a scratch on them. On the robber's side of the glass screen lay a pile of very flat .32 lead bullets and on the teller's side an even larger pile of equally flat .22 bullets.

The 'bandit-proof' glass had just been too good: all it had to show was a few lead smears.

The robber was arrested on the spot and put away for a long time, while the teller, far from being hailed as the hero he felt himself to be, lost his job and was banned from holding a firearms certificate forever.

By that stage my work at the Metropolitan Police Laboratory was telling on my body. The recoil from firing 15 or 20 rounds from sawn-off 12-bore shotguns virtually every day was wrecking the joints in my shoulder, elbows and wrists. Despite wearing double-padded earmuffs, the huge noise produced by these weapons was slowly destroying my hearing as the sound was being transmitted through the bones of my face and teeth to my inner ears. As a result, I suffered from constant tinnitus and the quarterly hospital checks showed an alarming deterioration in my high-frequency hearing. My blood-lead concentration was also reaching dangerous levels from firing so many rounds in confined spaces and I was worried about what permanent damage the accumulation of so much lead in my bones was doing to me. Was it time, no matter how much I enjoyed the job, to consider a move?

About a year before the Ealing case I had attended an interview for promotion, but was told that despite being the only person available and qualified for the vacant position my interview was not sufficiently good for me to be promoted. I was not happy: the train fare from Kent to London was becoming prohibitively expensive and the additional money from the promotion would have helped considerably. The lab had also moved to new premises in Lambeth and my journey time had increased from one-and-a-half hours each way to over two hours. I was getting pretty fed up with the travelling, the low salary and the huge workload. It was then that I saw an advertisement in the *Telegraph* for the position of forensic firearms examiner in the Royal Hong Kong Police Force. Nearly three times the salary; almost no tax; accommodation provided; how could I not apply?

Barbara was not at all impressed. She didn't want to go out to 'some foreign country where they don't speak English and I don't know anybody', but I was adamant. The interview was strange to say the least. Present were two, quite senior, Hong Kong police officers telling me that everything I liked doing in England would be impossible in Hong Kong and that I would find the heat and humidity unbearable. The third member of the board was a long-retired forensic firearms examiner from somewhere up north who asked me absolutely stupid questions. He was also as deaf as a post and couldn't hear a word anyone said, so having him on the board was a complete waste of time. Equally annoying was his insistence on calling me Mr King. He was, however, so deaf that no matter how many times I and the board told him that my name was not King but Heard, he continued to call me King.

I must have said something right; on the grapevine the word was that they wanted me urgently and were prepared to pay the top salary. All I had to do was wait for the formal offer to arrive in the post. Weeks went by, then months, but still no reply. In the meantime Barbara discovered that she was pregnant with our second child and, as the travelling was really getting me down, a move back to London was the only option. After much searching we finally found a house that suited our needs and was situated close to the Cockfosters end of the Piccadilly line. I could now be in at work within 30 minutes of leaving home, a great improvement on the previous two hours or more.

Word had obviously got round the laboratory that I had had an interview for the Hong Kong job and that I was expected to leave at any time. Eventually I was summonsed by the director of the laboratory to talk about the matter. I was told that my promotion was virtually secured, if I withdrew my application for Hong Kong. Barbara, now living very close to her mother, was more adamant than ever that she wanted to stay in England. So, with the promise of a promotion in the pipeline, I withdrew my application for Hong

Kong. After waiting five months for the results of the Hong Kong interview to come through, seven days after sending the letter withdrawing my application, the offer arrived in the post.

The day of the promotion interview came and the director, who was chairman of the board, slipped me a sly wink as I walked in. It went like clockwork. I had really prepared well, could answer all the questions fully and confidently and the half-dozen or so mock interviews which senior colleagues had set up for me really helped. I walked out of the room with a spring in my step, especially as the director gave me that knowing smile which said 'a good job done'. I had no fears and no worries. I was completely confident that I had passed.

Seven weeks later the director called me into his office for the result of the interview board and once again I can quote verbatim his words: 'Brian, that was a fantastic interview. If you had done the same last year you would have passed with flying colours and would now have been in the senior position for a whole year. Unfortunately, it was not good enough this year and you failed.' I was dumbstruck, lost for words and could feel the colour draining from my face. Fortunately, the Hong Kong office had been in touch with me the week before and sent me a letter asking if I would reconsider my withdrawal as they still wanted me to work there. So, after regaining my composure, I said the only thing I could: 'My letter of resignation will be on your desk within the hour.' Now who was dumbstruck?

Although Barbara was not without her reservations, she knew what terrible pressure I was under and about the low salary and bitter disappointment of not getting the promotion. So, after spending Christmas and New Year with family and friends, on Friday, 13 January 1977, we left in a blinding snowstorm for Hong Kong.

CHAPTER 13

THE MYSTERIOUS FAR EAST

At first, my job charter seemed quite reasonable and was to involve something I was not only quite good at but also looked forward to doing. Basically the Royal Hong Kong Police wanted me to train two officers who had been recruited from the general stream of the Criminal Investigation Department (CID), and to modernise the Ballistics Office (as it was then called). I was also to share the existing casework with the other ballistics officer who was already working in the bureau.

Unfortunately, it was not as easy as it sounded. The two recruits appeared to me to have little interest in the job, and had not had the benefit of an academic background. The office was a complete shambles, the few pieces of equipment that existed were 40 or more years out of date, rusty and with optics so mouldy they were useless. To top it all, the other officer, who had been running the office for the past three years, seemed to be uncomfortable with my presence which did not make my life any easier. As if that wasn't enough, there wasn't a penny available to carry out even the most basic updating that was so urgently required.

I don't think I have ever seen such an unprofessionally run office in my life. There was absolutely no filing system, a complete lack of proper exhibit-handling procedure, no attempt at exhibit continuity and the most antiquated and useless equipment I had ever encountered. Case notes and scene examinations were merely noted in a stenographer's pad; case exhibits were chucked into a large heap on the floor awaiting examination; and reports were thrown haphazardly into a filing cabinet.

A couple of days after arriving I was informed by the other examiner that he hadn't been on leave for nearly three years and was stopping work immediately and, after a three months' run-down (whatever that was), he would be taking six months' leave. I would now be doing the job of four examiners instead of merely three. So, for the next nine months I was on permanent 24-hour call for any incident which might arise.

The force had, unfortunately, become used to the ballistics officer turning out to every case imaginable and in my first week I was called out, at night, no less than 15 times. Not one of these call-outs could be considered worthy of a case file number, let alone a call-out: empty cartridge cases found in a rubbish bin, plastic toy guns, ball bearings found in the gutter, strips of caps for a toy cap-gun and so it went on. As well as being run ragged, turning out all over the colony at night, the same happened during the day. If that wasn't bad enough, every gun which did come in had to be entered into an arms receipt book, an arms ledger, an arms examination book and an arms log. After that lot, small card files had to be filled out: one for the gun's serial number, one for its police number (if it was a police weapon), one for its case number and one for the police case number. Each of these card indexes was cross-referenced, producing a huge, completely useless database. That was one of the first things to go. I then set about putting a number of what were, for evidential purposes, vital systems into place. These included such basics as a chronological system for filing and numbering cases, a case-management system whereby the progress of any case investigation could be tracked, an exhibit-tracking system so that the location of exhibits could be instantly ascertained and, most important of all, chain-of-evidence continuity procedures so that when one person handed an exhibit over to another it was signed off by one person and on by the next. If today one tried to take a case to court with just one of these systems missing it would be instantly thrown out.

Once the other examiner had departed on leave I thought I would look through the pile of exhibits on the office floor. It then became obvious that hardly a single case had been examined for the past three years. It was no wonder he had so much time to go out drinking and fill in stupid card indexes. There were over 500 outstanding cases, most of which – I must admit – were rubbish but were, nevertheless, booked exhibits with an officer somewhere in Hong Kong waiting for a report. Among the rubbish, though, there were cases of murder, suicide, armed robbery, gun snatching and every other type of case imaginable. What with the training, attempting to implement an efficient office-management system, updating the office, dealing with all the call-outs, case receipts and office administration, it took me nearly two years to deal with the outstanding cases.

At that time the office itself was really small and consisted of two rooms, one of which contained a truly antique comparison microscope and the other two steel desks. Off the room with the desks was a concrete cubicle measuring six foot by six foot, which served as the 'indoor range'. This was, unbelievably, used for all the test firing carried out in the bureau. Everything from an air gun to fully fledged sawn-off shotguns had to be fired in this pokey little hole. It had no windows or extraction system and after three or four rounds had been fired it became totally uninhabitable. Safety equipment consisted of one pair of completely worn-out earmuffs. What tools existed, and there were precious few, consisted of a few broken-tipped screwdrivers (the proceeds of unsolved breaking and entering cases) and the oldest hand drill imaginable (but no drill bits). Modernising the office was going to be something of an uphill struggle

The accepted routine for the trainees, who had been there for some time before I arrived, was the same every day. Roll in about 9.30am, read the paper, do the crossword and go to the bank or do a bit of shopping. At about 11.30am it was off to whichever police mess was holding a curry lunch and stay there drinking oneself silly until about 3.00pm. A quick call into the office to see what was happening, then at 4.00pm up to the police inspector's mess, conveniently situated a few floors above the Ballistics Office, to continue drinking until late in the evening. Fortunately, or unfortunately depending upon your point of view, I do not agree with drinking at lunchtime, especially if you have to deal with loaded weapons. This made me something of a social pariah, to say the least.

Casework was different from that in the UK, with much of it involving general toolmark examinations. Monday morning was toolmark day, and it was always the same, with a pile of requests awaiting my arrival at 8.00am. These were all really grotty jobs and I hated virtually every one of them. First on the list were those closest to Police Headquarters, which is situated in the centre of the so-called 'Red Light District' of Wanchai. Red Light District was a misnomer if ever there was one, for while it may have had a reputation in the R&R era of the Vietnam war, in 1977 it was just a run-down bar area which few people visited. Outside each of these establishments were notices proclaiming 'Topless Model Dancers Inside' and 'No Cover Charge', which I always thought hilarious for a topless bar.

Once you got inside the door, through the thick nicotine-infused curtains and into the bar you often found that you were the only customer. The topless model dancers consisted of a few bored women playing Majong or slurping their way through a bowl of nasty-looking noodles. The air conditioners were always set to 'Arctic' and to prevent the onset of pneumonia the 'girls' always had a thick jumper or coat over their shoulders. At the sight of a potential customer the coat would be thrown off to reveal their 'topless splendour' and a drink would be served at some horrendously inflated price. The 'topless model' would then make an attempt at being seductive and talk you into buying her a tiny glass of 7-up, usually costing around £30. When you told her where to go with her drink she would quickly don a coat and disappear to the other end of the bar, mumbling 'no money no honey', and carry on with whatever she was doing before you entered. If you were stupid enough to buy a drink it was downed in a trice and immediately refilled for another £30. In this way, bills of a thousand pounds could be run up in no time at all, and there was never anything on offer other than a few minutes of banal pidgin English conversation.

Walking into one of these establishments first thing on a Monday morning to look at their burgled safe was not a good way to start the week. The floor was so filthy the carpet stuck to your feet, every surface you touched was black with nicotine-stained grime and they always reeked of stale beer and cigarette smoke. The 'office' was filthy and as soon as you touched the slightest thing a million gigantic cockroaches scuttled out from their hiding places. I was always very quick to get those jobs finished: you never knew what you were going to catch.

Next were the office blocks. These were always 20 or more floors high and the burglar would either go up the back stairs, enter from the roof and work down or break in on the ground floor and work up. These blocks all seemed to contain thousands of small offices, often consisting of no more than one tiny room crammed full of desks. It was always the same, with each office door and desk having been levered open usually with a broken screwdriver. Silicone casts had to be taken from each and every scratch mark, just in case anyone was ever arrested. For some reason the officers in charge of these multiple burglary cases always wanted to know whether the burglar had worked from top down or bottom up. I never did understand why they required this information, but trying to work out the direction from subtle changes in the screwdriver's shape was a very time-consuming process.

In the three years before I managed to offload the toolmark cases on to the general forensic chemists, I don't think we had one significant positive case. The burglars made so much money from each job they simply threw the tools away and bought new ones with the proceeds.

The last on the Monday morning list were the butcher and herbalist shops. The herbalists I didn't mind too much as they were really interesting places, full of strange smells and weird plants. The dog penises, deer testicles, bear paws and other unidentifiable parts of various four-legged mammals I could, however, do without. I seriously tried to avoid the butcher shops if at all possible. They stank abominably, every surface was covered in animal blood and piles of intestines lay all over the floor. If matters could be worse, there always seemed to be a vast selection of skinned buffalo and cows heads hanging on hooks, their bulging eyes following you everywhere you went.

Some of the cases were, however, quite amusing. At one scene I found the biggest tin opener ever, with a cutting blade of 18 inches or more long. The burglars had tried to cut open a safe with this implement using a 10-foot scaffold pole as a lever. They did quite well, until they woke up a neighbour with all the noise they were making and had to do a runner. At another scene it was obvious that this gang had tried everything: drilling, sawing, explosives (which didn't go off), squeezing it with a hydraulic jack and wire hawser, even attempting to pick the lock. In the end they gave up and left empty-handed. During my examination I decided that I required a better look at some of the marks caused by the hydraulic jack so I decided to turn this six-foot-high safe on its side. Four of us carefully tilted this monster and as we did so the bottom just fell straight off. The safe had been in the same place for so long that the heat and humidity had completely rusted the base away. All the safe breakers had to do was tilt it and they would have been inside and the proud owners of several tens of thousands of dollars.

One striation-matching case I vividly remember solving involved a Triad 'chopping'. Now Triads may be a fairly vicious lot when it comes to territory war, but when it comes to people who do not pay their debts they are very cute indeed. They think that if you take someone out and kill them, the body will be quickly buried by family and friends and within a few weeks the incident will be forgotten. On the other hand, if you cut someone into ribbons, remove a few fingers and an ear, and slice up his face, but don't quite kill him, then he will be walking around like Frankenstein's monster for the rest of his life, as a warning to others not to mess with that Triad gang. It works well.

In this particular case they had used an 18-inch-long beef knife to chop off all his fingers, cut his back so badly it required 300 stitches, cut out one eye and remove his lips. As a final farewell they had hit him so hard over the head with the knife that the blade had stuck in the skull and it took two of them to free it. As they were attempting to stitch him up at the hospital, the needle grated against something hard in the scalp. On excavation it was found to be a tiny piece of metal, presumably from the cutting edge of a knife.

A few days later a suspect was arrested and all the knives from his kitchen were sent in for blood grouping. Not only was our suspect an extremely busy little Triad – there was blood from about 20 different people on the knives – but he was also extremely unhygienic: he had been using the same knives for cooking. During my examination I noticed that one of the knives had a microscopic chip out of the blade. After some quite difficult work on the comparison microscope I was able to prove that striation marks from where the knife had last been sharpened matched perfectly with those on the chip of metal. That proved beyond reasonable doubt that the knife had been used to cut open the injured man's skull.

Another call-out to a murder scene in the country provided what I thought was something I had no hope of ever seeing: the legendary 'Death by a Thousand Needles'. It is rumoured that, in times gone by, emperors of the old Chinese dynasties reserved a special kind of torture for those they wanted to suffer before they died. The torture, it is said, could last for months, with the victim screaming until his voice cords burst. It was the worst imaginable way to die.

The victim was tied to a plank and long, thin needles were slowly pushed into every part of his body where they were left to irritate and slowly become infected. It could take hours to insert one needle and, as the name would suggest, a thousand needles had to be inserted before he was allowed to die. Generally, it was reserved only for offences against the Emperor or his family, but since that could be for something as small and insignificant as looking at the Emperor, it wasn't all that uncommon.

My old boss in the UK once thought he had come across such a case when he arrived at the scene of the death of an old Chinese spinster. It turned out, however, that her cat had jumped on to the still warm naked body and had been 'pawing' the skin, thus putting thousands of small puncture marks in the skin. She had in fact died from natural causes.

My case was located on a hillside overlooking the east end of the harbour, at a place called Sai Wan. The hill itself was called Devil's Peak and was the site of one of the Second World War gun emplacements intended to protect Hong Kong from a sea invasion. The gun had long gone, leaving just the barracks and ammunition stores, but when operational it was serviced by hundreds of British soldiers. As the Cantonese call Europeans Gwai Lo, which means Foreign Devil, this could have been the origin of the hill's name.

The body was lying face down in the grass and there was an obvious bullet entry hole in the back of the head. He was naked from the waist up and had a large bruise on the back of the neck from being pistol whipped across the base of the skull. The bullet had gone straight through the skull exiting through the top of his forehead in typical Chinese-gangland execution style. What was fascinating, however, was the thousands of small puncture marks all over his body. No needles could be seen, but legend has it that for those who had committed particularly heinous crimes against the Emperor, the pins were pushed below the surface so that they could not be removed. The hapless victim was then released to slowly die in agony, without any chance of removing the pins.

At the mortuary we had the body X-rayed to see if we could locate the pins but there was nothing, not even a shadow on any of the plates. It wasn't until his trousers were taken off that the cause of the puncture wounds was finally discovered. There in his trousers were hundreds of one-inch-long ants, which had been biting his skin. So powerful were the enormous jaws on these ants that they had completely punctured the skin, leaving needle-sized holes. No Death by a Thousand Pins, unfortunately, just another Triad execution.

In my early days in Hong Kong, the place was run very much on a shoe-string budget. Everything that could be done on the cheap wasdone so, and if something could be purchased second hand it was preferable to buying new. Even some of the buses had been bought second hand from India who had bought them years before that second hand from the UK!

It was likewise very much the situation as far as the Zoological Gardens in Central was concerned. Not exactly a zoo, more a small collection of animals and birds, held in quite dreadful conditions, in a small area at one end of the botanical gardens. Amongst the collection was a thriving family of black panthers who were, despite their small concrete enclosures with rusty iron bars, breeding quite happily. That was until one day the keeper decided that the female, who was quite heavily pregnant, had a genetic disease of the hips and had to be killed. This genetic problem is not a life-threatening condition, merely something akin to osteo-arthritis of the hip joints. The keeper, however, decided that she must not be allowed to breed and killing her was the only option. I thought this was a little extreme, but I'm no vet so I didn't really know. What I did know is that the keeper had decided that the only way to kill this magnificent beast was to have it shot – and he asked me to do it. 'No way, Jose! There is no way that I am ever going to shoot such a wonderful animal. Let her give birth, look after the cubs and don't allow it to breed again.' When I refused, the other ballistics officer (who always fancied himself as a bit of a hunter back in his native New Zealand) piped up and agreed to do it the next morning. I wanted nothing to do with it at all, but went along to see what would happen.

His first mistake was deciding to shoot it with a 9mm sub-machine gun. No way was this gun/ammunition combination going to be powerful enough for a quick dispatch. A full-blown rifle round such as the 25-3000 or 7.62x51mm with a soft-pointed bullet was required. If not that, then a 12-bore shotgun loaded with solid slug. That would definitely do the trick at close range. No, he wasn't going to listen, the 9mm Heckler and Koch MP5 SD with a built in silencer was going to be the weapon of his choice.

The kill was going to be done at first light to ensure that no one else was going to be about. Also, as there was no special holding pen available, the panther was going to be shot whilst walking around in its cage. Absolutely everything was wrong about this. I knew in my bones that it was going to be terribly bad.

There were just four of us present, the ballistics officer, one of the trainee ballistic officers, the keeper and myself. The gun was loaded with just three rounds of plain military-style fully-jacketed ammunition and, when the animal stopped pacing round the pen, he stuck the muzzle through the bars and fired two shots at the head at a range of about twenty feet. In theory, either one of the shots should have penetrated the brain and killed it instantly, but the first shot merely glanced off the skull and the second missed completely. To this day I have no idea how this huge cat covered the distance so quickly, but with the loudest roar I have ever heard it was suddenly across the cage and had these huge fangs around the muzzle of the gun. The firer panicked, wet his pants, and as he pulled the gun out of the cat's mouth he sent the last round way up into the sky, which in crowded Hong Kong is not a good thing to do.

The cat was beside itself with fury – it was obviously quite badly injured and in pain. It just kept throwing itself against the side of the cage with an absolutely frightening series of roars, hisses and growls. Whilst the ballistics officer was sitting on the floor fumbling with the magazine trying to reload it, the trainee ballistics officer calmly got out his issue .38 Special revolver, which he had thankfully loaded with soft-point ammunition, and shot the animal dead with two, perfectly placed, shots to the heart. Suddenly it was all over, and the whole botanical gardens were plunged into silence. Not a bird sang or a cicada chirped. It was if every animal instinctively knew what an awful act had just been perpetrated.

Nowadays, such a thing would never be allowed to happen. Hong Kong has some of the most conscientious and capable veterinary surgeons available with state-of-the-art equipment, including, should it be required, the best tranquillising guns available. One of the best, and the man currently in charge of the zoological gardens, is Barry Bousfield. Coincidentally, the big-game hunter who originally supplied virtually all of the zoological garden's animals and birds was Barry's father. When, many years later, Barry arrived in Hong Kong and I told him about the way the panther had died he was beside himself with anger, for it had been Barry who had helped his father catch and crate up the panther for transport to Hong Kong.

Ladies' Nights were always big occasions in Hong Kong, with the men in their white dinner suits and the women in their long elegant ball gowns, and in my early days in Hong Kong the place to hold a Ladies' Night was in the old Hong Kong Club. It was a magnificent Colonial-style building dating from the late 1890s, with a sweeping central oak staircase leading to a minstrel gallery off which all the function rooms ran. The main ballroom was huge, with dark-stained rosewood floors, lofty ceilings and lazily turning fans and chandeliers by the dozen.

It was a beautiful late-autumn evening with no humidity, the temperature was a very manageable 28° and there was no more than a gentle breeze to stir the tropical vegetation. The dancing had gone on long into the night, the gin and tonics were flowing freely and everyone was having a wonderful time. Then my pager went off.

Leaving my wife to fend for herself, I quickly arranged for a 999 car to pick me up at the club; white DJ, medals and all, and with wailing sirens I was transported from a place of grace and refinement to one of blood, death and chaos.

The scene was on the first floor of a grotty building in the depths of Kowloon Tong, an area with very little to recommend it, other than the road out. The premises, a fairly large room with a small attached pantry and toilet at one end, was reached via a very narrow and steep wooden staircase from the rear of a dingy shop on the ground floor. The owner of this shop was obviously making some money on the side by renting out the room to an illegal gambling syndicate run by a local Triad gang. To ensure some form of security the Triads had hired, illegally of course, an off-duty detective police constable (DPC) to stand guard with his force-issue .38 Colt Detective Special revolver.

Their evening had been going well. There were more than 30 people gambling and about HK$800,000 (£75,000) in stakes on the table. Then in burst a rival Triad gang armed with several meat choppers and a number of guns. The DPC took cover in the pantry as the gang threatened the gamblers with the choppers and, just to prove they meant business, fired three warning shots into the ceiling. A gun battle then ensued with the three armed men firing eight shots at the DPC and him returning five before dropping dead.

As with all such incidents, by the time the police arrived there wasn't a single cent left on the table or a witness to be found anywhere, and at first it was a bit difficult to determine exactly what had happened. Tables were turned over, and there were patches of blood, bits of ceiling plaster, betting chips, broken glasses, spilt beer, food, and cards everywhere. At one end of the room, with his body halfway out of the pantry door was the dead DPC with blood pouring out of his nose, mouth and ears. Together with the pathologist I carried out a fairly comprehensive examination of the body, but we couldn't find a bullet wound anywhere. In desperation we sent the body to a local hospital to be X-rayed.

There was not much more to be done at the scene at that stage than to make a sketch map of the premises indicating where the various bullet holes, ricochet marks and flattened bullets had been found. By the time I had finished it was too late to go back to the party, and anyway my spanking-new white DJ was covered in the dead DPC's blood, which rather settled the matter.

At the mortuary the next morning we studied the dozens of X-rays and it was immediately clear that the bullet was inside the skull. But how did it get there? After a meticulous examination of the head we finally located a tiny entry hole in the corner of the eye, right through the tear duct. After cutting off the top of the skull we were in for another surprise: the brain flowed out like water. This had been caused by a bullet entering the skull cavity at such a shallow angle that it had skidded round and round the inside. In the process the bullet had effectively macerated the brain leaving a series of black lines on the inside of the skull as it went.

The bullet was obviously .22 calibre, but it bore no rifling and had been squeezed out into a long irregular shape only about 0.18 of an inch in diameter, indicating that it had been fired through a homemade barrel. On examining the bullets found at the scene it was obvious that homemade .38 calibre and .32 calibre revolvers had been used by the criminals, as well as what appeared to be two additional homemade .22 calibre weapons. On one of the bullets fired from the deceased's gun was a minute fragment of skin and what looked like bone, but who had he hit? One of the robbers or one of the gamblers?

Months later, through some brilliant detective work and lots of hard work, a gang of five suspects was arrested, but no guns were recovered from any of their addresses. After weeks of further investigation a 'safe house' was discovered, which was thought to hold the guns and the last of the suspects. The raid was carried out in deathly silence in the middle of the night, but it wasn't until we got within 100 yards of the house that we discovered it was in an abandoned pigsty which stank abominably.

Crashing through the doors with sledgehammers and tossing flash-bang stun grenades into each room, we soon had the occupants in handcuffs and looking terribly dazed. Flash-bang stun grenades explode with the most ear-piercing noise imaginable, then five or six small pellets of magnesium dust are ejected which burn with an incredibly intense light. The effect, if you happen to be anywhere near one of these, is completely disorientating. You can't hear, you can't see, you lose all sense of balance and usually just fall to the floor in agony.

For hours we slowly took apart this hovel of a place, until finally, hidden in a stud wall between two rooms, we found the guns: a .38 calibre revolver, a .32 calibre revolver and a three-shot palm pistol, all of which were homemade. I say 'homemade' but at that time they were fairly common in Asia. They were known as 'Palteks', and were made in small engineering shops all over the Philippines.

It was easy enough, even though there wasn't any rifling, to match the bullet from the DPC's head and the other two .22 bullets from the scene with the palm pistol. It was equally simple to match up all the fired .38 and .32 calibre bullets with the two revolvers. Only one outstanding matter: who had the DPC shot before being killed himself? A close look at the .38 calibre revolver from the pigsty showed a shallow furrow in the left side of the wooden grip which, if held in the right hand, would match up perfectly with the missing top joint and a half of the third finger on the right hand of one of the arrested persons. This tied in nicely with the supposition that whilst the gun was being held away from the body, almost definitely with the arm straight and pointing upwards at about forty-five degrees, a bullet had struck the left side of the gun's grip. The gun had to have been held away from the body, otherwise the bullet would, after striking the grip, have gone on to hit the body of the person holding the gun. As the fingers of the hand holding the gun would have covered this side of the grip, the bullet would, before hitting the grip, have removed the top joint of the third finger of that hand. The only other possibility was that the gun was held in the left hand, but then the bullet would have gone through the back of the hand and, after hitting the grip, most probably gone on up into the wrist and forearm. This would have caused terrible damage to that arm and as we had all the suspects in custody, none of whom had sustained such damage, it was an unlikely option. Likewise, as there were no dead bodies at the scene or bullet wounds on the bodies of those arrested, I came to the conclusion that the first option, with the gun pointing upwards, was the most probable scenario. After some questioning the man with the missing half finger admitted firing the gun at the ceiling as a warning and then nearly having his finger severed by a bullet from the DPC's gun. He also said that a quick visit to an illegal doctor in the Kowloon Walled City resulted in what remained of the finger being cut off with a pair of pliers and no anaesthetic; a painful experience, he recalled.

The trial went well, and it was mainly my evidence that convicted the gang of the murder. At sentencing, the judge called to the clerk of the court for a square of black silk, which he placed on the top of his wig while he pronounced the death penalty. I had never seen that before. It was rather a sobering thought that someone had been sentenced to death due almost entirely to my efforts.

CHAPTER 14

VIETNAMESE BOAT PEOPLE AND THE GOLD SMUGGLER

It was about this time that Vietnamese refugees started to arrive in their thousands. Some of them were obviously quite wealthy and came with the universal form of money: gold bars. It wasn't long before the South Sea pirates became aware of the potential wealth that was slipping through their fingers and the slow-moving Vietnamese refugee boats became their prime target.

Most of these boats had nothing on board at all, the refugees being poor farmers who had used up all of their money in bribes to get out of the country. That didn't matter: each and every boat they came across was stopped; the men and children were invariably thrown overboard and the women gang-raped, until they either died or the pirates tired of them. If they managed to survive, they were then sold into prostitution, making a fat profit for the pirates.

The refugees soon realised that if they were to get to Hong Kong in one piece, they had to arm themselves against the pirates. First of all it was just rusty pistols, then rifles and then full machine guns. With hundreds of thousands of guns lying abandoned in the fields just waiting to be picked up, weapons and ammunition were easy to come by.

One of my many jobs at that time was to meet these boats as they entered Hong Kong waters, and search them for arms and ammunition. A police boat would pick me up about five minutes' drive from my office and we would race out at full speed to greet the refugee boat as it entered Hong Kong waters. The boats themselves were generally only about 40 feet long, being very old inshore fishing boats with the typical Vietnamese raised and pointed bow. They always leaked like sieves and there was invariably one crew member frantically bailing out with an old GI helmet. It never ceased to amaze me how these things – often with no more than a simple single-cylinder diesel engine, usually well past its prime – made the perilous 1,000-mile journey to Hong Kong. I always wondered on seeing these boats how many had sunk for every one that made it safely to its destination.

These boats were vessels of abject misery. Many were scarred from shoot-outs with pirates, while others had obviously been boarded and the occupants forced to endure their brutality. Here were beaten men and savaged women, but these were the lucky ones who had not been thrown overboard to the mercy of the sea and sharks. Their faces, no matter what they had been through, always brightened with a smile on seeing the police boat racing towards them, because it meant that the horrors of their journey were over and they were now in safe hands. But did they have much to look forward to? They lived in cramped, hot and humid refugee camps run by vicious gangs from North Vietnam, who forced many of the women into prostitution. There was no work for the men, nothing to do all day, sparse education for the children and minimal food. Could this be better than what they had left? If so, I am glad that it was something my family and I never had to experience.

Despite the smiles, the boats always refused to stop, or even slow down, until berthed at the quarantine buoy on the outskirts of the harbour. As a result, boarding one of these heaving vessels as it raced through the choppy waters was always a pretty exciting undertaking. To add to the excitement, the decks were as slippery as ice from the diesel that was stored in leaky 50-gallon drums. The boats themselves stank terribly of vomit, faeces, rotten food and diesel fuel. Below decks, it was pitch black, stifling hot and full of exhaust fumes. After having visited a few boats I became aware of the usual hiding places, and it didn't take long to conduct a search, which usually turned up a couple of Colt 1911 A1 .45 calibre pistols, an M16 or AK47 assault rifle and some ammunition. The weapons were always in a terrible condition, but due credit must be given to their military design and ruggedness, because after minimal cleaning they would nearly always fire.

One thing that concerned me was the number of rats I encountered while searching the bilges and food-storage areas. Some time later it was discovered that the rats often carried bubonic plague and after that we were not allowed to go on to the boats unless we had been vaccinated against every disease imaginable.

Not long after I arrived in Hong Kong a small freighter wallowed into port, laden down with thousands of refugees. I don't think I have ever seen so many people crammed on to the decks of a single vessel. On boarding the vessel it became obvious that the deck cargo, supposedly 50-gallon drums of cooking oil, was nothing other than empty containers and that the boat had always been intended for the transport of refugees. One of the holds contained a mountain of rotting rice, and the whole boat stank abominably of this heaving, rotting, fermenting mass. Because there were not enough toilets to cater for the hordes of refugees, small wooden platforms were hung over the sides at 15-foot intervals. Due to the poor food, virtually everyone on board suffered from diarrhoea and, to make matters worse, there had been an outbreak of cholera. As a result, every square inch of the outside surface of the hull was covered in faeces and vomit. One of the holds had obviously been used to house those who were particularly ill and it was probably the most evil-smelling place I have ever entered.

My job, as usual, was to search the boat for weapons, but it was enormous, and to complicate things further it had begun to take on water and was listing badly. The power was off because the donkey engines were flooded and I had to do my best with just my small, failing flashlight. Down dark and dank corridors I went, with nothing but the yellowing beam of my torch and the groaning of the ship, as she wallowed heavy with water, to keep me company. I was sloshing about in water up to my knees. The humidity was so high it was like a Sixties London fog and all the time I was trying to avoid the hundreds of rats which were busily swimming back and forth, desperately trying to escape before the boat sank. I came to one hold which was half-full of water and so large the beam from my light wouldn't reach even halfway across it. Peering down into this inky echoing darkness sent shivers up and down my spine, but I had to go down and see what was there. Hand over hand, down the wet and slimy iron ladder I went, the torch between my teeth threatening to slip from my grasp at any moment. There was a sudden splash as my feet hit the water and the sound reverberated round the eerily quiet hold. Carefully probing with my foot, I tried to determine whether I could go any lower. Then, up from the murky depths below and into the small pool of light cast by my torch came a pure white arm, which reached out and touched my ankle. I nearly died. My heart was in my mouth and my legs were doing a fair impression of a Walt Disney cartoon character. Summoning all my resolve I shone the torch on to the arm. It was that of a dead refugee, brought to the top of the water as a result of the build-up of decomposition gases. Nonetheless, a terrifying incident.

Another ship arrived some six months later and like the first it was loaded to the gunwales with very sick Vietnamese refugees. The captain of the vessel said that soon after leaving port the engine had developed a fault and he was forced to anchor off a bay in Vietnam while a piston ring was replaced. During the night, he related, thousands of Vietnamese refugees swarmed on to the ship and forced him to sail to Hong Kong.

It didn't sound like a very convincing story, but how to prove that he was lying? Some bright spark pointed out that if the ship was in port and it had to be repaired, then the shipyard would use its own tools. If, on the other hand, it was forced to make repairs at sea then tools from the boat would be used. It should, therefore, be an easy matter to look at the toolmarks on the nuts holding the engine together to determine whether the ship's tools had been used recently. Not much hope of that, I thought, but I would have a look around the boat to see what I could find.

It was a relatively small ship, but I could not believe the size of the ship's pistons, they must have been at least two feet across. I climbed all over the engine, but there wasn't anything significant, in fact it looked as though the paint on the cylinder heads hadn't been disturbed for months, if not years. Next I had a look at the spare piston rings that were hanging on a steel rod welded to the wall of the workshop, and there, before my very eyes, was the proof we required: a thick, even, undisturbed layer of dust over the rod and all the rings. After taking some photographs I thought I would take a quick look around the boat's engine compartment and propeller tube, just for interest's sake. As I was walking down the propeller shaft tube, my eye caught a glint of something between the iron plates covering the bilges. Being nosey, I prised up one of the metal plates and there, shining in all its glory, was about $3 million worth of gold leaf. Piles and piles of thin sheets of gold were there, weighing in at over 3,000 ounces. This was obviously the captain's payment for giving the refugees safe passage to Hong Kong. He never saw that again and, as far as I know, is still languishing in jail for his sins.

Top: Tools of the trade. (*Clockwise from top*) Chinese type 56 (AK 47) 7.62x39mm assault rifle; Russian Makarov pistol 9mm MAK calibre; Chinese 'homemade' pistol .32" ACP; M40 7.62x25mm pistol, made for clandestine operations by Russia; Chinese stick grenade; Chinese Type 54 (Russian TT33) 7.62x25mm pistol; Chinese ball grenade; Harrington and Richardson .32 calibre revolver; 'Baby Browning' .25" ACP calibre; Chinese stick grenade and Philippines 'paltek' revolver .38" special calibre.

Bottom left: Converted and unconverted butterfly starting pistols.

Bottom right: A 'homemade' style gun.

Receiving the Police Meritorious Service Medal for my work in the field of forensic firearms examination.

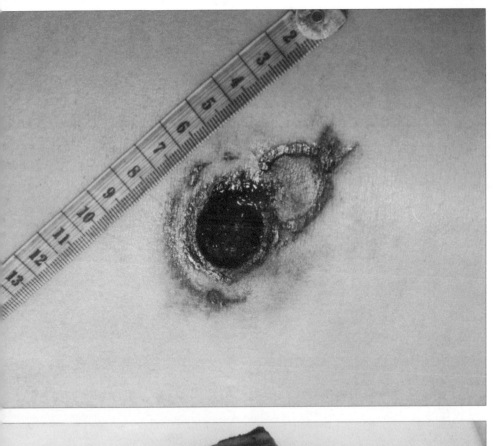

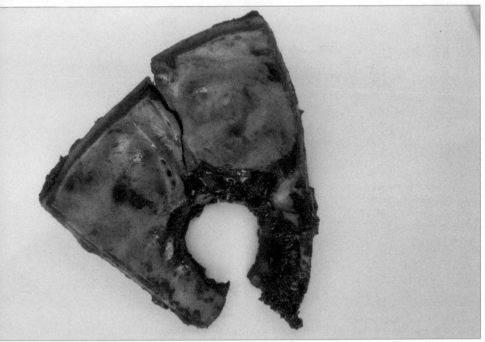

Top: The Chinese fisherman's contact wound clearly showing the mark left by the unfired top barrel and foresight.

Bottom: A large calibre entry hole in back of the skull of a triad execution victim.

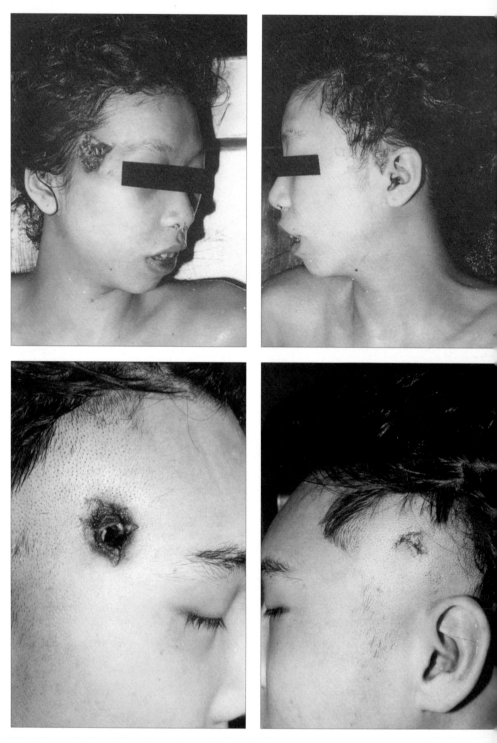

Top: The suicide of the detective's girlfriend, showing a large entry wound (*left*) and a small exit wound (*right*).

Bottom: A classic example where the muzzle of the weapon has been in tight contact with the head during firing, resulting in a much larger entry hole (*left*) than exit hole (*right*).

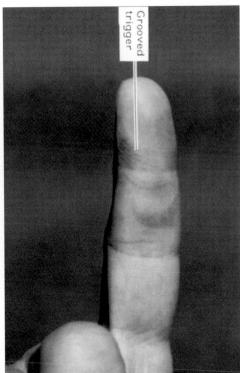

Grooved trigger

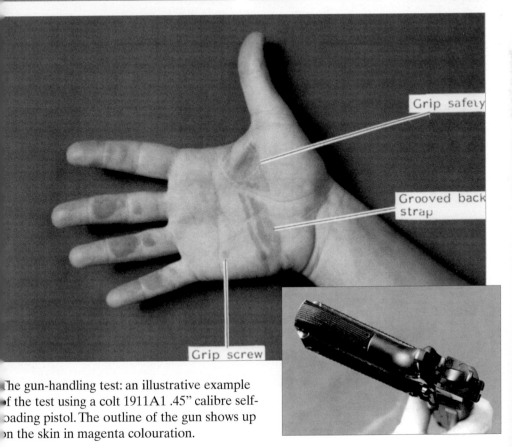

Grip safety

Grooved back strap

Grip screw

The gun-handling test: an illustrative example of the test using a colt 1911A1 .45" calibre self-loading pistol. The outline of the gun shows up on the skin in magenta colouration.

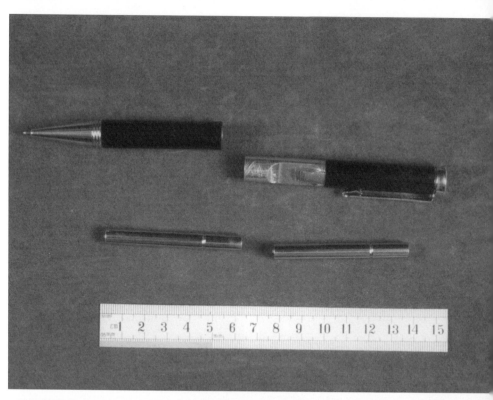

Top: Chinese pen pistol.

Bottom: Cigarette lighter gun.

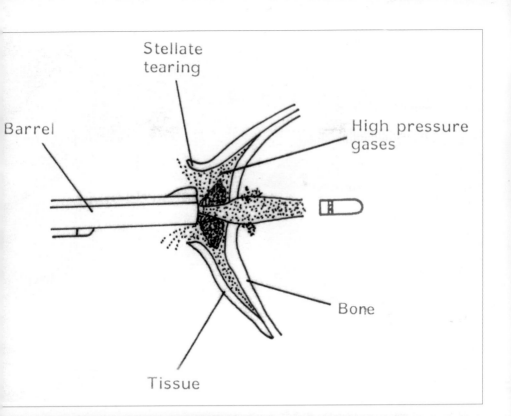

Top: Diagram showing how high-pressure gases burst back out of a contact entry hole giving a larger entry hole than exit hole.

Bottom: The gun-firing test. The microsecond flash shows the way in which the smoke produced on firing is deposited on the hands as gunshot residue.

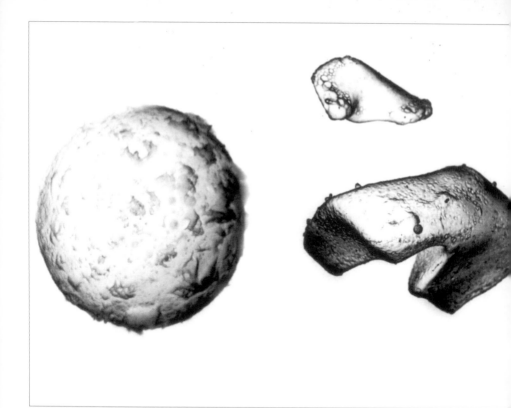

Top: Propellant particle removed from road sign with sub-microscopic gunshot residue particle adhering.

Bottom: A photomicrograph of a pistol's breech face, clearly showing how it was marked for identification.

CHAPTER 15

BIG-GAME HUNTING IN HONG KONG

In my early days with the police I had a lot of contact with the Sniper Unit, both as an adviser on arms and ammunition, and as a friend. There were about 10 officers in all, but the ones I had most contact with were Hugh Healy-Brown, a very good pistol shot but also good with a rifle; Sidney Chow, the best pistol shot I have ever seen; Murry Hoar, the best rifle shot I have ever met; and Mark Godfrey whose talents, apart from being a part-time stunt driver in the local film industry, I never did discover.

We spent some really great days on the range together, with me trying to hit the target and them trying to get all their shots into one hole. Once, Sidney carried out a quick draw as a butterfly fluttered past about 15 yards away. Just one shot rang out and the two wings fluttered to the ground, the body having been shot out from between them. I saw Murry put six shots from a heavy-barrelled AR

15 into one hole at 200 yards; something which, had I not seen it, I would have sworn was impossible with such a weapon. Sydney also shot a sparrow straight through the eye with a standard AR 15 at 150 yards, which seemed cruel, but showed impressive marksmanship.

Very rarely were they called out for actual incidents and when they were it was usually for something totally off-the-wall. On one occasion a circus had gone bankrupt, leaving five small elephants stranded in Hong Kong. Weeks passed, and without a proper diet the elephants were deteriorating fast. In the end the Government stepped in and paid for them to be shipped to Thailand. First, however, they had to be loaded on to the ship, so, using a barge with a crane on it, they were unceremoniously lifted into the bottom of a large lighter (a large, high-sided, flat-bottomed barge which has an onboard crane and which is used for the transfer of goods from offshore anchored ships to the docks). The lighter, being flat-bottomed, was rolling quite alarmingly, and soon the elephants started to panic: trumpeting, hollering and stamping around in the bottom of the ship. As they became more and more upset, diarrhoea set in. Believe me, five elephants with diarrhoea is something to steer clear of, if at all possible.

The bottom of the lighter was now really slippery, and the crew, fearing that it might capsize, called the police. Nobody knew what to do or who to call, so the Sniper Unit was ordered to go and make the lighter safe. With his standard AR 15, Hugh was sent to take control of the boat; a laughable situation if ever there was one. There he was, rifle cradled in his arms, crouched in one corner of the lighter, desperately trying to avoid the spray coming out of the rear of the five elephants, and wondering what to do. Luckily, before someone ordered him to shoot the elephants with the AR 15, which would have been about as much use as a pea-shooter, someone had the brainwave of dropping a couple of tons of straw into the lighter. The elephants now had food to keep them occupied and something to stop them slithering about, and peace was restored.

Later, the unit's skills were called on to deal with a runaway Asian bullock. These are huge: animals weighing 1,500lbs are not unusual. They are also built like bulldozers and have skin as hard as steel. Luckily, however, they are normally quite docile.

The animals were being imported from Thailand for slaughter in Hong Kong. As one of them was being unloaded from a lighter it decided that the slaughterhouse was not its preferred destination. It jumped out of the loading net, straight into the harbour and started to swim for its life. Several half-hearted attempts were made to capture it but with little success. On it swam until it reached the harbour wall in Tsim Sha Tsui where there was an ungated entry point into the underground storm drain system. It clambered into this tunnel and immediately disappeared into the labyrinth of tunnels under Kowloon.

We now had 1,500lbs of very upset buffalo thundering through the drains somewhere beneath Kowloon. It obviously couldn't be left there, as maintenance men were required to check out the drains on a regular basis and the last thing that they would want was a confrontation with a very irate buffalo in a pitch-black tunnel. So, who else to call but the Sniper Unit?

A systematic search of the tunnels was out of the question because it presented the risk of meeting this leviathan face to face, with no possibility of escape. All that could be done was to pull up as many manhole covers as possible and listen for the sounds of his hooves on the concrete tunnel. As there was a bit of water running through the drains, Mark thought it would be a good idea to float rafts of burning paper down the drains in an attempt to flush it out. Unfortunately, the paper kept going out and apart from clogging up several of the sumps with wet paper nothing was achieved.

For a long time nothing happened. Then, in the distance, they heard the patter of hooves coming towards them. Mark picked up a shotgun and, running down the middle of Nathan Road, tried to get far enough in front of the beast that he could clamber down one of the manholes. Ripping up one of the covers he leapt into the hole only to see the buffalo a mere 20 yards in front of him with flared nostrils and eyes ablaze. As the buffalo started to charge, Mark let him have three rounds at a range of less than 10 yards but, alas, nobody had bothered to check what ammunition the shotguns were loaded with. Three rounds of birdshot succeeded only in upsetting the animal even more. With a huge bellow the buffalo covered the remaining few yards in next to no time and Mark's fate looked sealed but, at the last moment he was grabbed by the shoulders from above and pulled from certain death beneath the buffalo's horns by two of his PCs.

We all stood there, stunned by how close Mark had come to being sewer rat food. Of the buffalo all that could be heard was the rapidly fading clip-clop of its hooves on the concrete tube below.

A couple of hours later we were much better prepared, with the best part of 100 officers looking down manholes for signs of the buffalo. And then we heard it again, trotting further and further into the labyrinth of tunnels that spread up towards Lion Rock and away from the harbour. Eventually we managed to get ahead of him and, holding Hugh by his ankles, we lowered him into the tunnel. As the buffalo went past like a train, Hugh let it have five shots on fully automatic mode, straight into the base of its neck. The buffalo dropped dead like a stone, never to move again. Then the water pressure built up around him and started to move the carcass back towards Kowloon. Now we had nothing to tell us where it was going, and too many branches and side tunnels to cover, even with all the men we had. Once again we had lost it, all 1,500lbs of, now dead, prime buffalo meat.

We searched and searched for days but found nothing, until complaints of a foul smell started to come in, and there it was washed up against the outfall grille where it emptied into Yaumatei typhoon shelter. It was over to Urban Services to get the rotting buffalo carcass out from behind the rusted solid grille.

Another Asian buffalo, but this time one which had escaped from an illegal abattoir in the New Territories was running amok, charging whatever came into view. A number of cars had been reduced to crumpled tin foil and several shops had been completely demolished. People were up trees, hanging on to lampposts, in fact anywhere out of reach of the beast's huge horns.

'Time to call the Ballistics Officer,' someone announced and duly I was called. I had read all the books about humane killers and where one should aim to kill a deer or wild boar when hunting, but this thing was like the county of Kent on four feet, with a set of horns more akin to a bulldozer blade than those found on any Bambi I had ever encountered. It must have weighed the best part of a ton.

There it stood in the middle of a field, snorting and bellowing whilst pawing the ground with its head lowered, ready to charge. Luckily we – that is the inspector 'in charge', a couple of PCs and myself – had found a stone wall to hide behind. There we all sat, without a clue what to do, until the inspector said: 'In police training school they showed us a diagram of where to shoot various animals, unfortunately that was 15 years ago and I can't remember a thing about it.' Thanks.

After 10 minutes of this, a PC came running up, cradling a pump-action shotgun that had been kept in the local police station to shoot the wild boars which are always raiding the local farmers' ginger plantations. 'It's loaded with solid slug,' he said. 'That should do the trick.' The inspector, despite my warnings about it being a completely unsuitable missile and weapon combination, decided that it was time for action, and with a call of 'Here Daisy' jumped over the wall to face the buffalo.

The buffalo, now with drool pouring out of its mouth, bellowed and charged straight at the inspector like an express train. The sound of its hoofs was like thunder, the ground was shaking and, with all the snorting and bellowing, all I wanted at that stage was a hole to crawl into. Suddenly there was a huge bang, then another, as the shotgun was rapidly fired, followed by an earth-moving crash and silence. Like gnomes, the two PCs and I slowly raised our heads above the wall, expecting to see a very mangled inspector impaled upon the buffalo's horns. But no, he was still standing, very white and shaking like a leaf, but still standing. Instead there was this huge mound of very still, very black buffalo with one horn deeply embedded in the earth. A thin trickle of blood came from each of two holes in his forehead.

'Whatever you do don't go near him,' I shouted. 'There is nearly eight inches of armour-hard bone and horn where you shot him and it couldn't possibly have killed him!'

'Nonsense,' said the inspector and proceeded to put one foot on the buffalo's neck, striking a pose for the press, who had just arrived. The flash guns were going off like strobe lights at a disco as the inspector first turned this way and then that, so that all were assured of a picture for the next day's rag. Suddenly, there was a deafening bellow as the buffalo came to and got unsteadily to his feet. In the time it took the beast to regain its footing, everyone had fled to shelter and we were back to square one.

Luckily, the buffalo had remembered that charging a human being resulted in a severe pain between the eyes and wasn't about to make the same mistake twice. But how long was that going to last? After a short while, the cavalry turned up in the form of the Marksman Unit and within a very short time the unfortunate beast had met his maker. A vet soon turned up for a post mortem and when we opened the skin over its forehead there were two extremely shiny discs of lead about an inch-and-a-half in diameter and a quarter of an inch thick. The solid lead slugs hadn't even scratched the bone, just flattened themselves on the armour-hard horn that covers it.

The ammunition which finally dispatched the beast were 7.62x51mm calibre soft-point rifle rounds of the same calibre as used by NATO forces. They had both been fired into the rib cage and were aimed at the area in which the heart was known to lie. On hitting the buffalo's tough hide the soft-nosed bullets had expanded to two or three times their original diameter, ploughing a huge wound track straight through the animal's vital organs, completely destroying the heart in the process. It had died almost instantly.

CHAPTER 16

KIDS WITH GUNS AND GRENADES

It was August, 37°C, 98 per cent humidity and tempers were rising. The kids had been off school for some time and were beginning to get restless, leading to all sorts of petty mischief. Poor-quality but exorbitantly priced plastic air 'rifles' were all the rage and the kids were forever shooting each other with them. They were very low-powered and the lightweight 6mm calibre plastic pellets they fired ensured that even a direct eye shot would cause little damage. However, less scrupulous toy shops were making a mint by replacing the springs with more powerful ones, changing the pistons and sealing rings, and even supplying heavier target pellets. The end result was the same: guns as weak as old knicker elastic.

Slowly, however, cases of wounding by these 'toys' started to come in: a very small calibre puncture wound straight through the upper arm, a festering puncture wound to the leg, then a completely punctured eye. When the eye was removed, embedded deep in the optic nerve, they found a large darning needle. An X-ray of the festering leg wound revealed another darning needle, lying alongside the bone. It wasn't until one of these bored youths was arrested that we realised the kids had been sticking darning needles through the plastic pellets. On firing, the pellet and needle left the gun together, but on striking skin the pellet had insufficient energy to penetrate and bounced off, leaving the darning needle to continue on. The darning needle, now no longer encumbered by the large lightweight pellet, penetrated the skin, travelling deep into the soft tissue below.

Just to test the wounding capabilities of this type of 'duplex bullet', I took a gun and some of the modified pellets to test on an unclaimed body at the mortuary. A few test shots showed that when fired at the leg the darning needle would easily penetrate to the bone. On hitting the bone it would slide down alongside it for several inches, ending up a long way from the impact site. When fired at the chest, the needle would, unless a rib was struck, penetrate to the heart and sometimes go straight through until stopped by a rib or the spine. An eye shot would burst the eye, often sticking quite deeply in the bone of the socket. This was obviously a very dangerous modification. It was amazing that nobody was killed.

Converted guns were also central to a foiled bank robbery in Mong Kok at around the same time. There was nothing particularly significant about the robbery itself, with a gang of four masked men armed with converted starting pistols inside the bank, a lookout outside and a driver. The robbery went fairly smoothly, with the gang getting away with about HK$300,000 (£25,000), no shots being fired and no injuries. The gang just disappeared after that, presumably changing cars once or twice then vanishing into the underground rail system on foot. I was, however, asked to review the surveillance tapes to see if I could identify the guns used. They were all 'Butterfly' brand Chinese double-barrelled starting pistols which had been converted to muzzle loading pistols. We were all so busy looking at the pistols that we nearly missed one of the robbers casually leaning up against a cash dispenser in a far corner of the bank. While two of the robbers were collecting the money from the tellers, he stuck the gun in the waist band of his trousers, got out his wallet, put his cash card in the machine, typed in his PIN number and drew out some cash. I was nearly speechless. Here was some moron robbing a bank of $300,000 and he decides he needs some cash for the tube train. We ran the tape back in disbelief and, yes, he was using his own bank card to obtain cash. There was a mad scramble for the records in the cash dispenser and within two hours we had the whole team and their guns under lock and key. The gang couldn't believe that we had caught them so quickly; to this day they don't know how we did it.

Converted 'Butterfly' brand starting pistols were common during my first few years in Hong Kong. They were fairly crude conversions which essentially turned the starting pistol into a double-barrelled, muzzle-loading, pistol with a crude percussion ignition system. The barrels were loaded with anything the owner could get his hands on. Sometimes it was fertiliser and sugar, other times firework powder and sometimes even propellant from shotgun ammunition. The missiles would also consist of whatever was to hand; a crude lead bullet, rusty nails, lead shot, even crushed glass. The degree of expertise involved in loading the weapons also varied wildly: sometimes the missiles just dribbled out of the end of the barrel, other times the whole thing blew up in a violent explosion. Over the few years they were in vogue several hundred of these things were used in robberies and something like 70 per cent of those fired ended up exploding. It was, in fact, not unusual to arrive at a scene and find parts of the converted pistol stuck in the ceiling and walls, with the odd finger or thumb attached. It was then just a matter of phoning round the local hospitals to see who had been admitted with missing digits and the case was solved. At one stage it was jokingly suggested that the criminals should be encouraged to use these converted starting pistols as the detection rate for armed crimes would be improved no end.

Spring is without a doubt the worst time of year in Hong Kong, when the cold winds coming down from China meet the hot humid winds coming up from the equator. These make for a truly miserable time with cloud (or is it mist?) to ground level, 100 per cent humidity and temperatures in the high twenties. Shoes left out of the heated wardrobe over night will end up with the insides coated in a thick carpet of green mould, and the smallest spot of soup or beer on a jacket will grow a thick patch of grass-like mould which removes all the colour from the cloth. In some of the flats high up on the Peak, you have to keep a stick in the bedroom to remove the mushrooms which grow overnight on the walls and ceiling. Luckily, that only lasts for five or six weeks until the furnace-like heat of summer arrives. I think it was Lawrence who said that the Arabian sun strikes down from the sky like a sword. Lawrence was dealing with the dry heat of the desert, but in the tropics it crushes you like an anvil: 38°C, 95 per cent humidity, and with the heat coming off the walls of the concrete jungle of Central, the streets in summer are not places in which to linger.

Escaping from the heat into my air-conditioned office, I was enjoying the relative calm of mid-summer while all the crooks were on holiday spending their ill-gotten gains, when the telephone rang with that special shrill tone. 'Brian, we've found an old cannon in the hills and we don't want to touch it until we're sure it's not loaded. Can you help?' asked Jamie Gill, an old friend of mine. I wasn't exactly sure what I was going to do with a cannon, but off I went up to the New Territories to meet Jamie and see what I could do for him. If anything it was hotter up there than in town and my jacket was soaked through within five minutes of getting out of the car. The location, it seemed, was high up on Tai Mo Shan, the tallest mountain in Hong Kong, and some way along a village path not accessible to a normal car. 'We will have to take the jeep,' said Jamie. Sounds good to me, I thought, some cross-country driving in a 4x4 off-road vehicle. How wrong could I be?

What was waiting for us at the station was not a muscle-man Land Rover, but a battered mini moke: essentially a flat platform with a wheel at each corner, a gutless 850cc engine in the front and four canvas chairs laughingly called seats. With no 4x4 and ground clearance less than for a normal car it was useless for anything other than a billiard table-flat tarmac road, but we all piled in and we were off. After an hour of ploughing up a very narrow path, crashing into potholes and having to get out and push at every turn, it finally ground to a halt and we had to start walking.

Another hour-and-a-half and we were at the 'scene', hunting round in the grass for the 'cannon'. By this time the sweat had soaked not only my suit jacket, but also down to the bottom of my trousers. I had been bitten to death by mosquitoes and smelt so bad I was having trouble living with myself. After disturbing a couple of really venomous snakes, several large lizards and some ground hornets, Jamie announced in a loud voice, 'Found it', pointing to a rusty lump of metal sticking up out of the rock-hard soil. After clearing the grass and some of the soil from the base, it took about two seconds to identify it as the bottom of an old streetlamp, but what was it doing so far from any road or habitation? A quick look at a map revealed that once there was a thriving village about half a mile further up the track. As there was no vehicular access to the village, the Government had put in some streetlights to help the villagers carry their produce up and down the path at night. As is often the case with such villages, the young people eventually left the land to work in the city, and the need for the streetlamps disappeared. What we had before us was all that was left of that row of streetlamps. Jamie was extremely quiet, but I made it abundantly clear that he owed me more than a few beers for dragging me so far off the beaten track for a rusty lamppost.

Old cannons were often found during harbour- or typhoon shelter-dredging operations, but it was only very occasionally that I went out to look at them, as the job was usually taken on by the Antiquities Board. One thing that I did see a lot of in those early days was ammunition and the remains of guns and bayonets from the Second World War. When the Japanese landed in December of 1941 they vastly outnumbered the British and Canadian troops and a hasty retreat was in order. Wong Nai Chung Gap, Repulse Bay, Stanley and a few other places saw some fierce fighting and some extraordinarily valiant action from troops hugely outnumbered by the Japanese Army. Usually, however, they retreated, dropping excess ammunition and supplies as they went. As a result, vast quantities of this ammunition, and occasionally weapons, were being found either by hill walkers or during excavations at building sites.

Normally, I refused to go to the scene as the ammunition and weapons were always in a terrible state and crumbled to dust as soon as touched. Once, though, I received a call from one of my wife's friends asking for some advice. This lady was living at Chung Hom Kok where, in the Second World War, there had been some very extensive barracks to house the soldiers looking after the huge artillery piece located at the tip of the peninsular. She wanted to know what to do with some rusty old bits of metal the kids had found while playing in the hills behind her house. She said that they had been rolling round in the car boot for a week or so and her husband was getting fed up with the noise and wanted them removed. I said that, rather than her getting involved with all the form-filling necessary if she were to report it to the police, I would call round that evening and get rid of whatever it was her kids had found.

About 6pm that evening I arrived at her house and after a quick beer and a chat I asked her to open the car boot for me. It wasn't, as I had expected, a few dozen rounds of very corroded .303 ammunition, but a full box of 25 Mills grenades. The box had disintegrated and the grenades were just rolling about in the boot. The most alarming thing about them was that the safety pins had all rusted through and each one had only a minute quantity of rust preventing the lever from flying off and the grenade from detonating. I immediately got everyone out of the house, cleared a 100-yard cordon and called in the bomb-disposal squad. They said that it was one of the most dangerous jobs they had ever handled and it took them a whole day to make the car safe. On searching the area where the kids had found the grenades, another 150 were found, all in much the same condition. They were, however, detonated *in situ* with a huge explosion.

Hong Kong is, even to this day, riddled with Second World War-vintage tunnels, either intended for use as civilian air raid shelters, command bunkers or ammunition storage. As the maps and plans showing their location have long since disappeared, they are always being discovered during excavation work for new building foundations. Normally these tunnels contain nothing other than mushrooms and a few mice, but on one occasion they found something quite unusual and I was called for assistance.

It seemed that the tunnel had been used as some sort of torture chamber, and chained to the wall was a skeleton in military uniform. There were also several pistols, boxes of ammunition and some radio equipment. I was told that the matter was 'highly confidential' and that, at the conclusion of my examination to identify the date of manufacture and origin of the items in the tunnel, I should never mention the subject to anyone other than the assigned officer. I waited all that day and the next but no call ever came. A few days later I made a few calls to see what had happened but everybody I had originally spoken to now denied any knowledge of the tunnel or its contents. Possibly a bit of a political hot potato, but somewhere in Western District the tunnel must still be there, presumably complete with its gruesome contents.

In one rare instance, ammunition of Japanese military origin was found. An old man of about 75 years old had just dropped dead in the street. First of all it was assumed that he had died of a heart attack or possibly just old age, but when they X-rayed him before the post mortem what should be found embedded in his spine but a bullet. Obviously this had become a murder case, but who would want to kill a virtually penniless old man of 75? The post mortem was being held at the Kennedy Town mortuary, a place I had always loathed. It smelt terrible, there were always piles of bodies lined up in the corridors and the place was infested with huge lazy cockroaches and bluebottle flies. Mortuary flies are particularly nauseous due to their size and lethargy, the results of feeding off cadavers. They always settle either on your lips or in your eyes.

We searched every square millimetre of this old man's parched, paper-thin, brown skin, but apart from a few sores and insect bites there was nothing, not a scratch. In desperation, the forensic pathologist opened him up and removed the innards, so that we could get to the spine, but the bullet was not to be seen. Eventually it was found embedded between two vertebrae and covered with a calcified deposit which had to be dug through to remove it. When it was finally out I identified it immediately as a fired Japanese 6.5mm Arisaka bullet in almost pristine condition. The odd thing about it was that there wasn't a spot of rifling on it, and when I applied even the slightest pressure to the metal jacket it just fell away in tissue-thin flakes. A more careful examination of his skin revealed a small puckered scar right on the edge of his navel, which was typical of a very old bullet wound. The old man had obviously been shot in the stomach by Japanese troops during the occupation of Hong Kong. The bullet had lodged in his spine and over the years the bullet jacket had literally been washed away by his body fluids, removing all traces of the rifling. The calcified deposit was the body's way of trying to assimilate the bullet into the bone structure. So not a murder, but an attempted one discovered 55 years too late.

CHAPTER 17

THE FREAK NAIL GUN INCIDENT AND THE LOVE MOTEL

I don't believe in fate, but sometimes something happens which seems so impossible that it feels like it is preordained. One instance of this involved a dead body found in among the huge stacks of containers at Hong Kong's Kwai Chung container port. It was found at one of the intersections of the road systems which provide access to these ten-high stacks of containers. The deceased had a hard hat on, but it was only made of plastic and didn't have much effect on the missile which had penetrated his left temple. On pulling off the hat, a slightly scratched, hardened-steel nail dropped out of his right temple. The nail had obviously been fired from a cartridge-driven industrial nail-driving gun, but what was odd was that even the lowest-powered cartridge would normally drive a nail straight through a human head and out the other side

with ease, and with enough remaining velocity for it to disappear into the distance.

On looking around the maze of containers, it emerged that, at the far end of the terminal, a few randomly placed containers had been converted into site offices for some work which was being carried out in the terminal area. In the side of one of these site offices was an obvious small-calibre missile exit hole, and on the inside a large, regular-shaped area of gun smoke typical of the mark caused by the shroud of a nail-driving gun. The problem was that the containers were nowhere near the dead body. On following the trajectory that a nail fired from inside the container would have taken, a ricochet mark was eventually found on another container at a four-way intersection about 70 yards away. After striking the container, the nail had then changed direction by nearly 90° and continued down another alleyway in the container city for about 100 yards until it met the victim, who was walking round the corner at exactly the right moment.

It was later discovered that workers returning an industrial nail-driving gun to the site office safe thought that they would test it on the inside of the container, just to make sure it wasn't loaded. Unfortunately it was. Also, the nail missed the reinforcing ribs on the outside of the container. Not only that but, if the victim had been a fraction of a second later walking round the corner, or if any of the containers had been a fraction of a degree out, or if the shot had been discharged a fraction of a second sooner or later, it would have missed him. Fate or what? It was a freak case, very similar to the one with the man on the ladder.

It is strange how cases often come in multiples. Shortly after the case at the container terminal, I had to deal with a case of suicide using a nail gun. Committing suicide with a nail gun is not easy, because the guns have several very strong safety mechanisms built in which prevent them being fired unless the barrel shroud is pressed hard up against a flat surface. The victim had, however, considerably modified the shroud's mechanism and, by using the back of a tubular framed chair, some string and a piece of wood, had managed to shoot himself in the centre of the forehead. The nail had gone straight through the head, through two stud walls, a bookshelf and a bed, before embedding itself in a concrete wall. It was a messy scene: the back of his head had been completely removed and brains were splattered all over the opposite wall.

I also had to investigate a case where the nail from one of these guns had ricocheted from a concrete wall, travelled across a really busy street, through the wing and engine compartment of a car before shattering the engine's distributor and stopping the car in its tracks. My job was to determine whether the gun had been used negligently, which wasn't too difficult. While I was looking at the damage caused and marvelling at the way the nail had missed the throngs of people crossing the intersection, I heard another loud bang, this time accompanied by a scream, from the other end of the street where some modifications to a shop's interior were being carried out.

I rushed along to the shop to find, still with a smoking nail gun in his hand, an obviously very dead worker all tangled up in the ladder on which he had been standing. Above where he was lying, a large scab of concrete was missing from the ceiling, exposing a reinforcing bar. From the damaged ceiling and the reinforcing bar, it was obvious that he had been fixing a nail into the ceiling with the nail-driving gun and, as a result of using an overly powerful cartridge, the nail had penetrated to the reinforcing bar, spalling off a large quantity of concrete in the process. The nail had hit the reinforcing rod and somehow ricocheted off the rod straight back towards the worker's head. Although the nail was by now fairly bent, it still possessed a huge amount of energy and had gone straight through his head, passed down through his neck and most of his torso, finally exiting near his genitals. It seemed an impossible scenario, but it was the only explanation, given the evidence.

In Hong Kong there are a plethora of so-called 'Love Motels'. With Hong Kong being such an overcrowded place there is, unless they have their own flat, little opportunity for two people to be alone. These motels, therefore, serve many purposes from two young people wishing to spend a few hours together, through adulterous liaisons to the odd steamy session with a lady of the night. A room can be rented in one of these establishments for a few hundred dollars an hour with privacy being the strict rule. No booking-in register, no names given or asked for, even car-parking spaces have plastic strip curtains to drive through so that the number of your car cannot be seen. They are usually pretty seedy places, although I am told that the better-class 'hotels' do change the sheets every hour.

I was called out to one of these establishments at 6'clock one morning for an 'open fire' case. When I arrived at the scene all the occupants were lined up against a wall being questioned; a sorry lot they looked. The sorriest of them all, and accounting for over 75 per cent of the patrons, were the police officers who were there with their girlfriends.

The scene was on the first floor and it was a pretty bad one. Lying on the bed was a naked female in her late twenties with a contact bullet entry wound to her right temple and a ragged exit wound to her left temple. The entry wound was by far the bigger of the two, the gases exiting from the barrel having torn open the skin round the entry hole. This is, despite the traditional belief that the exit hole is always the biggest, quite normal in a contact wound. The reason for this is quite simply that the gases produced by firing initially follow the bullet into the brain, but in the split second it takes for the bullet to pass through the skull, they burst back out of the entry hole, tearing open the skin and taking brain, tissue and blood with them.

The barrel of the gun in this case was plugged with brain tissue and there was also a considerable quantity on the girl's right hand. A large glob of brain tissue was also stuck on the wall where it had been forced out of the exit hole by the remaining gas pressure in the skull cavity. She had obviously died almost instantly and the bedclothes were soaked with virtually all of the eight pints of blood her body had once contained. In her right hand was held a .38 Special calibre revolver which belonged to her boyfriend. He was a detective constable.

The pathologist confirmed that death had occurred at about three o'clock that morning, but the strange part was that the DPC had not called to report the suicide until 7.30am. There was a complicating factor in that the girlfriend was pregnant by the DPC who happened to be married to another woman. His statement said that they had had an argument over him refusing to leave his wife and marry her, and that they had, after drinking heavily, both fallen asleep completely drunk. The next thing he knew, he said, was at 7.30am, when he woke up to find her dead beside him. The question was, no matter how drunk he was, how could he have slept through a two-inch barrelled .38 Special revolver being fired in the same room?

It was all looking slightly suspicious, but I thought I would do some experimentation to see what the effects are of firing a gun in tight contact with the head. Human heads are always in short supply and anyway I didn't really like using cadavers as I always had the impression that they were looking at me. The next best thing is a sheep or pig's skull, so I purchased three of each and proceeded to carry out shootings with the muzzle in tight contact with the skin, in loose contact and at a distance of one inch. It was a messy set of experiments, with brain, skin, bone and tissue everywhere, but in the end it answered the question perfectly.

When the muzzle of the gun is in light contact or very close to the surface of the skin the gases simply expand as usual and, since their rate of expansion is greater than the speed of sound, a huge bang is heard. When, however, the muzzle is in tight contact with the skull the gases enter the brain cavity behind the bullet. The brain tissue and the large volume of the brain cavity control the expansion of the gases until they are no longer supersonic and, when they do exit, there is little or no noise. It is in fact exactly the same principle as a gun silencer, which has internal baffles to slow down the expanding gases and reduce them to subsonic speeds. These experiments showed that the combination of the half-bottle of Cognac that he had drunk and the silencing effect of her brain cavity would have been enough for him to sleep through the whole episode.

Hong Kong is one of the few places in the world which can still boast a tram system. Originally installed in 1904 and running just from Happy Valley to Central, it now extends the whole length of Hong Kong island. At $2 for the trip from Western District to Chai Wan it must be one of the best-value rides in the world. The double-decker trams are a bit noisy, but they are a great form of transport and, as an added bonus, they are totally pollution free.

Apart from the main route up and down the island, there is a side branch which makes a detour to Happy Valley where the racecourse is situated. After going round the valley, trams then rejoin the main line for the rest of the journey down the island.

Usually a tram rattles past every couple of minutes like clockwork but as I was looking out of my window one afternoon I noticed this huge tailback of trams from the Happy Valley area. I was just thinking about nipping outside to take a couple of photographs of this unusual sight when the phone went. It was the Divisional Commander (DVC) of Happy Valley asking for my assistance to investigate what was obviously, in his opinion, a shotgun murder. Strange, I thought, we have never had a shotgun murder in Hong Kong, but you never know, perhaps he is right.

The scene was really unbelievable, hundreds of onlookers, reporters by the score, TV cameras and dozens and dozens of police, armed to the teeth and all wearing bullet-resistant jackets. Roadblocks had been set up all over the island and traffic was at a complete standstill. The DVC pointed the deceased out to me, on the top deck of the tram with what remained of his head resting on the sill of an open window. It was a pretty gruesome sight: the left side of his face and skull was missing, as was the majority of his brain. There was a lot of blood, both in the tram and running down the outside. Adhering to the rear of the window frame there was also a fair amount of brain material, but it was not enough to account for the quantity missing from the cranial cavity.

The wound was unlike any shotgun wound I had seen before. It was as though a large guillotine had sliced off half his head. In fact there was no question; it could not have been caused by a weapon.

Leaving the pandemonium around the tram, I decided to walk back along the tram's route and see if I could find the rest of his face. It didn't take long; about 400 yards back, there, stuck to one of the concrete poles that support the overhead wires for the tram system, was the other half of his head. A quick look from a rickety ladder and it was obvious that this was no case of murder but simply an accident. These concrete poles are situated very close to the tram tracks and he must have had his head out of the window, enjoying the cooling effect of the air as the tram rattled down the tracks at full speed. He obviously didn't see the pole coming and it simply wiped off half of his head. The press had a field day, printing the sort of pictures that wouldn't be allowed anywhere else in the world, and I went back to the office to ponder the problems we were experiencing with the force-issue guns.

CHAPTER 18

DODGY AMMO AND INFERIOR GUNS

It was not very often that the radio was switched on in the office, but just by chance we were listening to a local news station when the dramatic news came in of the hijack of a China Airlines jet coming out of Taiwan. The plane was not due to land in Hong Kong but there had been shots in the cockpit and an urgent request was put out for an immediate landing. It was obvious that my presence was going to be required, so, rather than wait for the inevitable traffic jams, I immediately arranged for an Emergency Unit vehicle with three outriders to take me to the airport. In those days the airport was at Kai Tak, which required a trip through the only, and inevitably congested, cross-harbour tunnel, then down through the normally very busy streets of East Kowloon to the airport.

The vehicle started off in a blaze of lights and four sirens, as did all three outriders. The noise must have been quite something, because the traffic, which usually ignores police and ambulance sirens, just melted out of the way. The Cross Harbour Tunnel Company blocked off one lane for us and we were through in a jiffy, but then everything ground to a halt. Every rubber-necked private citizen and newspaper hack in town had heard the radio report, and all of them wanted to see the first hijack ever to occur in Hong Kong. The roads were solid and it didn't matter how many sirens you had on, the traffic has nowhere to go so we were stuck. In the end the car took to the pavement, over a roundabout and up several one-way streets the wrong way and we were there just as the plane landed.

Several ambulances were on the tarmac waiting, and the pilot and co-pilot were whisked off the plane and off to hospital in no time at all. Next came the passengers and cabin staff, leaving the plane empty but for one dead body and the Taiwanese sky marshal, who was very much alive and, judging from the way he was bouncing around, running on pure adrenaline.

On being questioned, the sky marshal said that about an hour after leaving Taiwan the flight engineer had decided that he wanted to claim political asylum in China. Threatening the pilot and co-pilot with a peculiar long-handled hammer, he had attempted to divert the plane's flight path to China. A struggle ensued, during which he beat the pilot over the head with the hammer until he was in a coma with a severely broken skull. Not content with nearly killing the pilot he then proceeded to beat the co-pilot until he too was knocked senseless. This wasn't the most intelligent of things to do, because at that stage there wasn't anyone left who could pilot the plane. Hearing all the commotion, the sky marshal, who was in the main cabin, pulled out a small 7.65mm calibre self-loading pistol, pushed it through a letterbox opening in the cabin door, and shot the hijacker dead with two bullets through the heart.

After breaking down the door, the cabin staff managed to revive the co-pilot who finally got the plane down on to the ground, despite bursting two tyres in the process. Immediately after landing the plane, the co-pilot went into a coma and didn't come round for two days.

My job was to work out what the hijacker was doing at the time he was shot, and the range of firing. Determining what he was doing when shot was quite simple. The difference between the position of the holes in his clothes and those in his body showed that he was shot in the back, and at the time he had his right hand above his head, obviously striking the co-pilot with the hammer. The range of firing was a little more complicated as he was about three-and-a-half feet from the cabin door when he was shot.

At ranges up to about two-and-a-half feet it is possible to tell with considerable accuracy the distance from muzzle to target as a result of gun-smoke deposits on the target. Beyond that range the lightweight smoke particles fall away leaving only the relatively heavy partially burnt and unburnt propellant particles. These do travel out to nearly four feet but are relatively few in number, microscopic in size and difficult to see on anything other than a pure white shirt. The only way to determine the distribution of these particles is to stretch the garment over a piece of wood and examine it under a microscope. Every time a propellant particle is located, a dressmaker's pin is inserted next to the particle. After all the particles have been located the clothing is photographed from above using a flashgun. The heads on the pins reflect the light from the flash and stand out like miniature neon lights, making it very easy to determine the distribution of particles. This method showed that he had been about four feet away from the sky marshal when he had been shot, which fitted in nicely with everything else.

My next job was just to make sure that the hijacker had been shot with the sky marshal's gun. The bullets were easy, as the barrel was quite roughly finished, leaving deep score marks on the bullets, but when it came to the cartridge case there were some strange deep marks on the base. These marks corresponded to small chisel marks on the standing breech face that were imprinting themselves on to the base of the cartridge when it was fired. These marks had obviously been deliberately made, but not by the manufacturer. A few phone calls to Taiwan confirmed that the guns of all officers on special duties, such as sky marshals and undercover agents, were marked in a way that made it possible, without a comparison microscope, to determine whose gun had been fired.

This prompted me to carry out a little research to see if any other police force had used a similar identification system. One of the old ballistic officers, now dead, called Freddy Ewens, who was reputed to be a White Russian, told me that he had worked as a police officer in Shanghai prior to 1944. At that time the enclave was run, and policed, by four nations: Russia, England, France and America. With such a set-up it was extremely difficult to determine who had shot who in a shooting incident, because comparison microscopes were few and far between in those days, and China didn't have any at all. This made it necessary to devise a simple method of identifying who had fired what bullet and cartridge case. A technique of marking not only the standing breech faces but also the rifling of each gun was introduced so that with a simple hand magnifying glass it was possible to determine both the nationality of the person firing and the gun's number. I looked into the logistics of implementing such a system: for 100, 200 or even 300 guns it was feasible, but we had 25,000 police guns in Hong Kong and it would have been impossible.

In those early days the uniformed side of the Royal Hong Kong Police Force was using a Colt revolver originally designed to fire .38 Special calibre ammunition. For some unknown reason, I suspect it was financial, the revolvers had been factory converted to fire the very weak .38 Smith & Wesson calibre ammunition. For many years the .38 Smith and Wesson calibre ammunition had been universally recognised as being next to useless as a police or self-defence round, and insufficiently accurate for target use. As a result, nobody used it and the round was virtually unobtainable. The force was rapidly approaching a situation where it had guns but no ammunition. After much searching, a small European company agreed to make the quantity required and we were in business once more.

For the first month everything seemed satisfactory and then during a training session a gun blew up in an officer's hand. Slowly the situation worsened, with reports of some rounds producing a huge recoil and, strangely enough, other bullets only just making it to the end of the barrel. One gun sent in for examination contained not one but five bullets firmly stuck in the barrel. I went along to a couple of training sessions and the difference in the noise made by successive rounds was really dramatic with one being a huge explosion and the other a light 'pop'. I called for a few thousand rounds and carefully dismantled them. The results were absolutely amazing, with powder charges varying by anything up to 50 per cent.

Suddenly, we had another blown-up gun, then another, then another, and it was getting serious. I did some experimentation to try and duplicate the damage to the guns which had blown up, but it was extremely difficult, because modern revolvers are made with a huge built-in safety margin.

First I tried firing the gun with a bullet stuck in the barrel, but to no effect; then I tried with two, still nothing; then welding the bullet into the case, and again nothing; then a double charge of powder, still nothing. In desperation I tried to fill the cartridge case to the top, which was equivalent to three-and-a-half normal charges. On pulling the trigger – remotely, I might add – there was a huge explosion and the gun flew into pieces in exactly the same way as those during training had.

We contacted the ammunition company and they insisted that it was impossible for a cartridge to be loaded with even a small additional charge, let alone three times more than it should contain. We sent a representative to look at the manufacturing process and it really was crude, with most operations being carried out by hand. The worst process of all involved the measuring of the propellant, which was so bad that occasional double or triple overloads were almost guaranteed.

We dumped the remaining ammunition in the sea and eventually found another manufacturer with more modern equipment, but we couldn't take the risk of running out of ammunition again. It was obviously time to update our weapons, but what to choose?

I was off to the States on a conference and while I was there I visited a few factories to see what was on offer. At first the manufacturers were quite offhand, but as soon as I told them that we had 25,000 armed police in Hong Kong, I was treated like royalty. One of the most famous manufacturers, Smith and Wesson, offered to supply us with a stainless steel .357 Magnum calibre revolver at considerably less cost than the old Colt we were using. It must have been the deal of the century: a gun which was virtually impervious to rusting and requiring little or no maintenance, in the perfect calibre for police use and made to whatever specification we desired. The final icing on the cake, not that one was necessary, was that they would buy all our old revolvers from us! And the answer I got back from those above? 'We think that a shiny stainless steel gun looks far too threatening and the word Magnum sounds too dangerous. Altogether it will give the force a bad public image and the offer is therefore rejected.'

Unbelievable as it sounds, that was the decision made and the force ended up with a standard blue steel revolver in .38 Special calibre: just an average gun which rusts terribly in Hong Kong's humid tropical climate, firing a calibre of ammunition which virtually every other police force in the world had rejected as being useless 20 years before.

After the débâcle of the .38 S&W ammunition I had suggested that a slightly more scientific approach should be taken when evaluating ammunition submitted for purchase. It wasn't anything radical or esoteric, just a series of tests to determine the average velocity, standard deviation, reliability, presence of corrosive substances in the primer and – as we were using plain lead, i.e. non-jacketed, bullets at that time – the quantity and quality of the lubricant. The lubricant evaluation was included, as previous tests had shown that the bullets of some ammunition contained so much lubricant that the smoke produced made it impossible to see the target after three or four shots had been fired.

It wasn't long after I submitted my suggestion that the next exercise for the purchase of ten million rounds of .38 Special calibre revolver ammunition was announced. This was not an insubstantial quantity of ammunition and everybody and his uncle submitted samples for testing. Ammunition came from as far afield as South Korea, China, Germany, Mexico, Australia, Philippines, Singapore, France and Italy. It was a huge undertaking: firing 50 rounds from each batch for velocity determination; pulling another 50 for consistency of propellant load and bullet weight; examining another 200 for manufacturing defects, and so on.

Eventually most of the rounds were ruled out for one reason or another, leaving us with three of the well-known American brands from which to chose. They were, naturally, also the most expensive, but as I pointed out in my final report, you get what you pay for. Unfortunately, some bean counter decided that the cheapest brand submitted was more than sufficient for the force, especially as it had the words 'state-of-the-art construction' printed on the box. I pointed out that it was one of the most inconsistent brands as far as velocity went, had the most manufacturing faults and apparently had no bullet lubricant at all, but the bean counter had made his decision and the order went out.

Not long after the ammunition went into service it was noticed that the scores from the twice-annual revolver test, which every officer had to pass, had dropped to levels never seen before. It was also noted that all the revolvers used for these proficiency tests had what appeared to be molten lead dripping out of the barrel. It was at that stage that I was called in.

A quick look at the revolvers concerned immediately revealed the problem. The unlubricated bullet was literally soldering itself to the inside of the bore leaving a thick coating of lead with the passage of each round. After 20 rounds, so little of the rifling remained visible that the bullets were not being spin-stabilised and as a consequence they were coming out of the barrel sideways and tumbling completely out of control. After a couple of hundred rounds the barrel had been reduced from that of a .38 calibre to almost .22 and with so little velocity that most bullets didn't even reach the target.

The manufacturer was contacted and after some acrimonious exchanges they replied: 'The ammunition is coated with a state-of-the-art lubricant. Service use has shown it to be more than sufficient for the quantity of ammunition expended under operational circumstances.' Just to see what they were talking about I tried to recover some of this 'state-of-the-art lubricant' for analysis. I was using the most sensitive instruments then available but couldn't even get a response from 200 bullets. In the end, after subjecting 500 bullets to a really strong solvent, I obtained a tiny, tiny quantity of glue-like material which turned out to be ordinary varnish. 'State-of-the-art lubricant' my foot; it was useless.

We tried to get the company to take it back, but they refused, sticking to their story about the lubricant being more than adequate for operational use. In the end there was no other option but to throw ten million rounds into the sea. It was tempting to say, 'I told you so'; they never ignored my advice again.

It was soon discovered that the new .38 Special calibre ammunition wasn't all that much better than the old .38 Smith and Wesson calibre. So, after testing hundreds of different bullet configurations using gelatine blocks and other tissue stimulants, an improved type of ammunition was introduced, called .38 Special+P calibre. The ammunition had a semi-jacketed hollow-point bullet and, while it was a great improvement on the standard .38 Special round with a plain lead bullet, it still wasn't anywhere near as effective as the .357 Magnum the force should have chosen in the first place.

CHAPTER 19

SAVED FROM THE UK BY A SUICIDE

I finally completed the training of the recruits and, with the very meagre funds available, modernised the office to the best of my ability. It had taken five years, and as my contract was almost at an end I was readying myself for pastures new. There was nothing lined up on the job front but I was pretty sure I could get my old job back in London. Failing that, I knew that with my experience I could easily get employment elsewhere. Then, just as I was arranging for the packers to come in, the boss phoned to ask if I would stay on for another year. They had a couple of things they wanted me to finish up, he said. The pay was still good and I had nowhere else to go, so I agreed on condition that I had a few weeks' leave first. As it was probably to be my last holiday in the Far East, I made it one of those 'if it's Friday afternoon it must be India'

trips. In five weeks we visited Sri Lanka, India, Kashmir, the Maldives, Thailand, Greece and then London. Some holiday: I definitely needed a rest after getting back from that lot.

I was on the last leg of my stay in London and, whilst I had enjoyed the travelling, I was looking forward to getting back to work. It was eight o'clock in the morning, the paper hit the doormat with a thud, and I wearily struggled out of bed with bleary eyes and more than a bit of a hangover. Instantly I was wide awake as the front page headline of the paper jumped out at me: 'HOMOSEXUAL POLICE OFFICER FOUND DEAD IN HONG KONG. FIVE SHOTS TO THE CHEST IN A LOCKED ROOM, COULD THIS REALLY BE SUICIDE?' Now here was a case that required some very careful scene and bench work if ever there was one.

I knew the deceased officer quite well from cases we'd worked on together and, whilst I wasn't sure about his leanings, I had always had my suspicions. In those days, homosexuality in Hong Kong, even among consenting adults in private, was against the law and anyone with such a disposition became a prime target for blackmail.

There were, it emerged, 101 tales of why and how it happened, but the one which seemed to attract most attention was that Jim (not his real name) had been given the task of looking into the homosexual activities of very senior business people, magistrates, judges and even other police officers. It was a 'set a thief to catch a thief' scenario. Unfortunately, his and his homosexual friends' names kept appearing on every file he opened. Eventually, according to the gossip, the pressure and strain of dealing with this wealth of potentially dangerous information became too great and he chose what was, to his mind, the only way out: suicide.

The question was, did he do it? Complicating the matter was the fact that he was found with five bullet wounds in his chest. The press, pretty irresponsible at the best of times and outrageously so in this case, set upon the story like hounds after fresh blood. Headlines such as 'POLICE USE SPECIAL HIT SQUAD TO MURDER THE POLICE OFFICER WHO KNEW TOO MUCH' were run-of-the-mill, with a new 'revelation' appearing every day. That he was found in a room locked and bolted from the inside and with bars covering all the windows meant nothing, it was a juicy story and they were going to milk it for every drop they could.

One very prominent member of the community, who should have known better, came up with the following scenario to explain how he was found in a locked room: 'The hit man was an existing friend of Jim's and, while having a drink, he suddenly said, "I'm afraid that I now have to kill you, Jim" and, using Jim's own issue revolver, proceeded to pump shots into him until he finally died. To make it look like suicide, he placed the gun in Jim's hand, locked and bolted the door from the inside, then climbed into the wardrobe to await discovery of the body. The investigation team arrived together with pathologists, fingerprint experts and photographers and, when the room was full, he surreptitiously climbed out from the wardrobe, made some comment about having another investigation to attend to and left.'

By the time I returned to Hong Kong, everyone was climbing on the bandwagon, each with his own half-brained explanation for what had happened. 'Experts' were crawling out of the woodwork to prove whatever theory happened to be paying the most money at the time. It was a circus of gigantic, but pathetic, proportions. I tried to keep out of the frame as much as possible, since the crime scene, as far as forensic firearms evidence was concerned, had been very badly handled and I could do without any of the blame coming to rest on my shoulders. What everyone wanted to know was:

a) Could someone really shoot himself in the chest five times?
b) Would the impact from the first shot have thrown him backwards into the wall with the impact from the first bullet?

c) Could someone have got into the room and then out again with it being locked from the inside?

d) Could it be conclusively proved that he did or did not fire the gun himself?

The answers, as any competent forensic firearms examiner worth his salt could have confirmed, were:

a) He was using one of the old revolvers loaded with the .38 Smith & Wesson calibre ammunition, which has been shown time and time again to be an ineffective round. Also, as no vital organs had been hit by any of the bullets, death was finally caused by internal bleeding. Death by this means would have taken a long time: long enough for him to have fired all five shots.

b) Despite what you see in films, it is impossible for the impact of even the largest-calibre handgun bullet to throw someone backwards. The most basic laws of physics show that action and reaction are equal and opposite, so even if a bullet did have enough power to throw someone backwards, the firer of the gun it came from would similarly have been thrown backwards.

c) It was impossible for someone to have got out of that room leaving the doors locked as they were.

d) This was a different matter. While some very primitive chemical methods of detecting lead on the hands did exist, there was nothing available in Hong Kong which could prove beyond reasonable doubt that someone had fired a gun.

The case dragged on, charlatans came and went and arguments raged back and forth. Large blocks of gelatine were hung from the ceiling on strings and shot, weights were hung on triggers, visual aids of all shapes and sizes were bandied around and people got stuck in small windows trying to get into and out of the bedroom. It was a shambles.

Eventually a Royal Commission was established to look more deeply into the matter. After many months and millions of dollars, the judge decided that, while he was satisfied that Jim had committed suicide, there was no way that it could be proved conclusively. He also made a number of recommendations, one of which was that 'The Royal Hong Kong Police must have some method to conclusively prove whether or not a person has fired a gun'.

I was coming to the end of my extended contract and was, once again, in the throws of packing up to leave when I received a call from the Commissioner of Police. 'Brian,' he said, 'I understand that you did some early research in the UK trying to prove that a person had fired a gun. Do you think you could stay on here in Hong Kong and complete the research for us?' It was the job I had always wanted to do, and in a place I really liked working and living. How could I turn it down? So, for four years I was placed on attachment to the Government Laboratory's Scanning Electron Microscope (SEM) Section.

Those next four years constituted one of the busiest periods of my life, working all day in the lab developing and improving the techniques and then, as the SEM was being used during the day for other casework, working long into the night processing the samples. The director of the forensic laboratory was quite a good friend of mine and very supportive, but he was rather a stickler for timekeeping. I had a number of run-ins with him over taking the odd extra half-hour over lunch to play squash, but although I considered his attitude rather unreasonable I thought nothing more of it. On one occasion, however, I thought he really overstepped the mark.

I had arrived in the lab, as normal, at about 7.30am and had worked all day without a break until 5.30pm when the normal lab staff left and I could use the SEM. I had only been working on the instrument for about three hours when I was called to a crime scene involving an exchange of fire between the police and some gold-shop robbers. It was rather an important case, because we were not sure that those arrested were, in fact, the culprits. I took the samples straight back to the lab and worked on them until 4.00pm the next evening. The results showed beyond reasonable doubt that we had the right people, but I was exhausted after working non-stop for 40-odd hours. So, after reporting my findings to the investigating team I went home for what I felt was a well-deserved rest. The next morning the director called me into his office to carpet me for leaving early the night before. To add insult to injury he made an entry in my record of service to the effect that my time-keeping was lackadaisical and set a bad example to the rest of the staff. That entry followed me for years and significantly affected my promotional prospects.

Hundreds and hundreds of cases went through my hands during that period; Hong Kong was experiencing a crime wave of unprecedented proportions. I was also attending all police open-fire incidents, even if there were no arrests, to improve the breadth of my background knowledge on the deposition of gun-smoke particles on the hands of the firer. As a result, many of the cases I dealt with during that time have slipped from my memory. However, one case I could never forget was the Time Watch shop robbery.

The Time Watch shop is about halfway down Nathan Road, which is more commonly known as the Golden Mile. It is just one long row, well over a mile in length, of gold, jewellery, camera and electronic goods shops. A shopper's paradise, but also a place infamous the world over for ripping off tourists, and one that locals tend to avoid like the plague. The Time Watch shop is a really upmarket place, even for the Golden Mile, with few watches costing less than HK$30,000 (£2,500) and many closer to the HK$800,000 (£67,000) mark.

The Criminal Intelligence Bureau had information that a

particularly vicious mainland gang were planning to rob the shop and, from inside information, we knew, almost to the minute, when it was going to happen. Sharpshooters were placed on the tops of buildings and plain-clothes detectives were on every corner and in every shop for 200 yards on both sides of the road.

About two hours before the raid was due to take place the three expatriate officers in charge of the case thought that they would drive by, in an undercover taxi, 'just to make sure everything was ready'. But their informant had got the time wrong. Just as they were cruising past the shop, four armed men came running around the corner and the robbery began.

It had all gone terribly wrong: nobody was ready, the snipers hadn't got their guns in place and all the hidden detectives were out of sight for fear of giving the game away. There was no option: the three expatriate detectives together with the undercover driver had to act, and, after stopping the taxi in the middle of the road, they came out with guns drawn. What they didn't realise was that there was another armed lookout further down the road and yet another further up the road. The hail of bullets that greeted them from six men each armed with at least two guns was truly lethal. They had to take cover behind the taxi and return fire as best they could. After reloading their guns in the shop the robbers came out guns blazing and ran around the corner to their waiting van. The three detectives followed them and another gun battle broke out across the street. The gang got in the van and were about to drive away when one of the detectives ran in front of the van, pointed the gun through the windscreen at the driver and pulled the trigger. However, the round-nosed, plain lead .38 Special bullet was insufficient for the job and it merely cracked the screen and skidded off. In a cost-cutting exercise the Government had only issued each officer with six rounds and his gun was now empty with no spare rounds available. He could see his end was near.

The driver calmly got out of the van, pointed his .357 Magnum revolver at the detective's head, told him to spread-eagle himself on the floor, then calmly pulled the trigger. It didn't go off: the round had misfired. He pulled the trigger again but his gun was now also empty. Giving the detective no time to scramble away, he reached into the van, got another gun and once again pulled the trigger, but that gun was empty as well. With a grin he said to the detective 'must be your lucky day daai lo', then calmly got back into the van and the gang drove off.

Despite the detective's best efforts the gang fled with about HK$10,000,000 (£900,000) worth of watches. Roadblocks were set up and despite a short exchange of fire at one of them the gang disappeared. The taxi had been shot to pieces, there were holes everywhere and all four tyres were flat, but miraculously only the driver was injured, with a bullet wound through his thigh. One of the expatriate detectives also had a small wound, but that was caused by a small ricocheting lead fragment which had managed to slip through the gap in the side of his bullet-resistant vest.

The street was sealed off and I started my examination of the taxi, but just as I started to take notes, one of the taxi's remaining windows exploded above my head in a shower of glass. I stood up and there was an enormous bang and a whine as something ricocheted from the lid of the boot. Together with the officers assisting me, I ran for cover as a shop window nearby shattered into a million pieces. As we crouched in a doorway, a neon streetlight above us exploded in a shower of sparks and glass, and a police officer next to me fell to the floor as if poleaxed. He groaned and got groggily to his feet, and while more missiles ricocheted from the pavement I helped him to cover in a side alley.

There were four of us taking cover in this narrow alleyway as the fusillade of missiles ricocheted all around us. Just then I heard a loud bang from above, but when I looked up it was not another sniper as I had feared; someone from 20-odd storeys above had thrown a large black cat out of a window at us. The cat had hit a metal sign hung from the building and been deflected, but if it hadn't done so it would have landed right on top of us. As we ran out of the alleyway to miss the cat and the remains of the sign, another fusillade of missiles came at us felling another officer in the process. Back into cover once again, but it was obvious that we'd be there all night if something wasn't done and done quickly.

Tempting fate, I ventured out to try and ascertain where the fire was originating from. After a few more near misses I had it located on the third floor of a building across the street and about 100 yards away. After a bit of searching I found a couple of the missiles and they turned out not to be bullets but steel ball bearings, about 0.4 inches in diameter. Obviously they were not being fired from a catapult because they possessed too much power and were being fired very accurately, but what were they being fired from then? I had no idea, but in an attempt to stop the fusillade I sent a platoon of armed Special Duties Unit police to raid the floor. The culprit, unfortunately, heard them coming and fled, taking the weapon, whatever it was, with him. To this day I have never discovered who or what was discharging those lethal ball bearings.

Eventually I finished my examination of the taxi and, although it had been hit over 25 times, not one whole bullet was found; just tiny fragments of shattered lead. We then had a call to say that a shot-up white van had been found about a mile away. It was obviously the vehicle we were looking for, and bore more similarity to a colander than a van. Inside, there were hundreds of rounds of .38 Special and .357 Magnum ammunition just rolling around on the floor. The bullets were all covered in a peculiar, white crystalline substance. About half of them were hollow point and the nose cavity in these bullets was also filled with the same white crystalline powder. It wasn't until I got them back to the lab that it all clicked in place. The reason I hadn't been able to find a single complete bullet in Nathan Road was the white powder. It was obviously some sort of very sensitive high explosive and as soon as the bullet hit something the explosion shattered it into 1,000 pieces. From the look of the material I guessed that it must be mercury fulminate, an extremely sensitive and very high-powered explosive.

To confirm my suspicions I took 20 of the bullets, carefully wrapped individually in cotton wool, to one of the chemists for the powder to be analysed. I told him what I thought it was and explained how sensitive and violent it could be. I then went off for half an hour to see one of my friends while the chemist carried out his analysis. When I returned, I couldn't believe my eyes: he had scraped out the powder from the nose cavity of ten bullets and was in the process of re-crystallising it into a purer sample. In one hand he had a flask of the solution and in the other a rubber-bulbed pipette. On the bench was a wooden retort stand holding a filter funnel. I rushed over and told him to stop it at once as the purer the material got the more unstable it became. 'Don't tell me what to do,' he said. 'I am the chemist in charge of this case and I know what I am doing.' He obviously didn't want or value my advice so I, very quickly, retreated to the other end of the room. Just as I got through the door and out into the corridor there was the most incredible ear-piercing explosion, and then complete silence. I rushed back into the room expecting to find him dead on the floor, but no, he was still standing, completely stunned, but still standing. The front of his lab coat hung in tatters; the top half of the wooden retort stand had become thousands of wood fibres which were slowly settling like confetti; all the glassware had vanished; and all he held in his hands was the rubber teat from the pipette.

Some days later we recovered some of the watches from a hiding place in the hills and with them were five bullet-resistant jackets, all of which had been shot with police ammunition. We also learnt through informants that the ammunition had been modified in Thailand and a big batch of it had been brought into Hong Kong on a fishing boat. The white powder was, as I had suspected, mercury fulminate, and had been recovered from industrial detonators that had been stolen from a mine. We also learnt that at least two people had lost a hand extracting the fulminate from the detonators and putting it on to the bullets.

In succeeding months a number of cases appeared where similar ammunition had been used, but I had already sent a teleprinter message to everyone in the force to the effect that if they recovered ammunition with white powder on the bullets they were not to even touch it. Eventually all but one of the gang were arrested and sent down for life, which, in Hong Kong, really does mean life.

CHAPTER 20

PERFECTING TECHNIQUES, MAKING HANDS MAGENTA

One of the most important skills when analysing scratch marks on bullets and cartridge cases using a comparison microscope is the ability to adjust the lighting to such an angle that the maximum amount of detail is revealed. The principle is the same as when the sun goes down over mountainous country and the mountains are highlighted, until suddenly the sun gets too low and all detail disappears. It sounds very simple just to keep lowering the angle of a light until the best image is obtained, but it requires an enormous amount of experience to get it just right.

This experience was called on while I was on attachment to the Scanning Electron Microscope (SEM) section of the Government Laboratory. One of the senior chemists, Dr David Clarke, was dealing with a kidnap case and he and the police were not getting very far. A local multi-millionaire had been kidnapped and a huge ransom was demanded for his release. Unusually for the Chinese, the family refused to pay, so the kidnappers simply increased the ransom demand. Still the family refused to pay.

The kidnappers were obviously losing patience and sent a Polaroid photograph of the victim tied to a chair, beaten and blindfolded, just to prove that they did have the victim under their control. The family were not having anything to do with them, so in desperation the kidnappers cut off one of his ears, took another photograph of the victim, and sent it, together with the ear, to the family. The kidnappers now had the family's attention and, although the police told them not to, they paid the ransom. This was not a very bright thing to do. The victim was never seen again.

All we had to work with at that stage was two Polaroid prints, but until the scene could be located or the suspects arrested these were of little use. The numbers on the back of the prints were just batch numbers for the production run, which was of tens of thousands, and the chemicals and print materials could, likewise, tell us nothing. In the end, David asked me if I could use low-level lighting to see whether there were any production marks on the film itself. A quick look at the film under the microscope showed it to be composed of a normal photographic paper backing covered with a very thin film of a soft transparent plastic material. Between the two layers were the dyes and chemicals used to record then develop the print.

What we were hoping for were manufacturing scratch marks, such as those found on polythene bags. When such things as polythene bags and transparent adhesive tape are made they are extruded through a die. Slight imperfections in the die or even small pieces of debris adhering to the edges of the die result in microscopic scratch marks on the surface of the extruded material. These marks are often used in forensic evidence, for example to show that a piece of adhesive tape sealing a bag of heroin came from a roll of tape found at the suspect's address, or that a piece of plastic-covered wire found at the scene of an explosion was cut from a reel of similar wire found later at a suspect's flat.

The transparent material on the surface of the photograph did not, however, possess such manufacturing marks. There was something present but it was too fine to see using normal methods. After some experimentation I found that if the dense white smoke from a piece of burning magnesium metal was allowed to gently drift over the surface of the film, the coating so formed revealed the presence of exceedingly fine parallel lines on the top surface of the transparent layer. But where were the marks coming from?

A quick trip to one of the local photography shops produced two brand-new cameras and several dozen packs of film. After dismantling one of the cameras it was obvious that a thin piece of cut metal, which served to guide the film out of the delivery slot, was lightly pressing on the transparent top layer of the film, scratching it in the process. I ran some film through both cameras and it was obvious that the marks made by each camera were reproducible and that the marks made by one camera were completely different from those of the other. This was looking really good, but it was very difficult to obtain an even and reproducible coating with the magnesium smoke. Also, if you weren't very careful, the film caught alight from the heat produced by the burning magnesium. Obviously, some method other than smoking the film with burning magnesium had to be found.

Using polarising filters over the lens and in the light source of the microscope showed promise, but there was insufficient detail visible for a normal microscopic comparison to be conducted. The big problem was that the light was passing through the transparent layer and being diffracted by the backing material. It then struck me that a method caused Phase Contrast Microscopy might assist. This type of microscope uses a polarising filter in the light source and another in the lens system. It also has a focused light source that comes down through the lens system (co-axial) rather than incident lighting, which comes in from the side as on a normal microscope. Luckily we had a Phase Contrast microscope in the laboratory which was used for comparing the colours of fibres. After purchasing some special lenses and filters I had the microscope for the job. A quick look through the microscope and there were the striation lines standing out jet black against an off-white background, just like tramlines.

Polaroid HK were very helpful and supplied 150 cameras for us to test and each one produced completely different striation marks proving that this was a viable technique.

We had the technique, but as yet no suspect camera. Eventually, after a lot of informants' money changing hands, a suspect was located who happened to have a Polaroid camera exactly the same as the one we were looking for. Within 10 minutes I had a perfect match between the camera and the photographs of the kidnap victim. I didn't give evidence because it wasn't my case, but several months later a conviction for kidnap was secured and, as far as I am aware, he is still serving his 20-year sentence.

A couple of months later the same microscopic technique was utilised again but for a completely different type of case. It was about three-thirty in the morning when two police constables patrolling down Queen's Road Central heard a whining noise coming from a shop doorway about 200 yards away. As the PCs approached the shop a man came dashing out with a large bag over his shoulder and what looked like a large cylinder in his hands. After chasing him for half a mile the man dropped the bag and the cylinder and, now freed from the weight of what he was carrying, soon outran the two constables.

On examining the dropped bag they found a small motorcycle battery connected to a motorcycle starter motor. Welded on to the spindle of the motor was the chuck from a drill with a thin drill bit in place. Going back to where they first saw the now wanted person they found that a whole row of shops had been burgled by drilling out the locks on the front door. In one shop doorway was a broken drill showing that the culprit had to change drills halfway along the row.

A couple of hours later a suspect was apprehended but he denied all knowledge of the incident. What we now needed was some way of connecting him to the starter motor, and the starter motor to the drilled locks.

At that time I had been working on a method, called the Ferrozine or Gun Handling test, that could show whether a person had held, but not necessarily fired, a gun. This method relies on minute traces of the gun's metal being transferred from the gun to the hands via sweat. The traces are far too small to analyse, but even if they could be identified all it would reveal was that iron was present, probably one of the most common contaminants encountered. I had developed a chemical reagent which would bind with the metal traces on the hand to give an intense magenta coloration. As guns are fairly unique in shape and dimension it is, from the pattern left on the hand, quite easy to determine the type, make and often model of gun held. Using this technique it is, therefore, quite possible to say that an arrested person had held in his right hand a Colt Model 1911 A1 .45 calibre self-loading pistol and had pulled the trigger with his right index finger. While the technique had been used on many occasions to prove that a person had held a gun, I had never tried the technique on a drill chuck.

We sat the suspect down at a table in the Central Police Station, carefully explained what we were going to do and asked whether he had any objection to the test being carried out. Luckily, he said 'no' and carefully I proceeded to spray his hands with the reagent. Within a minute or two a deep magenta-coloured shape appeared on his right hand. It was clear from the dimensions and shape that it had originated from the castellations of a drill chuck, probably as a result of changing the broken drill bit. He was taken aback, but immediately said: 'That shows nothing, you can go to my home and you will find at least three drills there.' What he hadn't realised was that one of the castellations on the chuck had broken off, leaving a very distinctive shape which was perfectly reproduced on his hands.

The result proved beyond reasonable doubt that he had been in contact with the drill. Now came the difficult bit: proving that the drill bit had been used to drill out the locks on the shop doors. It is a well-known fact that minute irregularities on a drill bit will, if the hole is not drilled through, leave a circular set of striations at the bottom of a drilled hole which are unique to that drill. The problem in this case was that the drill holes were an inch deep and only three-sixteenths of an inch in diameter. The problem with trying to look down such a hole is that the internal reflections from the light source completely eliminate any shadows, making it impossible to see the striation marks.

Could I, I wondered, use the phase contrast microscope to see deep down into the drilled holes? I reasoned that as the light source is co-axial and focused on the object being examined, there should be little in the way of internal reflections. Even if some were present, the polarised light source should eliminate the worst of them. The method worked a treat and it was possible to show that the drill found in the chuck matched up perfectly with the last two shops burgled. It also showed that the shop before that had drill holes made by not only the broken bit found in the doorway, but also the one from the chuck. In addition it could also be shown that the broken drill had drilled the locks in three of the previous six shops which had also been burgled. He must have gone down for five or six years – I don't remember.

During my time in the Forensic Division of the Government laboratory it was still a small, close-knit, organisation with almost a family feel about it. Nowadays it has expanded way beyond recognition and is completely devoid of that which made it such a special place to work, but I suppose that is the price of progress. During those halcyon days, if a big complicated case was being examined everybody chipped in either with advice or help no matter whether they had any connection with the case or were even in the same section. One such case I remember exceedingly well gained notoriety by being the most gruesome murder case in Hong Kong's history. It has become known as the 'Jars Murders'.

The case started off when a photo technician in a Tsim Sha Tsui photo-developing shop came across a batch of very suspicious looking photographs. Photographs of naked women and even slightly pornographic snaps were quite common, but the woman depicted in this set just didn't quite look as if she had been alive at the time they were taken. His suspicions were finally confirmed when, at the end of the reel, he found a photograph of a severed breast.

The police were called and kept the shop under surveillance until a taxi driver came rushing into the shop to collect the prints. His name was Lam Kor-wan. Lam was arrested and, naturally, he denied all knowledge of having taken the prints, stating that he was merely collecting them for a friend. Back at his flat in To Kwa Wan it was, however, quite obvious that Lam had more than a passing interest in photography and that he wasn't merely collecting the prints for a friend of his. His bedroom was crammed full of thousands of dollars worth of sophisticated camera equipment and thousands and thousands of photographs.

The flat was a typical Government low-cost housing unit: a six hundred square feet concrete box with a tiny kitchen, living room and two bedrooms, one of which Lam shared with his brother. With his brother, father and mother in residence the place was depressingly crowded.

Lam's tiny bedroom was dominated by a bunk bed leaving a three-foot wide passage down one side. Every spare inch of the room was crammed full of Lam's equipment and possessions, including one of the largest collections of highly pornographic magazines that anyone had ever seen. Rolls and rolls of developed negatives, thousands of photographs, reels of movie film, pile upon pile of video tapes and, under his bed, rows of glass jars and plastic Tupperware boxes.

The officers carefully pulled these jars and boxes out from under the bed and it was at this stage that Lam started to become very nervous. Opening the first box nearly had the officer gagging from the stench of formaldehyde. After a few moments to catch his breath he once again peered inside and there, floating in the liquid, was the severed breast. Opening the next jar with trepidation the officer was confronted with the neatly excised complete pubic area from a woman. And, so it went on, jar after jar, box after box of female human body parts. Here, they knew, was a slaughterhouse.

The police eventually seized over 1,500 colour slides, 1,000 colour negatives, over 2,000 prints, dozens of home videos, films and nearly 6,000 pornographic magazines.

Police arrested Lam, his brother and father on suspicion of murder as they were convinced that it would have been impossible for any one person alone to keep such a secret in such a tiny flat. Eventually, after much questioning Lam admitted that he had acted alone and that his father and brother knew nothing of what he had done. His confession took days to take down and resulted in one of Hong Kong's most disturbing cases.

Although Lam shared this tiny flat with his family it wasn't that difficult for him to keep his perverted secrets from them. He only worked nights, so when he got up they had already gone to work, and when he returned home they were already in bed. Little did they know that he had his own porn studio in his bedroom.

Initially, Lam merely re-photographed his porno magazines, blowing the photographs up to life size. Eventually, however, he tired of this and wanted something a little closer to the real thing. For his jollies he would lock himself in the cubicle of a women's toilet and either take photographs and videos through a hole in the wall or from under the cubicle door. This, however, started to become risky as notices were being posted on the walls to warn of his presence and on several occasions he had been nearly caught.

He had had enough of being chased down the streets by irate women with their knickers round their ankles and so, on the 3rd February 1982, Lam decided it was time to became more than just a voyeur. He was half way through his normal night shift, business had been slow and his imagination was starting to wander. Outside a girlie bar in Tsim Sha Tsui he was hailed by a very drunk bar girl who wanted nothing other than to get home and sleep off the excess alcohol. Waiting until she fell into a deep sleep, he stopped in an isolated layby and calmly strangled her with a piece of wire. He wasn't far from his flat and the streets were deserted. Slipping by a sleeping night watchman he carried the corpse into the lift and up to his floor. Lifting up the settee he carefully hid the body underneath, making sure nothing was showing, then quietly went to bed. Feigning sleep, he waited until the rest of the family had departed for work whilst he eagerly planned his next move.

When the coast was clear, he dragged the body out. After carefully setting up his cameras, he had sex with the body in all the many ways he had learnt from his magazines. During this sex session he took dozens of photographs and several videos. When he had finished he carefully covered the floor with plastic then, still filming the process, cut the body up into pieces with an electric saw. These he took to a local river where they were eventually carried out to sea.

Two weeks later he struck again. It was a hostess, and, as before, he strangled her with wire. This time his sexual extremism took even more bizarre turns as he had sex with the body as he was cutting it up.

Very few people have been allowed to see all the tapes and photographs of these sexual mutilations as they were considered too disturbing for anyone to see. Even the judge and jury at his trial were not allowed access to the majority of the photographs and videos. I saw them, however, and some of the images were distressing beyond belief. To this day I cannot talk about them.

In the end he admitted to killing four women, but from remains found it is most probable that the number was more like six or seven. It was, however, academic and he was committed for life to Siu Lam, the prison for the mentally insane. I have been there on official business and believe me – it is not a good place to be spending the rest of your life.

The Ferrozine or Gun Handling test, which I developed during my time in the Government Laboratory, really has been a boon for the investigation of armed crime incidents. One case involved the armed robbery of an antique-watch shop in Central District. It was about 10.30pm and I had just had a good meal at home washed down with an excellent bottle of red wine and was ready for bed when the phone went. It was a really good friend of mine Paul Smith, a police superintendent with whom I had been playing squash for many years. After apologising profusely for disturbing me so late, he proceeded to describe the case and ask if I could help. It was a simple case where an illegal immigrant, supposedly armed with a self-loading pistol, had walked into the shop demanding cash. The shop owner was definitely not going to part with any of his money and after a bit of a struggle the culprit fled empty-handed. A suspect was picked up fairly quickly and Paul asked whether I could first have a look at the gun which had been found in the back of the shop and then see if I could find anything on the suspect's hands with the Gun Handling test.

I usually like to carry out the spraying of the hands first, so that you have no preconceived ideas about what you are looking for. It is so easy to imagine a grip screw here or a stippled finish on the back strap if that is what you know should be there. So I went directly to Central Police Station where the suspect was being held.

Central Police Station is a wonderful building and one of the oldest police stations in Hong Kong. With beautiful rosewood planking on the floor of all the offices, wide verandas circling each floor and lots of Victorian filigree ironwork, it is one of the few remaining architectural classics in Hong Kong (it also houses the head of the last wild tiger to be shot in Hong Kong).

I proceeded to spray the suspect's hands. At first he was calm and collected, but once the magenta coloration started to appear, he started shaking so much I thought he was going to fall off the chair. He had been holding something metal all right; the problem was that the marks on his hands looked nothing like any gun I had ever seen. An irregular patch of colour here, another there; it just couldn't be the pistol as described to me by Paul. I told Paul that it didn't look right and that he might as well be released. However, as he was an illegal immigrant, Paul had him detained in custody prior to a court appearance and deportation.

As the shop was quite close I walked down with Paul to unload the gun and make it safe for delivery to the office the next morning. The shop was extremely small and sitting at a desk, with hands as steady as a rock as he repaired a watch, was the owner. In broken English he described to me how this ruffian walked into his shop demanding money. 'I could see it was a toy,' he said, 'so I wrestled with him until I had the gun, then threw it in the back room and locked the door.' Climbing over all sorts of junk in this back room, I finally located the gun underneath some old clothing. But this was no toy; it was a fully loaded and cocked Chinese Type 54 pistol. The shop owner didn't realise quite how close he had been to being shot and killed.

On examining the gun I could see that it had been painted with black paint, but in a number of areas the paint had flaked off, leaving bare metal. Those areas corresponded exactly with the magenta-coloured areas that showed up on the suspect's hands, proving beyond any reasonable doubt that he had held that gun.

After four years of really hard work in the Forensic Division of the Government Laboratory, I transferred back to the BFIB to set up my own small section, dealing with gunshot residue cases. As the BFIB was fairly small I also took my turn on the call-out rota, so I was dealing with normal cases as well.

Over the years I have dealt with many cases where a person's injuries were so serious that he or she should have dropped dead on the spot. Perhaps the strangest of all involved an exchange of fire in Tsim Sha Tsui, Kowloon. Police had information that a mainland gang called the Dai Heun Jai (Big Circle Gang) were about to carry out a robbery on the fourth floor of an office building where several million dollars' worth of gems were being held. The informer said that they were going to come up the back stairwell, carry out the robbery and exit via the front staircase into a waiting car.

The police were in place and ready for the robbers' arrival. Men were out at the front covering every possible escape route, several cars were placed at strategic points to block the getaway car and officers were ready at every junction with tyre deflators, just in case. To stop them escaping back the way they had come, six men were ready on the next floor up, and six were hiding in the offices on the floor below. The premises were, as they say in the trade, 'as tight as a drum'.

Right on time the four-man gang crept up the back stairs, carefully covering every possible hiding place to make sure that there wasn't an ambush. Our men were, however, well out of sight and it wasn't until the gang was on the floor to be robbed that the trap was sprung. The men from above and below suddenly appeared and shouted for them to drop their guns, but they were obviously in no mind to be arrested so easily, and a huge gunfight broke out. In the concrete stairwell, bullets were ricocheting everywhere and the noise was almost overwhelming, but the adrenaline was running and the fight continued. The gang was armed with .38 Special calibre revolvers and Chinese Type 54, 7.62x25mm pistols. The .38 Special revolvers and ammunition were pretty similar to those carried by the police, but the Chinese Type 54 pistols fire a terribly penetrating round. Eventually, two of the gang fell to the ground with bullet wounds and a third put his hands up and surrendered. The fourth, however, managed to get through the swing doors into the office corridor. He turned round with his back to the wall and was just about to shoot one of our detectives in the face when another detective opened fire and shot the would-be robber/murderer in the left temple. The man immediately put his left hand up to his left temple and ran down the corridor for about 50 feet, until he reached a window, which he climbed out of. As he got on to the windowsill he lost his footing and fell to the ground, dead.

The scene was a nightmare, bullet stripe marks, ricochets, cartridge cases and flattened bullets everywhere, but strangely no blood in the office corridor. Assuming the crumpled heap lying on the podium below had been shot through the head, how on earth did he manage to run down the corridor, let alone climb out of the window? The shot should have been an almost instantly fatal wound.

The body was in a terrible state. Not only had he been shot several times, in addition to the shot in the temple, but he had hit an air conditioner and a very large concrete planter on the way down. Bones were sticking out of his arms and legs from compound fractures and his ribcage was a most peculiar shape from hitting the edge of the planter. It was, however, his head that was most odd: there was a classic entry hole on the left temple and only a bruise and abraded skin on the right where there should have been an exit hole. It was obvious that I had missed something of importance in the office corridor where he had been shot, so I went back up for a second look.

There on the wall, at head height and in the place where he was standing when shot, was a small dent in the plaster with some very small fragments of skin attached. The corridor was completely clear of blood as far as the window. Then there, on the left side of the window, was a huge spray of blood, and another on the outside wall of the building. I thought that I now had it sorted, but I needed to see the skull of the deceased to confirm my suspicions.

At the mortuary the pathologist peeled back the skin from the skull, always a grisly sight, and there was my confirmation: the bone under the bruise on the right temple was completely crushed but not penetrated. The top of the skull was sawn off and, not that I needed further confirmation, there was further proof. The bullet was not lying next to the bone but was someway back inside the brain.

The Hong Kong Police were still using .38+P Special calibre ammunition, which is quite a penetrating round of ammunition and, unless it hits something beforehand, it will normally pass straight through both sides of a human skull. In this shooting, however, the bullet was prevented from exiting the head because it was hard up against the wall. This accounted for the dent on the wall, the bruise on the temple and the crushed bone underneath. After crushing the bone up against the wall the bullet still had some energy left and it bounced back through the brain. Why he did not die immediately is a question I cannot answer, but I suspect that it was something to do with the quantity of adrenaline flowing through his body after the gunfight in the back stairwell. I also suspect that, as there was blood on his left palm, the lack of blood in the corridor was due to him holding his hand up to the wound to stem the flow. When he reached the window, however, he had to use his left hand to open the window so that he could climb out. This released the pressure of blood built up inside the skull, causing the huge spray of blood over the wall to the left of the window frame. I would think that he died as he climbed out of the window.

We also came across a Chinese immigrant with a death wish but nine lives. In Hong Kong, unlike most of the world, the police still have very powerful stop-and-search powers: a great way of picking up crimes that wouldn't otherwise be detected. A case in point involved a Chinese man who was stopped early one morning by a couple of beat police for no other reason than he looked a bit shabby. The beat police were obviously correct in their assumption that he was acting suspiciously as he turned out to be an illegal immigrant who obviously didn't want to be returned to mainland China. His first mistake was resisting arrest by getting into a scuffle with the police officers. His second, and almost fatal, mistake was in drawing out an imitation gun with which he threatened the two police officers. As he was backing away he tripped over some rubbish and while he was trying to regain his balance the two officers drew their weapons and fired, shooting him in the stomach and arm. I am told that, of all the places to get shot, the stomach is by far the most painful. Apart from the entry, and sometimes exit, hole the bullet passes through loop after loop of intestine. As leaky intestines can lead to fatal septicaemia the whole lot has to be removed and carefully examined for puncture wounds, each of which must be carefully sewn up. When the intestines are replaced, they never go back quite in the same order, and it takes weeks for them to sort themselves back into the correct position.

When he was fit for interrogation it was discovered that he had been living in a filthy hovel of a stone hut, because he couldn't afford to rent a flat. On searching the hut we found two cartridges similar to those used in the Time Watch shop robbery. We never did find out how he came by the cartridges, but that was how I became involved in the case.

While this man's wounds were not life-threatening they did keep him in hospital for a long time. It was about three months into his stay and he was just about to be released back into police custody when he decided to try and escape. Unfortunately, he hadn't done very much in the way of planning and it wasn't until he had jumped out of the window that he discovered it was on the third floor. Fortunately he didn't die, but he broke both legs and his pelvis, effectively putting an end to his escape plans.

He then had to spend another six months in hospital, this time in a full custodial ward, handcuffed and chained to the bed in a locked cage. Slowly he regained his health and strength and was transferred to a holding prison to await trial. Eventually the trial date was set and I duly arrived at court ready to give my evidence. At the last moment, defence counsel decided to accept my evidence but I thought that I would just sit in court for a while and see what sort of sentence he would get. For resisting arrest, possession of an imitation firearm and possession of two rounds of ammunition, I thought he'd get eight years at most.

He was brought up from the cells, pleaded not guilty and while the clerk of the court was reading out the charges he jumped out of the holding box, through a window, ran across the lawns outside the court and on to the dual carriageway outside. We were all standing there, stunned, when there was a terrible screech of tyres, a huge crunch and then silence. He had been run over by a lorry and was now stone dead. I suppose some are destined for a sticky end and after several false starts he made it.

CHAPTER 21

SCAMMING HONG KONG STYLE

Some of the scams I have encountered whilst working in Hong Kong have been so ludicrous that it is incredible that people not only fall for them, but continue to do so even after they have been publicised time and time again in the press. I have never been in charge of a scam case, but during my time on attachment to the general forensic science laboratory I was peripherally involved in quite a few. Often it would be no more than determining whether a pile of paper had been cut by a particular guillotine, or the elemental analysis of inks on fake banknotes or of imitation gold, using the scanning electron microscope.

There is one scam that, after 20-odd years of publicity, still catches five or more people out each month, and that is only the number that own up to having been taken for a ride. Every month, hundreds of letters are sent from Nigeria to anybody in Hong Kong who might be considered even slightly wealthy. Basically the letters are to this effect:

Dear Mr........

I am the secretary to the Nigerian Minister for Oil [or some other fictitious post]. As I have access to the Minister's official chequebook I have, over the past few years, managed to embezzle US$10,000,000. Before I am discovered with this money it must be moved out of Nigeria.

To release this money I need two things: firstly an overseas bank in which to deposit the money, and secondly US$50,000 dollars to bribe officials in the Nigerian Treasury Department so that I can send the money overseas.

If you would be willing to open a bank account in our joint names and deposit the required bribe into the account I will, once the money has been transferred, give you US$1,000,000 for your help. Please send me the account details once you have opened it and I will proceed from there.

Yours sincerely

Anybody in their right mind would see through this in an instant, but if the contents of the letter were not enough, the return address, which would normally be something like 'Bus stop No. 3, Main Street, Lagos, Nigeria', would give it away in an instant. However, every month, several reports are made by very distressed local citizens to the Commercial Crimes Bureau complaining that their deposit has disappeared and they would like action to be taken. Other than giving the details to the Nigerian Consulate, there was nothing that could be done, leaving one very happy bunny in Lagos and a very upset one in Hong Kong.

Another famous Nigerian scam is the 'Black Note' trick and it is normally targeted at businessmen staying in five-star hotels. Basically the conman shows the businessman a suitcase full of neatly stacked wads of black paper, reputed to be US$100 bills. The notes, they say, are part of a money-laundering process and they have been blackened by a hi-tech process to make transport less risky. To prove it, they take a note from the top of one of the piles and, after carefully cleaning it with a chemical, a genuine US$100 note is revealed. The chemical is, the conman explains, very rare and expensive, but, if the businessman would care to lend him US$10,000, then they could buy more of the chemical and share the proceeds with him. The case full of 'cash' is left with the businessman as 'an act of good faith' while they go off to buy more of the chemical. The case, of course, is full of cut-up pieces of black paper and that is the last the businessman ever sees of his money or the conman.

Another truly great con was perpetrated on one of my friends, VJ Diswani, who has a small business selling specialist cloth for the clothing trade. This really is a cut-throat business, with small profit margins, but VJ works hard and manages to make a reasonable living.

One day a Nigerian walked into VJ's shop wanting to buy US$200,000 worth of cloth for export to Nigeria. Now that was a large quantity for VJ, and he was not willing to take the risk of supplying so much cloth to a customer he didn't know. However, as a measure of good faith, the Nigerian put US$5,000 in cash on VJ's desk and said that he would be back. Three months later he duly returned and the same thing happened, with VJ now having US$10,000 of the man's money. On the third occasion, VJ thought that he must be for real as he now had US$15,000 of the man's money on his desk. A sale was agreed on the condition that the balance would be paid when the goods were delivered. And that was the last VJ ever saw of his US$200,000 worth of cloth. I suppose that he did still have the US$15,000, but that was small compensation for what he had lost.

Another great one involved a 'doctor' who phoned up a woman informing her that her husband had cancer of the penis and that it was going to fall off, probably with fatal consequences. The woman was distraught and asked the 'doctor' if there was anything that could be done. The 'doctor' said that the only way to prevent her husband's penis falling off was to record her moans during sex. We never did get to the bottom of why the husband needed to hear her moans while having sex with another man, but the next day he called back and, using a voice distorter, pretended to be a woman whose husband had been cured by the same method.

The 'doctor' met the woman in the park the next day and said that he was a sex therapist recommended by her husband's doctor. At his request she performed oral sex on him in the park then, later that afternoon, they had sex for which she paid HK$3,000. Presumably she was quite satisfied with the cure as her husband's penis never fell off, but she did tell the police and the 'doctor' was jailed for four years.

Another scam along very similar lines involved telling a woman that her husband had cancer of the stomach and needed special antibodies which the 'doctor' had in his body fluids. The only way that her husband could receive these antibodies was through sex, but first the doctor would have to give them to her via sex. It would, he pointed out, take six or eight sessions before sufficient antibodies were transferred, but then the husband would be permanently cured. Once again it all fell through when the woman asked her husband how his doctor thought the cancer cure was proceeding.

A 'pimp' persuaded some 60 police officers that they could make loads of extra cash by working as gigolos, but first he required some 'titillating' pictures to show to his prospective clients. In all he took some 5,000 photographs of the police officers, most of whom were wearing little more than a belt and holding a truncheon provocatively. Police, not looking for extra work I might add, came across the photographs when they raided the flat of the 'pimp', suspecting he was running a male prostitution racket. It turned out that there was no male prostitution racket and no wealthy women waiting to pay large sums of money for sex with boys in, or possibly out of, blue. Most of the police officers involved were either dismissed or asked to retire but strangely the 'pimp' was never prosecuted.

The last six months of 1999 saw an unprecedented number of chickens running around with no heads bleating about the Millennium Bug. The press had a field day and predictions of doom and gloom filled the pages virtually every day. The scammers, of course, had a field day and cleaned up in a big way. Their MO was always the same: stand on a busy street corner with a briefcase containing nicely labelled pills and have 10 or so of their accomplices crowding round supposedly clamouring to buy the bottles of pills. Eventually some mug would take the bait and eventually be sold a packet of 'Anti-Millennium Bug' tablets. Allegedly, these were to be fed into the floppy disk drive where they would cure any problems the computer might have. If the mug looked particularly stupid then the scammer would offer to sell the whole suitcase at a big discount so that the mug could make a huge profit for himself. Of course, the tablets were usually no more than aspirin and definitely not capable of fixing any Y2K bug that a computer might have.

The odd scam was found closer to home. Central District at lunchtime has been likened by Billy Connolly to London's Oxford Street on the day before Christmas, and with all the shops having a 50 per cent sale. It is wall-to-wall people moving up and down the road, and in and out of the shops, and all this on a normal weekday. The pavements are so packed that in places the pedestrians can be three or four abreast not only on the pavement but in the road as well. It was into this chaos that four armed robbers carried out a daring robbery on the biggest gold shop in Central.

While most Hong Kong gold shops sell very expensive watches and the odd diamond ring, pendant or necklace, their main trade is in pure gold. Not 9-, 12- or 18-carat gold but 'five nines gold' as it is called locally, which is 99.999 per cent pure. None of the items have a price on the tag, just a weight. On the wall are two prices: one for gold coins and ingots and the other for worked gold; there being very little difference between the two. As to the items themselves, there are thousands of items in glass counters with no security other than small, hinged flaps on the back. If you ask to see a necklace they will bring out a bunch, weighing probably 2lbs in total, all tied together with a piece of string. The shop will also have a very large selection of extremely tacky gold 'ornaments' in the form of dragons, tigers, bullocks and any other animal which takes their fancy. All the shops are open-fronted and often have no alarm system at all. It is no wonder that these are the favourite targets of local, and mainland, criminals.

Normally, robbers will jump over the counter and simply scoop up as many gold necklaces and bracelets as possible, often getting away with 10 or more pounds of pure gold in a few moments. Selling the gold on is the easy part, since gold shops will willingly take it back at a 10 to 20 per cent discount over the 'fancy gold' price advertised in the shop. It was rumoured that one gold shop made millions by 'making it known' that they would have extra gold on display but fewer than usual assistants. After the robbers had fled, the shop would make an insurance claim for 50 per cent more than was taken and then arrange to buy back the stolen gold at a 20 per cent discount with no questions asked.

After one of these gold-shop robberies has taken place there is gold everywhere for, in the process of scooping up whatever comes to hand from the display cabinets, many small items, such as earrings and pendants, fall to the floor or fall out from the mass which has been taken. Having been to many of these gold-shop robberies, I am always very careful not to touch these items or tread on any of them. It was, however, during a spate of robberies in Tsim Sha Tsui that I noticed one particular police photographer who kept turning up to take the photographs. This is a bit unusual as they are normally on a rota system and it is infrequently that one sees the same photographer on two consecutive days. One other thing I noticed was that he always wore these shoes with really thick crêpe soles, similar to the ones worn by the Teddy Boys in the Sixties. At one scene I noticed that he was walking backwards and forwards over all this gold, time and time again. At the next scene he was doing the same thing and so I paid close attention. I couldn't believe my eyes; his shoes seemed to be hoovering up the small gold pieces as he walked over them. On the third occasions I saw him do this I just had to mention it to the officer in charge who had surveillance put on him when he left the scene. As soon as he got back to his car, off came the shoes and, stuck on to the bottom of each crêpe sole, was about an ounce of small gold ornaments.

Later I had a chance to examine his shoes and found that he had treated the soles of his shoes with benzene (a rubber solvent) until the rubber became really sticky and picked up everything he trod on. Back at his flat were found in excess of eight ounces of gold and his bank account showed large cash deposits two or three days after each of the gold-shop robberies he had attended. He doesn't work as a police photographer any more.

CHAPTER 22

MESSING ABOUT
IN BOATS

Sometimes the evidence that a shooting happened in a particular way is overwhelming yet people still argue. One such case concerned the shooting of a fisherman. It was a classic case as far as the wounds were concerned and I wrote it up in my previous book (*A Handbook of Firearms and Ballistics – Examining and Interpreting Forensic Evidence*, J. Wiley) as an illustration of a tight contact wound with a double-barrelled shotgun. However, one of the book reviewers said I had misinterpreted the cause of the shotgun wound, and concluded that the book was dangerous for the misinformation it contained, recommending it never be purchased by anyone. It was, however, a classic case of a 12-bore shotgun contact wound and if I hadn't been sure of my facts it would never have been written up as such.

Before delving into the case, some brief background information on the mechanisms involved. When a double-barrelled shotgun is fired with the muzzle held in very tight contact with the skin, the huge volume of gases produced during firing is forced into the body cavity causing a temporary, but violent, inflation of the area around the wound. This crushes the skin against the muzzle of the other, unfired, barrel, leaving a clear imprint in the skin. If there is a foresight or top rib present, this can also leave an imprint on the skin. And that is what happened on this occasion.

The deceased had taken his fishing boat, probably illegally, down to the waters off the coast of Vietnam as the fish stocks there are very large. After a long trip with a full hold, the boat was on its way back into Hong Kong's waters when is was boarded by four armed mainland Chinese men from a motorised inflatable speedboat.

Mainland pirates were, at that time, quite common in the waters surrounding Hong Kong and were utterly ruthless. They would take anything they could get their hands on: radios, compasses, mobile telephones and, especially, cash. The captain, however, wasn't having it, as he was having a hard time paying off his debts. He put up a violent struggle. During the fighting, one of the pirates stuck a 12-bore shotgun into the captain's rather rotund stomach and pulled the trigger, killing him almost instantly.

I was called to the boat to examine the scene but there wasn't much of importance apart from the body. To preserve it, the body had been buried in ice with the fish in the hold and I wasn't going to go down there to examine it. Back at the mortuary it was obvious that he had been shot with the lower barrel of an 'over and under' 12-bore shotgun. At the time of the shooting the muzzle of the barrel had been in tight contact with the skin and the unfired barrel and large winged foresight had left clearly visible imprints on the skin. I had seen such winged sights on weapons made in China and was fairly certain that this was the origin of the gun used. This was further reinforced when the pellets and wadding were recovered from the body cavity as these were also clearly of Chinese origin.

Just to make absolutely sure of my facts I interviewed the captain's family who were present at the shooting and they confirmed that the shotgun barrels were pushed deep into the captain's stomach at the time the shot was fired, and that the gun was of the over and under type with a folding stock. Although they didn't see the foresight the rest of the description fitted exactly with that of a Chinese-made weapon.

The next day an inflatable boat was intercepted by the Hong Kong Marine Police which contained four men, several pistols and one 'over and under' 12-bore shotgun with a winged front sight and a folding stock. I examined the gun and found it to be loaded with Chinese ammunition with the same wadding as that found in the body of the deceased. I also found that the lower barrel had been fired within the last couple of days. At an identity parade, the family of the victim picked out the four men instantly and further identified the one who had shot the captain. Just to make absolutely sure I obtained a dead pig and shot it with the muzzles of the recovered 12-bore in tight contact with the pig's belly. It produced exactly the same imprint as I had seen on the body of the deceased.

I had the gun, the wound, the eyewitnesses, the ammunition and even test firings on the dead pig, which perfectly duplicated the wound, yet still I was accused of not knowing what I was talking about. A moot point, but possibly it might be worth noting that I was giving evidence as a forensic firearms expert before this reviewer was even born!

In my time in Hong Kong I have had occasion to deal with many fishing-boat cases, most of which involved ground already covered: the smuggling of illegal immigrants, antiques or old Chinese silver coins. One exception, however, occurred in the waters just off the south-western coast of the Philippines and involved a huge fishing junk. I was telephoned early one Saturday morning to say that this fishing boat was limping into Aberdeen typhoon shelter as a result of being shot at, and that I should get there as quickly as possible as it was likely to sink at any moment. This was new to me, as a boat has to be shot a very large number of times, even with something as big as .50 Browning or 12.7mm cannon, before it will take on enough water to defeat the bilge pumps.

When I arrived, the boat was surrounded by builders from the various shipyards and a small vessel with a huge pump was desperately trying to empty the bilges. It was obvious that some makeshift repairs had been carried out at sea, because part of a mattress and some planks of wood were poking up above the waterline. After an hour's frantic pumping, the boat slowly righted itself and regained its normal level in the water, but the bilge pumps were still removing huge quantities of water.

Eventually, it was declared safe and I was allowed on board to see if I could determine what had caused the damage. The captain became really animated, describing how this jet fighter swooped out of the sky and started to fire at the boat. The firing was followed by a huge bang and the boat began to sink. To illustrate how strong the four-inch-thick teak wood decking was, he swung a three-pound ball hammer way over his head and brought it crashing down on the deck. I was amazed, hardly even a hint of a dent, the hammer just bounced off. He then took me to look at a six-inch-diameter hole in the roof cover over the main deck with an equally large hole through the decking below. Obviously no pistol or rifle bullet caused this damage. Looking through the hole I could see the engine room with the now silent 'donkey' engine.

Going down into the engine room was a real experience for this boat was truly cavernous. In the engine room were two enormous six-cylinder diesel engines to power the boat and a donkey engine which was bigger than any bus engine ever made. The engine was there to power the bilge pump and provide electricity for the refrigerated fish hold, lighting and air conditioning. Whatever had gone through the deck had also taken out part of the 10-inch by 10-

inch deck support beam, after which it had gone straight through one of the, almost half-inch-thick, stainless steel engine mounting plates. After destroying the mounting plate the missile had continued straight through the four-inch-thick teak hull and disappeared into the sea below.

The captain recounted how the boat was taking on so much water that in a few minutes the donkey engine was flooded and the whole boat was listing so badly that he thought it was going to turn turtle. To add to the problems there was a six-foot swell and gale-force winds. He said the only thing that would stop the water would be to put something over the hole from the outside and let the water pressure form a seal. That meant, however, that one of the crew had to dive down under the boat to fix a mattress and some old sail material over the hole. By the time the plug was fitted and some planks had been nailed into place the hold was six-foot deep in water and the boat was close to sinking. Luckily they had a small two-stroke engine as a back-up bilge pump and with that and three handpumps they were able to keep the boat afloat until they reached port.

With all the damage that had been caused I was sure that there must be some remains of the missile but there was nothing around the hole in the deck other than some smears of grey paint. Climbing down under the engine, I found a small piece of heat-blued and twisted metal embedded in the edges of the hole. By this stage I was, however, soaked to the skin as the water was forcing its way through the hole at really high pressure and spraying out like a geyser. Crawling under the engine to have a better look at the hole was difficult with all the salt water in my eyes and it was almost impossible to see what I was doing. But there, wedged between the mattress and the hull, was a grey-coloured tail fin assembly. I pulled and pushed and levered, until finally it sprang out of the hole accompanied by what seemed like the whole of the South China Sea. Still wedged under the engine I was, however, slowly drowning as the bilges were now filling up with water faster than the pumps could remove it. There was a mad scramble on deck to get the donkey engine started, while two detectives were pushing and pulling on my legs trying to get me out. For a few minutes I really thought that I was about to meet my maker, but suddenly the donkey engine coughed to life, the water level started to fall and I was able to wriggle free.

Back to the lab with my precious cargo, but what was it? Obviously a tail fin from something, but this was well outside of my normal line of work. After a few hours with some reference books it was obvious that I had the tail stabilisation fins from an American air practice bomb. Luckily it was not one filled with explosives but lead dust, to give it the characteristics of the live item. The thing weighed almost 15lbs and when it hit the deck it must have been travelling at close to the speed of sound, giving it tremendous energy. A few phone calls to the local consulates and it was clear that there were no American planes in the vicinity, just a few Philippine fighter bombers which were carrying out some exercises against floating targets. Obviously one of the pilots had become bored with dropping practice bombs and shooting paper boats and had decided to go looking for more interesting targets. We never did find out which plane actually dropped the offending bomb, but through the grapevine we heard that a fighter pilot had suddenly been transferred from active duty to a desk and demoted by several ranks.

It was not just fishing boats that came within my remit. In the mid-Eighties, car smuggling was the crime on the tip of everyone's tongue. Huge speedboats called Dai Feis (Big Fast) fitted with five, 300 horsepower outboard engines were being built just to transport cars back to mainland China. Over 40 foot long with hulls armoured with quarter-inch-thick stainless steel, and capable of speeds in excess of 100mph, they were, even when fully loaded with a Mercedes 500, almost impossible to stop. They could easily outrun the launches and speedboats of the police and even the helicopters had a job keeping up with them. A few of these huge boats were seized in various raids and were given to the British Marine Commandos who were then stationed in Hong Kong. These men were all built like barn doors and completely fearless which they needed to be considering their tactic for stopping the smugglers. After long chases with both boats at speeds close to 100mph they would intercept then ram the smugglers' boat. During the few seconds that the two boats were locked together the Marines would jump into the smugglers' boat and cut the fuel lines with a knife. My only experiences of travelling in a Dai Fei has been at about half its maximum speed and even then the boats spent more of their time out of the water than in. Crashing through the waves, jumping from crest to crest in them it is almost impossible to stand up. The thought of jumping from one to another when they are doing twice that speed is mind-boggling.

At that time the smugglers were stealing cars to order and delivering them to wealthy businessmen across the border and by necessity they had to have their operation down to a fine art. Once an order had been received a local contact would scour the car parks to find the correct make, model and colour of car with whatever accessories were required. Once the car had been located, the Dai Fei was called to rendezvous at a convenient location, usually a building site by the sea. A lorry with a small on-board crane fitted with fabric lifting straps would then be waiting for delivery of the car at the location. Once the car had been broken into and was on its way to the delivery site, the Dai Fei would be called by mobile phone and given the exact time of arrival. The car would be driven on to the fabric straps and immediately lifted up and swung over the sea just as the Dai Fei arrived. The boat would momentarily stop, the car would be dropped into the hull, the straps would be cut and the boat with the car now on board would roar off at full speed. Within five minutes the boat would be in Chinese waters and in 10 more the car would be off-loaded and would disappear on to the mainland. The operation was so slick that they were almost impossible to catch.

The Marine Commandos did intercept many of these boats, but a more reliable and less dangerous method was required to ensure that the smugglers could be brought to a stop without the life-threatening tactics of the Marines. Attempts were made to waterbomb the boats with firefighting buckets, but it was almost impossible to keep up with them, let alone accurately drop a couple of tons of water in their hold. As the bilges of these boats were always awash with petrol from the maze of pipes and homemade petrol tanks, it was considered that a flare fired into the boat might dissuade them. Once again, trying to fire a flare accurately from one boat to another whilst both crashed through the waves proved almost impossible. A couple of successful attempts were made, firing the flares from a helicopter with spectacular results, but this was eventually abandoned as well because it was hazardous for the helicopter.

In the end a bright detective named Kevin Laurie came up with a way to stop them once and for all. His method involved the placing of a heavy police presence at all the normal sites used for the loading of the cars. This drove the smugglers further and further away until the only sites open to them were in a long narrow inlet called Tolo Harbour. Across the entrance to this inlet was strung a half-inch-thick steel hawser supported just below the water on buoys. In the centre of the inlet was a gap in the hawser, patrolled by police boats, through which law-abiding citizens could pass unhindered. On the way there, the smugglers would slip through the gap ostensibly as a normal unloaded pleasure boat. On the return journey, however, they would not risk being stopped by the police and would attempt to drive through at top speed. Once the police were aware that a boat was making a run for it, a length of hawser would be brought up from the depths to plug the gap. Not knowing that the hawser was now in place, the smugglers would attempt to drive through the gap at top speed, only to be brought to a grinding halt as all five of their engines were torn off by the hawser.

I witnessed a couple of these 'stoppings', as they were called, and it really was a spectacular event. With a roar like thunder the smugglers' boat would come hurtling out of the blackness with a huge phosphorescent bow wave and a 20-foot-high cock's comb of spray behind. Being an inlet, the sea was as smooth as silk and the boat seemed to be supported by no more than the propellers alone as it skimmed along, complete with Mercedes, at well over 100mph. Suddenly there was an awful splintering noise as the propellers struck the hawser and the engines back-somersaulted in the air, screaming as the last drops of petrol in their carburettors were used up. Almost simultaneously all five engines would hit the water with a great splash and immediately sink from sight as the boat slowly cruised to a halt with its very bemused crew still scratching their heads.

Eventually legislation was passed banning the manufacture and use of these boats in Hong Kong and severe restrictions were placed on the number and power of the engines a speedboat could use. As China did not have the technical ability to make these highly specialised boats the supply finally dried up and they disappeared. I did in fact deal with one of the last cases involving the use of a Dai Fei to smuggle a vehicle out of Hong Kong but it didn't have its engines ripped out, it was high and dry on an island.

Unlike Hong Kong's authorities, China takes a much more pragmatic view when it comes to stopping a Dai Fei. All this chasing, jumping from boat to boat and stringing hawsers across channels is too much like hard work as far as they are concerned. They reason that, no matter how fast a Dai Fei might be, it is never going to out run a speeding bullet. If, after being warned, a boat refuses to stop, then they just open fire with their 7.62x39mm calibre Type 56 (AK47 variant) fully automatic rifles. If that doesn't get the attention of the smugglers, and it usually does, the covers come off the 12.5mm cannon.

In this case the boat, which was loaded with a Pajero 4WD, had slipped past the marine police and was well into Chinese waters when it was spotted by the Chinese Navy. They were hailed to stop and the floodlights were turned on, but knowing that the penalty for smuggling in China is death there was no way they were going to put their hands up. The boat made a full 180° turn and headed like a bat out of hell back to Hong Kong waters, where, its occupants knew, the most they would face would be a few years in jail. The Chinese gunboat wasn't going to give up that easily though and chased them right into Hong Kong waters with all available men on deck firing their fully automatic rifles.

Despite its armour plating, the Dai Fei was taking hits left, right and centre, and two of the engines, both on one side, had stopped working. The boat was limping along at only 80mph now, and the bullets continued to pour from the Chinese gunboat. Knowing that it was only a matter of time before the Dai Fei either stopped altogether or the cover came off the 12.5mm cannon, they pushed the throttles to full and lashed the wheel to make the boat continue in a straight line. Despite the speed of the boat, all four crew members then jumped overboard.

The boat continued for about another mile before hitting the rocky foreshore of a small island. There was a firework-like display of sparks which ignited the petrol now freely flowing from the smashed engines. The boat careered across the rocks and straight up the hill in the centre of the island, finally ending up nearly 100 yards from the shore, leaving a blackened trail of burnt grass behind.

When I examined the boat it was a very sorry sight. Lying on its side, riddled with holes, two smashed engines, no propeller blades and the Pajero still in the boat, but absolutely shot to pieces. The Chinese military 7.62x39mm calibre rifle ammunition has a bullet with a hardened steel core, which is designated as a semi-armour-piercing round. These bullets are terribly penetrating, and had gone through the length of the Pajero, smashing everything in their path. Some had hit the car's engine compartment and the carburettors, distributor and generator had all been destroyed. Those bullets which had hit the engine had also broken lumps off the engine block and the rocker box cover was smashed to pieces as well. All in all it was a complete write-off.

As for the smugglers, several must have been hit, as there was a considerable amount of blood in the cockpit, together with two fingers. A few days later two bodies containing bullet wounds were washed up on one of the islands, but that was it. What became of the other two members of the crew was never discovered, although there is some suspicion that they were picked up by the Chinese gunboat. If that is so, then they are unlikely to surface again.

The forensic pathologists are usually very reliable and hardly ever take issue with my findings. There was, however, one occasion during which we nearly clashed over the identification of a bullet hole.

A fisherman had been fishing illegally within Vietnamese territorial waters. The problem is that after years and years of completely unrestricted fishing with extremely fine gill nets, the fish stocks in Hong Kong's waters have been completely exhausted and there is nothing left for the fishermen to catch. On the other hand, years and years of war, during which hardly any fishing took place, have left the coastal waters of Vietnam with one of the richest fishing areas in that part of the world.

The local fisherman in this case had been illegally fishing and when spotted by the Vietnamese Navy made a run for international waters. The Vietnamese immediately opened up with their fully automatic 7.62x39mm rifles and 12.7mm deck-mounted cannon. The fishing boat sustained dozens of bullet impacts both from rifle and cannon, with the cannon inflicting a tremendous amount of damage but, not wanting a lengthy stay in prison for himself or his crew, he did everything in his power to get away from the gunboat which was bearing down on him at a great rate of knots. Most of the crew was in the bilges trying to avoid the hail of bullets crashing through the boat's superstructure. The captain, however, was almost unprotected in the wheelhouse and eventually a bullet sliced through the thin woodwork, fatally wounding him in the process. Another crew member took over the helm and eventually the fishing boat managed to reach international waters at which point the Vietnamese Navy boat gave up the chase. To preserve his body, the captain was laid among the ice and fish in the hold, while the boat made its way back to Hong Kong at top speed.

My first job was to have a look at the body before it was moved from the ice. It was not a pretty sight. The back of the body, where it had been lying on the ice, was perfectly preserved, but the front, which had been exposed, was dark brown and starting to blow up with decomposition gases. The face was very distended, the skin was black and peeling, and the eyes were nearly popping out of their sockets. I rolled the body over but there was only one bullet hole visible, so I instructed the body-removal team to take it back to the mortuary for further examination.

There was not really all that much I could do with the boat either as it had been shot about 50 times with 7.62x39mm rifle bullets and 15 times with a 12.7mm cannon. Most of the cannon shells had gone straight through the boat, but one had hit some metal reinforcing round a particularly large beam and the missile was still inside. I removed as many of the 7.62x39mm rifle bullets as I could, not in the hope that eventually we would recover the guns which had fired them, but more for the sake of completion and to determine how many guns had been used. The cannon shell was a bit more problematical as some seriously important pieces of the boat had to be removed in order to retrieve the missile. That I left up to a boat yard.

Back at the lab I examined the bullets under the comparison microscope which revealed that there were only four guns involved, all of which were probably Russian-type RPD light machine guns.

The 12.7mm was probably a deck-mounted Russian NSV heavy machine gun or some homegrown variant. The bullet is, in fact, still in the bureau's index of fired ammunition from unsolved crimes but, as we don't receive many 12.7mm cannons for examination, it is likely to remain there for a very long time.

First thing the next day I paid a trip to the mortuary to check on the state of thaw of the body. The front was blackening by the minute and the build-up of decomposition gases was causing it to blow up like a balloon. The eyes were on stalks and I was sure that any moment they would jump out of their sockets with a large 'pop'. The back was, however, still semi-frozen so the PM examination was put off until the afternoon.

Considering the state of the body I thought it best to miss lunch just in case it made a reappearance halfway through the examination. I did, however, ensure that I had a pocket full of extra-strong mints and some eucalyptus oil to put on my facemask. The pathologist measured the body and carried out a preliminary examination before declaring that there was just a single bullet entry hole in the lower back, indicating that the bullet must still be inside. The hole was, however, very clearly an exit hole, which I pointed out to the pathologist. Unusually, he became quite offensive and told me that I didn't know what I was talking about, it had to be an entry as there was no other hole. We turned the body over and over and closely examined every square inch of his body, but there was nothing else, just one hole in the back that I knew, with absolute certainty, was an exit hole.

Sticking the scalpel into the stomach cavity released the pent-up gases with a loud raspberry noise. The smell was absolutely appalling and the mints and eucalyptus had very little effect, leaving me gagging. Out came the bloated intestines so that the 'entry' hole might be examined from the inside and its trajectory followed. After finding very little, the pathologist concluded that the bullet must have entered at an angle to the body, struck a bone and been deflected down into the hip and legs area of the body. The body was turned over and a series of non-existent wound tracks were then followed down into the right leg which was then filleted from the bone in an attempt to locate the missing bullet. Absolutely nothing, so the other leg was dealt with in the same way, but still nothing. Up until then I had remained silent, but the thought that this could go on forever made me ask whether we could turn the body over and have another look at the stomach. By now the body had become very wet from the continued washing to remove the blood, and the top layer of sunburnt skin was absorbing water and becoming wrinkled. When examined more closely it became obvious that this really thick, leathery, weather-beaten layer of skin had become detached from the underlying layers during the putrefaction and in the process had wrinkled up. This wrinkling of the skin had completely closed over a bullet entry hole. When I straightened out the skin it was plainly obvious that the entry hole was just above the navel and that the hole in the back was the exit. The internal organs were put back in place and then the wound track could easily be followed from the front, through the internal organs and out of the back. Once again, all was not as it had at first appeared.

CHAPTER 23

NEAR-DEATH
ON THE EDGE

For the past four years, Quenten Ford (a solicitor with the HK Government) and I had been working hard on the production of a guidebook to rock climbing in Hong Kong. It was a labour of love; the interest area, as far as climbers were concerned, was far too small and localised for it to sell very many copies. I had, however, enjoyed so many years of climbing in Hong Kong that I wanted to put something back into the sport. As the last guidebook had been written some 30 years before and was terribly out of date, I thought this would be the ideal vehicle.

Every weekend we would be out scouring the hills looking for unclimbed pieces of rock or rediscovering ones written up in the old guidebook. Development in Hong Kong being what it is, we would often find a housing estate where a 200-foot-high cliff should be. On other occasions we would find a magnificent 300-foot face completely missed by the original writers. After spending all weekend climbing new routes or rediscovering old ones, the next week would be spent writing them up for the guidebook. I'm not quite sure how I fitted work into such a schedule, but I must have done somehow.

We could have gone on adding new routes to the book forever, but at some time it had to stop and 'Swan Song', a magnificent route which Quenten and I were the first to discover and climb, was going to be it as far as the book was concerned. The route was on a huge cliff, dropping straight into the sea on an island way out in the New Territories. A couple of climbs had crept up the outside edges of the cliff, but the massive centre of the face was so intimidating that nobody had dared even touch it. The cliff itself was composed of three slabs, the top one being just off vertical and nearly 300 feet high. This slab overlapped the next, forming a huge roof of between 10 and 30 feet across. This second slab was at an easier angle and only about 70 feet high. The second overlapped the lowest slab, which fell straight into the sea and was black with sea algae and as slippery as ice.

Fixing one end of a 480-foot rope to a tree, we threw the rest over the edge and slowly abseiled down to the bottom of the first slab, where we found a small ledge about six inches by six inches, which we used as a 'platform' to start the climb. The climb back up the slab was very hard indeed, with the crux being at the end of 150 feet of climbing. This climb consisted of a completely blank and vertical wall with a small peapod-shaped crack about three inches long in its centre. The only way across this blank section was to place the knuckle of the middle finger in the peapod slot and then bend the finger. This made the knuckle expand and, if you were lucky, it provided enough friction to support your weight while you swung across to more positive holds. Not a move for the faint-hearted.

The climb was completed, inserted into the relevant section of the book and the manuscript sent off to the publishers. A couple of weeks later a friend of mine, Martin Lancaster, who is a very strong climber, said that he had managed to climb a new start to Swan Song and asked if I would like to try it out with him. The climb started by abseiling way out to the right of where I started and down on to the second slab. After a hair-raising abseil we traversed into the centre of the slab underneath this huge roof, formed by the bottom of the top slab. We were always aware of the huge quantity of rock above. It was a very dark and foreboding place to be and I wanted out as soon as possible. At one point there is a break in the roof where it narrows to only 10 feet and that is where Martin had climbed the new start to Swan Song.

I let Martin lead so that I could watch carefully where each hand and foothold was. Climbing upside down across this 10-foot ceiling was going to be terribly strenuous and I had to get the moves right first time otherwise I would fall off through lack of strength. Martin was quickly across the roof, then disappeared over the lip and continued climbing to another small ledge about 40 feet further up the face. The rope tightened round my waist, signalling that it was now my turn to climb. I hate climbing across roofs because there's no room for mistakes, and if you hang about your arms tire in minutes and you fall off dramatically. The sequence of holds has to flow in one continuous movement until you are back on merely vertical ground and can take a rest.

I had all the holds, what few there were, spotted and launched myself out under the roof. It was going like clockwork, not tiring, just slowly moving from hold to hold ensuring that my feet stayed on something to reduce the weight on my fingers. Only one more hold then I would be at the lip, but it was just out of reach. Martin, being four inches taller than me, had a distinct advantage. There was only one thing for it: move one foot out on to another hold to give me a bit more reach, then a quick lunge. Nothing to it, I would soon have it in the bag.

How wrong could I be? The hold sloped the wrong way for the

hand I was using and there was nothing to get hold of. Suddenly I was off with a half back somersault, falling upside down, facing out from the cliff. The sea was coming up to meet me and then, all of a sudden, I stopped falling and was gently yo-yoing up and down on the end of the rope. My heartbeat must have been at least 300 beats per minute and I am sure that my system was running on pure adrenaline, but I had to calm down and sort myself out. I was in a really difficult position, hanging 10 feet out from the face, upside down and slowly rotating. It was, at the same time, quite mesmerising looking down at the sea some 200 feet below, watching it slowly turn round and round. But I had to fix this situation as quickly as possible, because Martin was taking the whole of my weight on his waist and it could be slowly dragging him off the cliff face. Equipment hanging everywhere wasn't making it any easier to right my position, but I slowly started to rearrange myself and was just in the process of trying to get the right way up when I suddenly dropped another 20 foot! I nearly died with fright.

As I fell I thought it must be the end; either Martin had fallen off or the rope had been cut through by the sharp rock. But then I stopped falling with a jerk and started to yo-yo again. This time there was no hanging about. I quickly righted myself, swung into the rock, grabbed hold of a flake of rock and started climbing. I got back to the roof, but this time I had to get it right as my arms were shot and I didn't have any energy left. I made a quick move up, then out under the roof, moved across and then lunged for the hold, this time with the correct hand. Swinging in space with just one handhold is no place to stay, so I put one foot on a hold and reached over the lip to an unseen one-finger jam. Letting go with everything else and swinging into space on just this one finger was also unnerving, but not as unnerving as seeing the rope lying in tatters like the white entrails of some monster, halfway between Martin and myself.

Later I discovered that, as I was hanging on the rope below the overhang, the rock had slowly sawed through the rope until it suddenly gave, but for a few strands. My weight on such a thin piece of nylon had caused it to stretch almost to breaking point but, as luck would have it, I managed to get hold of the rock before it broke completely.

Martin very calmly advised me to take it slowly and make no mistakes. Being in such a position concentrates the mind quite amazingly and, slowly regaining my composure, I performed a very controlled and smooth one-armed pull-up, still relying on this one-knuckle jam. At last a good hold was within reach and I could move up in relative safety. The rest of the climb was no picnic, since we only had half a rope to climb with, but after a couple of hours we were at the top, completely drained of energy and emotion. I had had too many lucky escapes; this was the last one as far as I was concerned, and Swan Song with the direct start was the last serious climb I ever made.

As a footnote, two weeks after my epic, Martin was climbing the same route with another partner who fell off before reaching the overhang. He wasn't too worried as it was only about 40 feet straight into the sea, which he entered with straight legs. What he didn't realise was that, just three feet below the surface, there was a huge rock which he hit with legs locked straight. He shattered both hips, had compound fractures of both legs, crushed a number of ribs, broke one arm and all but severed a foot. He survived, but only just.

CHAPTER 24

THE DEAD CAPTAIN, CARELESS MARKSMEN AND ACCIDENTS ON PURPOSE

For some unknown reason, the Hong Kong Government still insists that its staff should work every other Saturday morning, which is nearly always a complete waste of time. Admittedly it is quiet and the phone hardly ever rings, but you can be assured that if you need to speak to someone else in the Government it will either be his Saturday off or he will be out doing some shopping and not available. It was my 'long week', as it is called locally, and I had a few things to do on this particular Saturday, so thought I would sort those out before going to the bank to draw out some money for what remained of the weekend. I was just walking out of the door when the phone rang with urgency.

It was the commandant of the Shek Kong military camp to say that there had been a murder and could I come and 'do your forensic bit as soon as possible'? From his description of the scene it sounded like a case for the bomb-disposal unit, but I knew from bitter experience that it is always better to go and have a look just in case.

The camp was chaos: HK Police, military police, military CID, every bit of military brass you could imagine, helicopters landing and taking off, scores of press reporters, forensic pathologists, military doctors, military pathologists, in fact virtually anybody you could think of. Eventually, I was led into a captain's office and it was immediately obvious that it was not going to be my case.

The captain, or what remained of him, was still sitting behind his desk, but the centre of the desk was completely missing, with matchwood-sized pieces of it all over the room. Above the desk, embedded in the ceiling, were hundreds of pieces of shrapnel. Both hands had fingers missing and his face was pretty torn up as well. The worst part, however, was his legs; they had both been blown off above the knees and what remained of them was lying on the floor under the desk. His upper legs and the bottom of his torso were also in bad shape with some quite large holes in his abdomen through which poked large loops of intestine. The traumatic amputation of his legs had allowed the heart to completely pump his body dry and all ten pints of blood were slowly congealing into a lump on the floor.

A quick look under the desk and it was obvious what had happened. There on the floor was the fly-off lever from a British military grenade, together with some wires which had held the grenade in place. Attached to the drawer was a length of wire which had pulled the pin out of the grenade as it was opened, killing the captain almost immediately. Everybody and his uncle were questioned, everything in the office down to the last piece of paper was fingerprinted, but nothing. Not a shred of evidence. All that came out of the investigation was that the captain was universally hated and it had only been a matter of time before somebody did something pretty bad to him. There were a few suspects, but insufficient evidence to even consider making a case against anybody, and to this day the murder remains unsolved.

Before Hong Kong was handed over to China in 1997, when it became a Special Administrative Region of China, the China News Agency in Happy Valley was the de facto Chinese embassy. Never was there a news hack in sight, however, nor was any report ever generated, but there was a veritable forest of antennae on the roof and a huge number of very important looking mainland Chinese men in dark suits came and went.

The place was, especially as the handover date came ever closer, almost akin to holy ground with a constant police presence and lots of undercover surveillance to make sure nobody or no group of anti-China activists came too close. Of course, there were people sitting around with protest banners, lighting joss sticks for political prisoners, but it was always very peaceful as almost all protests in Hong Kong are.

All was well, until one evening when, as a couple of so-called CNA 'newspaper reporters' were about to pack up for the day, two bullets came crashing through their office window and embedded themselves in the opposite wall. Panic, pandemonium, headless chickens running around in circles, and senior police with eyes like dinner plates waiting for the Damoclean sword of China to fall and World War III to begin.

As far as I was concerned the scene was quite simple: two holes in the glass, two corresponding holes in the wall and two 9mm Parabellum pistol bullets fired from a pistol with six right-hand groove rifling. But where had they come from? The line of sight indicated a low-flying aircraft or possibly even an aircraft at altitude, but about 1,000 miles away! While I was lying in bed that evening pondering the problem, another two bullet holes appeared in the glass of an office three rooms away from the first. If nothing else, that dispensed with the idea of an assassination attempt on one of the officials, as nobody could be so bad a shot as to be three offices out.

The scene was very similar to the first, just two bullet holes in the window and two bullets in the wall, but this time from two different .357 Magnum revolvers. The trajectory was the same as before, coming from way above the rooftops.

The next morning I was going through the morning reports which list all the crimes and incidents over the previous 24 hours. I noticed a report from down in North Point regarding the sounds of gunfire. Now we hear very little of that in Hong Kong and the incident had been written off by the local police as a car backfiring or some other loud noise. That's a bit strange, I thought, so I checked on the previous day's reports. There was another call from the same area reporting similar sounds. This was looking a little more than coincidental, so out came the series of ballistics computer programs and I started to enter the data: a 115 grain bullet fired at 1,200 feet per second at an elevation of 15° from the top of a ten-storey building with 15- and 20-storey buildings in between. No, it wouldn't work. Try it the other way round: a bullet at the end of its trajectory descending at an angle of 30° travelling at 300 feet per second. Would that be enough to take it over the buildings?

After a couple of days' work I had narrowed down the area from which the rounds could have been fired to a 200-yard radius in North Point. Being a highly congested area there were, however, about 20 blocks of flats in that small radius. We had no option but to search them all laboriously. And then the leads started to come in. Residents of four blocks in one square reported the sounds of gunfire; then the resident in a flat on the top floor of another said they sounded as if they were coming from the roof above his flat. Sure enough, there on the roof was a fired 9mm Parabellum cartridge case. A blanket search of every flat in the block turned up a 24-year-old Chinese youth who had been educated in America. Under his bed was a veritable armoury of brand new weapons together with hundreds of rounds of ammunition.

It seems that the youth had been a keen shooter while studying in the States and had accounts at several gunsmith shops. When he finished his studies and returned to Hong Kong he kept up the accounts and simply had them mail out the guns either in parts or as whole weapons. While the postal checks for such things are very good in Hong Kong, they cannot check each and every one of the thousands of parcels that arrive each day and these weapons had slipped through without being noticed. There was no criminal intent; he was merely shooting at targets placed on the wall surrounding the roof. It just never entered his head that the bullets had to land somewhere and, in densely packed Hong Kong, that was bound to be a building. In this case it just happened to be the New China News Agency.

Another case in a similar vein started off with a call from my old friend Paul Smith who was then working as Assistant District Commander in Central Police Station. Paul explained that he had just received a phone call from a very good friend of his who was the security manager in an expensive five-star hotel just across the road from police headquarters. It seems that the hotel had been having a poolside barbecue a few days before when the guests started to comment that there was something very crunchy in the curried lamb. When they checked the food it was found to be full of minute shards of glass. As they pondered the origin of this glass, more started to rain down from above. Panic ensued, the pool was cleared and every room on that side of the building was checked. In four of the rooms it was found that the toughened glass had been shattered by some form of missile and it was the broken glass from these windows that was ending up in the curry.

The Wanchai Police were caled in but were of the opinion that nothing could be done by the ballistics officers as the damage had been caused by small steel balls fired from an air gun. They would, however, make a note of the incident in their report book. Under normal circumstances they would have been perfectly correct in their assumption, as that type of missile is usually fired from low-powered air- or gas-operated guns which rarely have sufficient energy to penetrate the glass. Being toughened glass, the impact of such a non-deforming missile over such a very small area is, however, sufficient to craze the glass and all one is left with is a very small hole with a cone of glass knocked out of the glass on the side opposite the impact. It is, therefore, usually impossible to obtain any directional information.

Paul phoned to say that his friend was beside himself as it was costing the hotel tens of thousands of dollars a day in lost room rental to say nothing of replacing the glass. Could I just have a look as a favour? Being an old friend, how could I turn him down?

During the night another three windows had been broken, making seven panes in all, which at HK$55,000 (£4,600) each was turning into quite an expensive bit of vandalism. It was a difficult job, because the windows were spread out over several floors and right along one side of the hotel. I asked the manager if I could be left alone with the problem for a couple of hours and be given the keys to the rooms concerned, together with those of some of the rooms which had not sustained any damage. Slowly a pattern began to emerge by determining where the shot could *not* have been fired from. It was narrowed down, block by block, floor by floor, until I had the building and then the floor and then one of two possible flats about 50 yards away.

Then we had a bit of a problem: the block belonged to the British Army stationed in Hong Kong and it was occupied by very senior married officers. This was quite a serious offence, so search warrants were obtained for raids to be carried out not only on the selected two flats but also, just to be absolutely sure, the two above, two below and one on either side. At the appointed time our Police Tactical Unit carried out simultaneous raids on all eight flats and, in one of the two which I had originally identified there was a BB air rifle together with a box of steel BBs, which belonged to the residents' teenage son. No guns were found in any of the other flats. There was absolutely no way of determining whether that was the gun which had caused the damage, as steel BBs are too hard to take on the bore characteristics. However, the purpose of the raid was to let whoever was doing the shooting know that we had the flats under surveillance. The youth's father was obviously not impressed, as he could see his army career coming to a very rapid halt. The raid obviously did the trick, there never was another window broken in that hotel, and a week later my wife and I enjoyed a very nice meal with Paul and his wife, compliments of the manager.

The late 1980s saw a dramatic increase in armed crime incidents in Hong Kong. Many reasons were given, but it appears it was connected with a number of Triad 'organisers' making contact with a ruthless gang of criminals on the mainland called the 'Dai Huen Jai' or Big Circle Boys. The contact was not made directly, but through an intermediary in one of the Special Economic Zones (SEZ), which made it almost impossible to trace the 'organiser'. Once a target was chosen, the mainland contact would arrange for the gang to be transported to Hong Kong in a Dai Fei. They would be picked up by car and taken to a prearranged hotel where they were given the target. The weapons they brought down from China usually consisted of at least one pistol each, several Chinese Type 56 assault rifles (same as the Russian AK47), a number of Chinese hand grenades and lots of spare ammunition and magazines. At one stage it was also rumoured that they were using weapons which had been taken out of Chinese military armouries. After the robbery was finished, the weapons were put back in the armoury, making them impossible to trace. This was, however, never proven one way or the other.

After casing the target the gang would contact the intermediary with the time of the robbery. The intermediary would then arrange for the Dai Fei to be standing by, ready to whisk them back to the safety of China. The robberies themselves were always carried out in the most ruthless way imaginable, with the streets being sprayed with fully automatic fire from the Type 56 assault rifle and people being shot dead just for being there. If the police did arrive before the robbers had fled, grenades would be freely used, with innocent bystanders being wounded and killed without a thought. This diversionary tactic allowed them to get into the MTR (underground rail) system where they would disappear into the crowds in seconds never to be seen again. These men were utterly ruthless; they knew that if caught they would either be incarcerated here for life or be sent back to the mainland for certain execution. They had nothing to lose.

The intermediary would arrange for them to be picked up at a convenient outlying station where they would be relieved of the gold and given a cash payment equal to several years' normal salary. The Dai Fei would them have then back on the mainland where they would disappear until they ran out of cash and were once again in the market for another job.

The ammunition being used in the Type 54 pistol (a variant of the Russian TT33 Tokarev) consisted of a lead core with a thick steel jacket. The bullet was leaving the muzzle at a velocity of about 1,400 feet per second (about 960mph) and with that bullet construction it is an extremely penetrative round. After a few months, however, we noticed that the ammunition being used was of a slightly different type, the bullet being made from a solid piece of steel. Being solid steel it did not deform on striking most materials, and was even more penetrating than the steel-jacketed bullet. In one case the robber shot an innocent bystander and it didn't just go through the bystander, it went straight through the manager who was standing behind, completely smashed the arm bone of a woman standing behind him and then went on through a wooden door before finally stopping in a heavy wooden desk.

Having seen at first hand the penetrative power of this bullet I was a little concerned about the reliability of the bullet-resistant vests (BRVs) that were on issue to the Royal Hong Kong Police at that time. I drew a couple out of stores, and, with the aid of a very large lump of plasticine to simulate a human body, I arranged for the top brass to witness the effectiveness, or otherwise, of the BRV against this new type of ammunition. The label on the BRV said that it was proof against 9mm Parabellum and .357 Magnum calibre ammunition and everyone was convinced that it would perform well.

Not being a particularly good shot, I stood just a few yards from the BRV to make sure that I didn't miss. There was a huge bang, and loads of sparks and smoke, but the target didn't move even a fraction of an inch. Everyone was falling about laughing over my missing the target, but I was convinced that I hadn't. All the brass gathered round while I took the BRV off the 'body' and there was a neat hole straight through the front of the vest, and through all 10 inches of plasticine. The bullet had not, however, stopped there. It had continued straight through the back of the BRV and through three telephone directories which were being used as support! Suddenly it was very quiet; the laughing had stopped. Just to prove a point I put both BRVs on the 'body' and shot it again. Once again not a flicker of movement from the 'body' and when we checked the bullet had gone through the front and back of both vests as well as the plasticine. Silence reigned.

The police were now in an extremely precarious position for they were issuing BRVs which they knew would not stop the ammunition being used by criminals. If one of their men were shot and killed while wearing one of these BRVs there would be very serious repercussions, to say nothing of legal liabilities. We phoned all the major BRV manufacturers in the world, but nobody had even encountered such a bullet. Something had to be done. As a stopgap method, thick heavy steel plates were issued which fitted into pockets at the front of these jackets. Although they did stop these bullets, they only covered a small part of the chest area, and were heavy and cumbersome. In addition, if a bullet hit the plate at a slight angle it would either go ricocheting off into the distance, potentially hitting an innocent bystander, or, if the shot were in a slightly upwards direction, it would go through the chin and out of the top of the head of the wearer.

I had built up a very good rapport with the BRV manufacturers and, by offering our range and laboratory as a testing facility for their research and development, we soon had a vest which would reliably stop two hits from the solid steel round in a very small circle. However, no sooner had we received our first supply of these new BRVs than the criminal started to use the Type 56 (AK47) rifles in earnest and, to make matters even worse, they started to use a semi-armour-piercing round with a steel core. Once again we were into developmental testing, but the only answer this time was for a titanium alloy plate which was big enough to cover the vital organs. This plate was sewn into a pocket in the front of the BRV. We did consider a plate at the back as well but, in theory, a policeman should always be facing his adversary, not running away. To reduce the ricochet potential we had several layers of Kevlar bullet-resistant material bonded on to the strike face of the plate which did the job quite well. As a result of all this developmental work, the Hong Kong Police probably had the best BRV on general issue to any civilian or military force in the world.

In the early developmental stages of titanium alloy supplementary BRV plates, a very well-respected European anti-terrorist squad decided to carry out live testing of the BRVs on one of their men. The BRV was proof against 7.62x51mm NATO armour-piercing ammunition, but just to be on the safe side they decided to only use a 9mm Parabellum machine gun for the testing. The target strapped on the vest and, with a very gung-ho 'do your best', instructed them to start firing. First one shot: 'Nothing,' he said. Then two: 'Still nothing.' Then the rest of the 30-round magazine.

Then, appallingly, halfway through the magazine, the man's bottom jaw fell off, together with his tongue. On hitting the titanium plate, the bullet had shattered into pieces of razor-sharp copper zinc alloy, jacket material and lead fragments. The fragments sprayed out in a 360° arc with those going towards the ground and to the left and right hitting nothing. However, those fragments which went upwards slowly sawed through his chin and then the jaw until it and his tongue fell off. Luckily, the doctors were able to sew his tongue back on and the bone successfully regrew after the bits were screwed and wired back in place. I saw him several years later and, whilst he had some horrible scars and talked with a distinct lisp, he was well and running a bodyguard business in the Middle East. The anti-terrorist unit did, however, learn its lesson and, apart from banning the live testing of BRVs, now has a chin guard fitted to all its vests.

Many crimes around that period of time involved the use of Chinese and Russian hand grenades and I always wondered how on earth the criminals could be obtaining these things in such large numbers. That was until the day my wife and I decided to take a short weekend break in Macau, a Portuguese enclave about 40 miles down the coast from Hong Kong. For a short break, Macau is a wonderful place, it has a completely different atmosphere from Hong Kong with a distinctly Mediterranean feel about it. The food and wine, being predominantly Portuguese, are out of this world and as a result the restaurants are wonderful.

We had risen late, having had a fantastic evening meal in a small Portuguese restaurant the night before, with copious quantities of wine and a bottle of chilled Portuguese White Port to finish. Once up, we took a stroll through the streets, before deciding where to lunch. Was it to be the Poisada de Santeago, a 300-year-old fort converted into a stunning hotel and restaurant, or Fernandos, on the furthest and smallest island from Macau but serving the most fabulous food you could ever imagine, all cooked over wood fires?

While pondering, idly drifting along, doing some window shopping and looking at the wares being sold by the street vendors, we almost knocked over an old lady with a tray hanging by a piece of string round her neck. With profuse apologies, I made sure she was not hurt and idly had a look at the contents of her tray. There, rolling about, were 10 Russian-made F1 anti-personnel hand grenades. She was selling them on the street corner for the equivalent of about HK$200 (£8) each. Of course, by the time I had managed to find a police officer she had long disappeared.

When I had worked in the Metropolitan Police Laboratory, apart from D11 the marksman unit and a few officers on protection duty, guns were only issued to the police in exceptional circumstances. You could almost guarantee, however, that on each occasion they were issued I would receive a very sheepish phone call the next day asking if I could help with a replacement round as a gun had gone off 'accidentally' during the operation. The amount of paperwork involved in officially reporting such an accidental discharge and the trouble that it would cause the officer concerned was always totally out of proportion with the event. As a result, after carefully investigating the case and ensuring that there was nothing more sinister to the incident, I would often surreptitiously exchange the fired round for a live one. It was amazing how many bottles of scotch and unsigned thank you cards appeared on my desk each Christmas as a result of these little acts of assistance.

In Hong Kong, considering that there are some 15,000 guns on issue on any one day, there are a surprisingly small number of so-called 'accidental discharges'. There is always going to be the odd cowboy practising quick draws in the toilet when the gun goes off, accidentally shooting the bathroom mirror, or the gun that goes off while being cleaned, but in general these incidents are very few and far between. There was, however, one case involving an expatriate friend of mine that resulted in him accidentally shooting himself in the hand!

This particular officer hated guns and almost refused to wear his issue weapon even when on operational duty. He still, however, had to take the quarterly range test and, despite loathing guns of any sort, always passed with flying colours. So he was quite capable with weapons. On his return from the range the gun was, however, always securely locked in his safe, not to see the light of day until the next range course came round.

Being in a headquarters unit, he very rarely became involved in operational duties, but on this particular day he had to conduct a raid on a premises where an armed robber was suspected of being holed up. Going unarmed was not an option on this occasion, so the gun was removed from the safe and loaded with six rounds of .38 Special ammunition. As he pushed the gun into his holster, which he was holding in his left hand, there was a huge explosion and his left hand started to pour with blood from a bullet that had gone through the bottom of the holster and then through his hand.

The hand was in a hell of a mess; large chunks of the holster and partially burnt propellant had been driven into the muscle. No bones or major tendons had been hit, but the hand swelled up like a football and it was more than six months before it subsided and he regained full use again.

An examination of burn marks on the internal surfaces of the holster showed that the gun was not fully home when it went off, something that was easy to duplicate with firings in test holsters. That meant that the finger, which must have been on the trigger when the gun was pushed into the holster, became trapped on the top edge of the holster as the gun was pushed home. As the gun was pushed down into the holster the finger exerted pressure on the trigger until it fired.

The gun in this case, a Colt Detective Special, can be fired either by a long relatively heavy pull on the trigger which cocks the hammer, rotates the cylinder then drops the hammer all in one action, called 'Double Action', or by first manually cocking the hammer and then a short relatively light pull on the trigger, called 'Single Action'. The pressures required are generally in the region of 14lbs for double action mode and 4lbs for single action.

Trying to duplicate the set of circumstances which led to the firing showed that it was almost impossible to push the gun into the holster with the finger on the trigger and have it fire by double action; the force required was just too great. Doing the same thing after first cocking the hammer, i.e. in single-action mode of firing, and the gun went off with relative ease.

I interviewed the officer on a number of occasions and he was adamant that he never cocked the gun before putting it into the holster. As it happened, an unexplainable 'accidental discharge' resulted in no more for him than a rap on the knuckles.

Another alleged accidental discharge involved a dispute over a karaoke disc in a rental shop in Chai Wan. It seems that a DPC was particularly keen on having the latest karaoke laser disc for a singing session he was having with his friends that evening. However, on arriving at the shop he saw the last copy of the disc being taken by another man. He tried to cajole this person into giving him the record, showed him his warrant card and threatened him with arrest, tried to fight him for it and, when all else failed, pulled out his gun and shot him. I thought it a bit over the top just for a karaoke record, but then it is a pastime in which I do not indulge.

I was asked to examine the scene and determine the sequence of events, which I thought a little unnecessary as there was unlikely to be much for me there. On the way, I contacted the officer in charge and he said that the injured person had been rushed to hospital for emergency surgery which I also thought a bit strange for what was reported as a minor flesh wound to the upper arm.

On arriving at the scene the arrested DPC was looking very sorry for himself, even though he now had the karaoke disc by his side. I took gunshot residue samples and conducted the gun-handling test, which showed that he had pulled the trigger with his index finger and had fired the gun. I found the bullet some distance away, quite damaged through ricocheting from the marble-clad walls and floor.

At that stage I was still a bit confused about why a flesh wound to the upper arm was considered worthy of emergency surgery, until I located, in a big pool of blood, a two-inch-long piece of the injured man's upper arm bone. The bullet had obviously struck the bone and taken it out through the other side of the arm, causing a massive exit hole which nearly cut his arm in two.

Later on, I examined the shirt, which showed that the range had been in excess of three feet, thus eliminating any possible question of a struggle for the gun. The incident did very little for the officer's promotional prospects and he is still languishing in Stanley Prison. As for the injured man, he received some money from the police force, but now has to have his suits made with one arm two inches shorter than the other.

CHAPTER 25

THE GREAT CHASE LEADING TO HAPPY VALLEY

As was usual in those times of high crime, the pager went off just as I was sitting down for a sandwich hastily snatched between case examinations. The officer in charge explained that there had been an armed robbery in the Chow Tai Fook jewellery shop in Queen's Road Central and several innocent bystanders had been injured, including an off-duty police officer and two tourists.

Looking out of my window in police headquarters, which is only about a mile from Central District, I could see the traffic jam beginning to back up from the crime scene. No point in taking the car, I thought, it will be quicker to walk. Within 15 minutes I was at the scene and there were hundreds and hundreds of people milling around trying to get a look at what had happened. Being lunch hour, the streets were packed anyway, but because the street was completely blocked off at both ends, there was a wall of people, dozens deep, all of them either trying to see what was happening or desperately trying to get back to work.

It seemed that four masked robbers, all armed with pistols, had robbed the shop of gold and expensive watches to the tune of about HK$10,000,000 (£900,000). They fired a couple of rounds into the back of the shop and to deter any would-be heroes and in the street they fired another seven or eight rounds into the crowd that had formed outside. They then disappeared into the underground railway system.

The results of the rounds fired into the crowd were a European off-duty policeman shot through the thigh, a shoe-repair man sitting on a stool shot through the side of the chest, one tourist with an upper arm shattered and another with a flesh wound to the waist. Considering how many shots had been fired and the very large number of people thronging the streets at that time of the day I was amazed at how few and how relatively minor were the injuries.

The injured had been taken to hospital and the bullets fired into the back of the shop were firmly embedded in the false walls so, leaving instructions for the bullets to be recovered, I took the two cartridge cases that I found on the pavement back to the office for comparison against any other unsolved crime ammunition components.

It has always amazed me in Hong Kong how few fired cartridge cases and bullets are found at the scene of a shooting. Reliable witnesses will often report 10 or 15 rounds having been fired from pistols or automatic rifles, but a thorough search of the scene might, at best, reveal a couple of fired cartridge cases and some bullet fragments. My theory is that bystanders at a scene will collect them as souvenirs that are then sold as, for example, 'lucky bullets from the Fat Boy murder case' for a vast sum of money.

The cartridge cases I found didn't match up with any of the fired ammunition components from previous unsolved crimes and I thought that was going to be the end of it. That was, until 11 o'clock that night. The phone woke me with a start. Years of such awakenings have taught me to be instantly awake, pen in hand, ready to take down details of the case. A police officer on patrol had been shot in the legs during a routine stop-and-search down in North Point. There was nothing for it but to struggle out of my warm bed, drag on some clothes and get down to the scene as quickly as possible.

By the time I had arrived the PC had been taken to hospital and nothing at all was left at the scene, not a cartridge case or fired bullet. By the time I had got back to bed it was two o'clock in the morning and I had just fallen into a deep, deep sleep when the phone went again. This time it was a call from Chai Wan, which is a bit further on from North Point. They had got four men holed up in a construction site. 'Bring your gun, they are all armed and we think it is the same team which did the Central robbery yesterday and the PC shooting earlier this morning.' Now, I don't usually carry a gun, but this seemed like an opportune moment to start, so, after strapping on the Model 60 stainless-steel Smith and Wesson which I had always kept loaded with a potent mixture of ammunition for just such a case, I was out of the door and running for the car.

The construction site was part of a very large residential complex, some of which had been completed but was not occupied and some of which was still wasteland. The area in where they had the robbers holed up was a two-acre square of land destined to be a park. Luckily it had high walls surrounding most of it, but one end was covered with really dense tropical undergrowth and that was where the robbers were thought to be hiding.

The main observation post was on the roof of a multi-storey car park which looked straight down on the end of the site containing the undergrowth. Earlier in the evening there had been a number of shots fired and everyone was keeping their heads well down for fear of losing them. My job was quite simple, if a little dangerous; I had to try and pinpoint the robbers with the infra-red night-vision binoculars and determine what weapons they had. Our anti-terrorist unit, the Special Duties Unit (SDU), would then use that information to determine what action to take once dawn broke.

All night I was up moving from one position to another, climbing from rooftop to rooftop, trying to locate the robbers. Once or twice I had fleeting glimpses of man-sized objects and then I thought we had one of them scuttling across open ground. The snipers on the rooftops had seen the same images, and actions were being cocked from all angles and ladders readied for an assault over the wall. In then end it turned out to be a stray dog, but was it a stray dog disturbed by something or somebody?

Dawn broke, and by this time everyone was very weary indeed from the stress and strain of the previous evening. On the site, nothing, not a twig or branch, had stirred for hours. The SDU were all kitted up in their balaclavas and with their Heckler and Koch sub-machine guns tightly held to their chests with elastic harnesses, ready for instant use. Now that it was light, the snipers could be seen on every available rooftop and canopy surrounding the site and there were many more who could not be seen hiding behind drawn Venetian blinds. At an unseen and unheard command, the SDU assault team was up and over the wall in a flash, taking up strategic points round the patch of vegetation. Slowly and methodically they advanced through the vegetation, searching out every square inch for any possible hiding place. Gradually they moved forward, with the vegetation so dense and high that at times all that could be seen was the stirring of leaves. After a nail-biting 45 minutes, they all emerged unscathed but without any arrests having been made.

From the vegetation they moved to the open area of the site, dodging from one patch of cover to the next. Small buildings dotted the site, the doors of which were kicked off, one at a time, and the rooms thoroughly searched, but still nothing. At one point they came to an uncovered opening for a large storm drain and without a second's hesitation one man dropped down into the drain and disappeared for a never-ending 10 minutes, after which it was declared 'clear'. Part of the site was obviously destined for an artificial river system, with bridges and waterfalls. Each and every possible hiding place was searched but still nothing. The wait was agonising and everybody was obviously experiencing the same nail-biting, hair-pulling tension.

The search continued until suddenly, at the point where a number of small open drains emptied into a large pit, they stopped. The message came over the system that the ballistics officer was needed at once. For a second it didn't register that they were calling for me! No not me, it can't be, that is really dangerous down there and I could really do without going. But I had to, and with just an SDU man who met me at the gate I walked across the site feeling more exposed than I have ever done in my life.

When we got to the pit they all backed off and, while not being paranoid, I got the distinct impression that these 'supermen' didn't want to be near whatever they had brought me over to. There, in the bottom of this drainage pit, was a small canvas backpack, partially submerged in water. It was just about at arm's length. I reached down, grabbed the straps and started to pull, but it just wouldn't budge. I repositioned myself to get a better grasp on it, idly noticing as I did so that the two SDU men moved even further away. 'Not a good sign,' I said to myself.

Taking a deep breath I pulled really hard and the bag began to move, but I still couldn't get it out. It must be stuck on some obstruction, I thought, so I gave it all that I had and slowly it came up out of the drain until I had it by my side. Carefully I opened the straps and peered inside, to see a whole bunch of wires, three cocked guns, some cardboard tubes and a lot of glinting gold. My first action was to carefully extract the guns and make them safe. Two Type 54 Chinese 7.62x25mm pistols and a Colt 1911A1 .45 calibre pistol, all fully loaded with one in the chamber and cocked, ready to fire. Next came a small paper bundle containing two syringes full of liquid, some white powder, metal foil and matches; obviously two of them were drug addicts. Next there were wires and card tubes which I recognised as being Chinese military explosives and detonators, luckily not connected. I removed them and, apart from 60-odd rounds of ammunition, the rest was pure gold: 40lbs of it. The bag was not stuck, as I had thought, it was just that I hadn't anticipated how heavy a 15-inch-diameter ball of gold was. There were also two watches which were solid platinum with every surface completely covered in diamonds which, I was later told, were worth HK$800,000 (£65,000) each!

The rest of the site was searched but nothing else was found. Unbeknown to everybody except the criminals, who had obviously selected this site in case they were surrounded, over in the far corner was a completely hidden storm drain which lead under the adjacent roads and blocks of flats to the sea wall some 200 yards away. At some time during the night they had slipped across the site, down into the drain and on to a waiting boat, making a clean escape.

Another lunch was interrupted when a call came saying that there had been a huge cash-in-transit robbery with over ten million in Hong Kong and American dollars stolen. Just a couple of rounds were fired and I was busy, so I let someone else in the office deal with the case. The next thing we knew was that the gang had hijacked a taxi and was being followed by police in cars and a helicopter. After a mad chase through Central, Wanchai and Happy Valley, the taxi eventually became stuck in a traffic jam in North Point and the gang fled on foot, firing at anything and anybody who got in the way. At one point the police had them surrounded, but they managed to shoot their way out, injuring a couple of police officers and two bystanders in the process. Through the maze of small streets they ran, firing three shots into an open-fronted shop in the hope of deterring or slowing down the police. One man fell dead on the spot, shot straight through the heart, another sustained a serious wound from a 9mm bullet which went through the frame of a tubular chair, then a metal desk, then through the lower abdomen, before dropping to the floor behind the injured person.

The chase continued, with reinforcements trying to surround the gang by anticipating where they were going. At one point a teacher, unaware of the gun battle in progress, turned a corner to confront the gang at a range of no more than a few yards. Two shots were fired: one missed and the other struck her in the centre of the forehead. The bullet went straight through her head, killing her instantly. The bullet finally stopped after hitting a wall on the other side of the road.

The gang turned the corner, and ran up an incline where they met 20-odd police who were just getting out of their vehicles in a dead-end side road. A huge gun fight erupted during which two grenades were exploded, injuring several policemen, but once again the gang got through unscathed. They fled into a multi-storey car park where we thought we had them cornered. What we didn't know was that they had stored a getaway car on the first floor and there was no way they were going to be caught. Just as the police started, gingerly, to enter the car park, out came this Mercedes S500at full throttle, crashing into two police cars as it made its escape.

The chase continued, closely followed by the helicopter, round the island and up towards the Peak. There they stopped the car, jumped over the edge of the road and disappeared down into the dense tropical jungle below. The helicopter circled for hours, hundreds of police combed the hillside, but it was so dense there was no way of knowing which direction they had taken. We had well and truly lost them.

Some of the ammunition used by the gang was pretty unusual and, by looking at the elemental composition of the firing residues on the base of the fired bullets, it was possible to tell which cartridge had fired the bullet that had killed the teacher. At that stage, though, it didn't mean anything because we had no guns and no arrests. Even if we did arrest somebody, the time lag was by now so great that all the firing residues would have been lost from their hands.

About two weeks after the incident some workers were clearing out the storm drains about halfway between the Peak and Central, when they found a pile of clothing, some masks, five pairs of cotton workman's gloves, two broken guns and about 100 rounds of ammunition. A quick check showed that the guns had been used in the robbery but had been abandoned after breaking, but with a lack of fingerprints, how were we ever going to tie them up with any suspects? One of the gloves, however, had a small spot of blood on the inside of the palm next to a tear in the fabric. Obviously one of the robbers had cut his hand during the escape. I took some adhesive lifts from the outside of the gloves and found firearms gunshot residues on all of them, the distribution of which showed that they had been worn by someone while firing a gun. One glove, however, had residues of a very unusual composition, the like of which I had never seen before, other than on the ammunition which killed the teacher. It also just happened that the residues were on the glove with a small spot of blood on it. Now we were really getting somewhere, all that was needed was a suspect.

A couple of months later, news began to filter in through informers that the gang we wanted was holed up in a flat in Happy Valley, but the information also said that they were very heavily armed and extremely dangerous. The flat, which was at the end of a long corridor, was kept under heavy surveillance for a further week, during which we monitored who was going in and out so that we knew exactly how many people we were dealing with.

Early one Wednesday morning all was set: our SDU was ready, and with great stealth they emptied every flat on the two floors above and the two below. We were now ready to pounce. The back-up Police Tactical Unit quietly surrounded the building while the whole SDU team regrouped on the ground floor. What nobody had bothered to check out was whether the building had security cameras fitted so that the residents could see, on their own TV sets, who was entering the building and who was on each floor. This building did, and the robbers, therefore, knew every move we were making and were awake, armed and ready.

Nearly all flats in Hong Kong are fitted with a steel security grille external to the normal front door and this one was no exception. As the SDU were counting on the element of surprise, there was no way that a lock picker could spend five minutes clicking away. So their first attempt at opening the door relied on a shotgun being fired at the lock. This was not too successful; all it managed to do was shoot off the top of the finger of the officer firing the gun. It was obvious that a little more force was required, so they decided to use Cordtex (high explosive in string form) to cut off the hinges, and plastic explosives to take off the door lock. Unfortunately, they were a little enthusiastic with the explosive and the grille, which weighed all of 200lbs was sent down the corridor with such force it embedded itself in the concrete wall at the other end. The wooden door, which itself was quite substantial, was blown to shreds and I couldn't find a piece larger than a matchstick. After this ear-shattering explosion, flash-bang stun grenades were thrown into the flat.

But, the robbers had a good idea of what was going to happen and were safe and sound in the bedrooms whilst all this thunder and lightning had been going on. The first SDU officer to enter quickly moved to the right of the door expecting to meet no resistance. What he did meet was a hail of about 40 rounds of ammunition of all calibres imaginable coming from the bedroom doors. The SDU responded with fire from automatic pistols, sub-machine guns, shotguns, tear-gas rounds and tear-gas grenades. The fire fight went back and forth until, eventually, the robbers ran out of ammunition and surrendered.

I attempted to carry out a normal scene examination to determine who had been standing where and firing what, but it was impossible. I had never before, nor have I since, seen so many bullet, shotgun pellet, flash-bang and tear-gas canister strike marks. There were ricochet marks everywhere, where the bullets and missiles just kept going from wall to ceiling to wall until they ran out of velocity and fell to the floor. Possibly the most amazing thing in the whole room was the wall which the first SDU officer had his back against when he entered the room. The wall was completely covered in bullet strike marks, except one man-shaped and man-sized area where the officer had stood. Not one bullet had hit or even scratched him.

Eventually the robbers had their blood grouped and we then knew who fired the fatal shot. He was charged with murder and the rest were charged with aiding and abetting murder. They were all sentenced to life with no possibility of parole.

CHAPTER 26

MASTERING MY METHOD

It was a warm sunny day, and a **PC** who was walking his beat in **Central District** was enjoying the low humidity and unbelievably bright blue skies of a typical Hong Kong autumn. A little further along the street, however, he spotted a man outside a jeweller's shop behaving suspiciously. Quickening his step, he shouted out to the man to stop, whereupon the man turned round and fired a shot from a pistol at the **PC**. Taking cover in a shop doorway the **PC** warily looked out to see the man extract a hand grenade from his coat pocket and throw it into the middle of the road. It went off with a huge roar, spraying the street with shrapnel and leaving a large hole in the tarmac road surface. On hearing the noise, three armed men came running out of the shop, jumped into a waiting car and and all four disappeared into the distance.

I was called to the scene very soon after the incident, as there was some question about whether a round had been fired at the PC. It didn't look totally convincing; there wasn't a fired cartridge case or bullet to be found anywhere, nor was there any obvious sign of a bullet hole. When I questioned the PC further he said that he was standing underneath a very large road sign at the time he claimed to have been shot at. I carried out a thorough examination of the road sign but failed to find anything even remotely similar to a bullet strike or ricochet mark. The only mark on the sign of any significance was an elongated dent that looked as if it might have been hit by a ladder. I did, however, have the distinct impression that the PC was telling the truth and thought that I should look at this strange dent a little closer.

The sign itself was about 15 foot square, a little too large to fit under a normal microscope, let alone into the chamber of an SEM, so I asked for the bit containing the dent to be cut out. Each road sign is, obviously, unique and must be individually made for a particular junction. The one that I was proposing to have cut into pieces was huge and was going to cost a fortune to replace. The traffic engineers were not at all happy, but if the case was to be solved, then they were going to have to cut up their precious sign whether they liked it or not.

After a few hours of arguing they turned up with a power saw driven by a large, powerful four-stroke engine. 'No,' I said, 'you can't do that. Cutting it out with a power saw could contaminate or damage the sample, it's got to be removed with hand tools.' I wasn't making myself popular; the dent was nearly in the middle of the sign and it was going to take hours to cut out the couple of inches I wanted.

Eventually I had it on my desk and under the microscope, but it still looked more like a scrape than a bullet ricochet or impact mark. The only thing to do was take some adhesive tapings of the scrape mark and, using the SEM, find out what made it. It took about 20 minutes on the SEM to locate a minute scraping of lead covered with steel, which had a very thin layer of copper on the top. Also on the taping I found a small particle of partially burnt propellant particle with an even smaller sphere of firearms gunshot residue on its surface.

The firearms discharge particle was obviously from a round of ammunition, but why was it stuck on a propellant particle and how did it get inside the scrape mark? When a round of ammunition is fired, the hot gases from the burning propellant can leave firearms gunshot residues and, very occasionally, propellant particles adhering to the base of the bullet. However, when the bullet strikes something, it does so nose first and the particles on the base are not transferred to whatever it strikes. An analysis of the particle, using an energy-dispersive X-ray analyser (EDX) attached to the SEM, showed that the ammunition from which it came was of Russian origin and 7.62x25mm calibre. That type of ammunition would normally have a bullet with a copper-coated steel jacket covering a lead core. If that had struck the sign point first, all that would be present was steel covered with copper. But we had lead smears as well.

It was then that it all became clear. The bullet had struck tail, and not point, first, leaving some of the lead core of the bullet (which is exposed at its base), some of the copper-coated steel jacket and a piece of propellant and firing residue which had stuck to the base during the firing. The bullet had struck tail first as it had been tumbling, rather than travelling point first which would indicate an unrifled barrel, i.e. a homemade weapon. The lack of cartridge case at the scene would also suggest that it was a poorly made weapon and the fired cartridge had stuck in the chamber rather than being ejected as it should have been.

I ran the elemental composition of the residue particle through the residue database, and while it was obviously Russian in origin there had never been a similar composition used in an armed robbery in Hong Kong. If we could find a suspect we might be lucky and recover some similar residues from his pockets.

About eight weeks later a suspect was found and, after going back through the witness statements, several pairs of trousers fitting the description of those used by the robber were located in his flat. After a couple of weeks of really hard work I eventually found, in the right pocket of a pair of trousers, just two particles of gunshot residues whose elemental composition matched exactly those found on the sign. This was pretty good presumptive evidence that he had fired a weapon in his right hand which had been loaded with Russian ammunition of the same type as that fired at the scene. But we needed much more before it could be taken to court.

Eventually a gun was found in a stone hut that the suspect was believed to have used as a hideout. The gun was a homemade smooth-bored weapon in 7.62x25mm calibre. I took tapings from inside the barrel, the results of which showed that the last round of ammunition fired had a bullet with a copper-coated steel jacket. These tapings also showed that the gunshot residue of the last round fired had exactly the same elemental composition as those on the sign and in his trousers pocket. The gun was fired for test purposes and it was found that soon after leaving the barrel the bullets started to tumble. It was also found that the cartridge cases would not eject from the chamber after firing, due to the poor design and manufacture of the gun. In another flat which the suspect was known to have used was a round of Russian ammunition, complete with the suspect's thumbprint on the side. This round had a copper-coated steel-jacketed bullet and gunshot residues that matched those in the gun, in the pocket and on the road sign. The suspect was charged with attempted murder of a police officer and sent down for life, largely on the basis of the results from the SEM examination.

During the same period there was an attempted armed robbery

of 'a cash in transit' van and a big gun battle had ensued between the police and the three robbers. The battle was over fairly quickly, with one robber being shot dead, one seriously wounded and one having escaped in a waiting car. The injured person had been found with a gun lying on the floor next to him, but as no weapon was found on the body of the deceased it was really important to determine whether he had in fact fired a gun or whether he was an innocent bystander caught in the crossfire.

Rather than risk contaminating myself with firing residues from the scene, I had my driver take me straight to the Kowloon public mortuary which was located in Tsim Sha Tsui. It was just about midnight by the time I arrived and there wasn't a person to be seen anywhere. All the doors were firmly locked and there wasn't a light on in the place. From past experience, I knew that there was always a reserve mortuary attendant on duty for the receipt of late arrivals, all I had to do was get him out of bed. I rang the bell, hammered on the door, but nothing. I rang and rang again and in desperation kicked the door as hard as I could which finally did the trick as I heard a grunt and the click of a light switch. Shuffle, shuffle, shuffle, and with a loud theatrical 'creak' the door opened just a crack.

Now in my time as a forensic scientist I have been to many hundreds of post-mortem examinations and have had to work alongside more mortuary attendants than I could count. I am not quite sure what drives anyone to become a mortuary attendant as the work is the worst imaginable and the pay is terrible. What all these men have in common, however, is that they all look as if they have been put together from spare parts found at work. Not once have I ever come across one who could be called 'normal', and this one, lurking behind the door, must have been the model from which all the rest were copied. He was bent over and hunchbacked, dragged a leg, one eye was higher and larger than the other, the few teeth he had were either black or yellow and one arm was longer than the other and a little twisted. To cap it all, he appeared to speak no known language, communicating by way of a grunting wheeze.

In my best Cantonese, which is terrible, I explained who I was and that I wanted to carry out an examination of the dead robber's body. Actually my Cantonese couldn't have been that bad because he grunted and opened up the door for me to enter. With a dreadful wheeze he pointed to the end of the corridor and shuffled off back to bed, leaving me to it.

I merely had to take some adhesive lifts from the palms and backs of each hand and then spray the hands with the Gun Handling reagent. This was difficult to do by oneself, because the fingers had to be stretched out straight for the taking of the lifts and the spraying. I called to my PC driver to come and help, but all he did was lock the car door and shake his head violently. I could have ordered him, but knowing how adverse the local Chinese are to touching dead bodies I thought it better to do it myself.

Now, I am not superstitious or afraid of the dark, nor do I believe in ghosts and spirits, but a mortuary full of dead bodies at midnight, especially where there is almost no lighting, is really, and I mean really, really spooky. The corridor had nothing more than what seemed like a 10-watt bulb at one end, sending out a yellowish glow which did nothing for the complexion of the bodies stacked one on top of another all the way along its length. At the far end of the corridor I could see the cutting tables, also full of bodies. Finding the one I was interested in among so many was not an easy task. Eventually, I saw a white shroud with a big patch of blood spreading across its surface and I knew that had to be my man.

Stripping the shroud off I could see two bullet wounds, one to the centre of the forehead and one in the chest. He was obviously dead, but what I didn't like was that he was still very warm. There is something about examining a warm body that I find distinctly off-putting. It is one part of the job I really dislike.

They must have had a really busy day, or perhaps the pathologists were all on holiday, because the place was packed out with bodies. There was blood everywhere and I had to be particularly careful where I put my kit and bag down in order to avoid taking them home covered in blood. Eventually I found a semi-clean spot and soon had the tapings, spray bottle reagents, tweezers and clipboard all ready to begin. Taking the tapings from the back of the hands wasn't too difficult and I soon had the two tapings in their sealed and labelled bottles. Turning the wrist over so that I could get to the palm was harder, because the low temperature in the mortuary was rapidly cooling the body. But now came the difficult bit: I had to keep the hand turned over at the same time as straightening the fingers with one hand, while taking the tapings with the other. Eventually I had the fingers spread, but trying to keep the hand from turning back was difficult because I didn't have a very good hold. I then discovered that I hadn't taken the taping out of its container.

Concentrating hard, I had just got the top off the tube when the deceased's distinctly warm hand closed round mine! I screamed and, just like a cartoon character, jumped straight up with my feet pawing the air for purchase. As soon as my feet hit the floor, I was down the corridor and out into the car park, gibbering. It was the scariest thing that has ever happened to me. Eventually I had to go back in and complete my work, but not before I had ordered the PC to stand at the door with his flashlight on and his gun drawn. I never did discover what had caused the hand to close over and hold mine, but it could have been rigor mortis setting in and contracting the muscles. Whatever it was, I have never worked on a warm body since.

The tests were both positive. He had held a Chinese self-loading Type 54 7.62x25mm calibre pistol in his right hand and had pulled the trigger with his right index finger. The presence of discharge residues showed that he had fired a gun in his right hand

and that the ammunition fired was of Chinese manufacture and the same make, origin and age as some of the cartridges found at the scene. All in all, a pretty positive case.

For some time I had been trying to extend the period over which I could detect firing residues on the hands of a suspect. The big problem was that there are very few residues deposited on to the hands during the firing of a weapon and they are not embedded in the skin or attached by some 'magic glue'-type compound. The particles are merely resting on the surface and are thus very easily removed by everyday activities. If there is one thing in their favour as far as retention goes, it is the small size of the particles. Being exceedingly small, too small, in fact, to be seen with even the best optical microscope, they become trapped in the microscopic folds of the skin and fall down into sweat glands and hair follicles. Under normal circumstances, the few particles which are deposited on to the hands fall off within about three hours. Finding a suspect within such a short time frame is somewhat unusual and, unless you are dealing with a dead body, the technique is generally of little use

Over the course of time, I had tried all sorts of techniques, from washing the hair with petroleum spirit and filtering the liquid to pushing swabs up people's noses to find somewhere that the residues might be deposited and retained for longer than 3 hours. Nasal swabs gave surprisingly good results, but I didn't really like raking out all the green snotty bits, and the suspects objected to me pushing a cotton bud on the end of a long stick up their nose.

I had to go back to basics and think like a criminal during and after an armed robbery to determine what he would be doing and how and where the residues might be deposited. I asked as many operational officers as I could about what they did during and after an exchange of fire, reviewed what tapes were available showing armed robberies in progress and even talked to the force clinical psychologist about his theories. In the end I came to the conclusion that, once the adrenaline rush of the robbery was over, the gang would probably go back to a safe house or hotel room, relax and talk about the robbery over a beer or cup of tea. Watching people recreate the scene almost always ended up with the person leaning back in the chair and putting his hands in his trouser pockets. That was exactly what I was looking for, somewhere that the residues were being deposited and would remain for periods exceeding the three-hour limit we currently had.

Hundreds of control tests showed that the residues were always transferred from the hands to the edges of the pockets. Eventually it was found that the residues worked their way down into the pocket where they remained for weeks, even months. In all the tests I carried out, even washing or dry cleaning the trousers did not remove the residues from the pockets.

In the USA, where everybody has access to a gun and every piece of clothing is likely to be contaminated with firing residues, the technique would be totally useless. But in Hong Kong, where private ownership of weapons is almost non-existent, a person found with firing residues in or on his clothes has a lot of explaining to do. Months were spent refining the test, carrying out lifts from the general population to see what the background contamination levels were (nil in every test performed) and then I was ready for my first case. It didn't take long in coming.

About six months earlier there had been a particularly callous armed robbery in Muk Wah Street, Kowloon. A gang of five had raided a gold shop with three of them standing guard outside with hand grenades, AK47 assault rifles and self-loading pistols while the other two, also heavily armed, carried out the robbery. Anybody who moved was shot at, and dozens of rounds were fired into the street. The gang made good its escape and we didn't hear anything about them for months.

Nearly six months later, as a result of some excellent detective work by Laurie Poots, suspects were arrested. The arresting officers also found some long black raincoats, which fitted the description of those worn by the gang. There were also other little bits and pieces to tie them to the scene, but there was precious little concrete evidence.

As a result of DNA fingerprinting of hair and blood on the coats it was possible to determine who had been wearing which coat; all that was needed then was to determine whether they had fired a gun while wearing the coats. The officer in charge was Laurie Poots, a good friend of mine who is now a barrister working in Hong Kong, and he was desperate for something which he could take to court. 'What about this new technique of yours, surely it's just what we need for this case?' said Laurie. It was, however, six months since the shooting and I had only managed to obtain positive results for up to four months. Still, in theory it should work, I thought.

It took weeks, because special holders had to be made which were then covered in a very sticky material called Vistanex, which happens to be one of the major components of bubble gum. After taking the samples from the pockets, the Vistanex was dissolved from the holder in an ultrasonic bath and passed through a two-stage filter. The first stage of this filter is quite coarse and is there to remove normal pocket debris such as hair, fibres and general dirt. The second filter, which is there to capture the particles of firing residues, is so highly specialised that the holes in it can only be made inside a nuclear reactor. After filtering out the residues, the filter has to be dried in an oven then go through a process called 'low-temperature, oxygen plasma ashing' which removes the last bits of organic material, leaving, hopefully, only the firing residues. The final process, which has to be carried out manually, is an examination in the Scanning Electron Microscope. All told, each pocket takes an average of six days' full-time work to examine, and as I had five coats, each with two pockets, I had to work for over two months to get a result.

In the end I found firing residues in the pockets of three of the coats, all of which were Chinese military 7.62x39mm (AK 47 type) ammunition. One of the coats had residues which were slightly different from the other two, which was found to be from much more modern ammunition which we had never seen before in Hong Kong. It just happened that this ammunition had only been used in one of the three guns and it was that gun which had been used to kill a woman at the scene. It tied in perfectly and was enough to convict him of murder for which he received a life sentence. The other two were charged with being his accomplices and also given life sentences.

There was a whole series of daring and very violent robberies over the next few months, many of which were suspected, or known, to have been carried out by the missing robber. One of the robberies concerned a whole series of adjacent gold shops that were robbed, almost simultaneously, while three men armed with grenades and AK 47 assault rifles stood guard outside and sprayed the street, and anything which moved, with a hail of bullets. One of the shots went straight through the steel post of a road sign and then hit a nurse who was running for cover, going in through her right temple and out of her left. As the bullet made its exit from the steel pole it began to tumble and made terrible wounds, killing her instantly. That was a most disturbing post-mortem examination.

The next time the police came across the fifth robber, who by then had become the most wanted man in Hong Kong, was about 18 months after the Muk Wah Street robbery. It was close to midnight, with a new moon, making everything not illuminated extremely difficult to see. Two PCs patrolling the streets of Kennedy Town had stopped for a short break as one of them needed a pee. Moving into the shadows by the sea wall he was going about his task, when he heard the burbling growl of powerful outboard motors. Peering over the wall he saw a Dai Fei with five men on board pulling up to the steps by the sea wall. Knowing that the use of Dai Feis had been prohibited in Hong Kong for some time, it was obvious that they were up to no good. Creeping back to his partner, they edged round until they were about 20 yards away from the top of the steps and waited for the arrival of the boat's occupants.

The boat was obviously very close now, and a sudden surge in the intensity of the exhaust note signalled the use of reverse gear to slow and park the boat. There were a few muted words, the noise of metal touching metal and heavy bags being lifted, and then the sound of footsteps coming closer. The PCs had their guns out and ready in anticipation of trouble and, as the men reached the top of the steps, the PCs shouted for them to put up their arms and surrender. The men were not giving up that easily and a fierce gun battle erupted. Dozens of shots were fired, with one man finally going down as he was struggling to get something out of his shoulder bag. Two of the men, hearing the wail of police sirens, knew that reinforcements were on the way and put up their hands in surrender while the other two fled, taking with them several guns and a bag.

With two suspects handcuffed at the station being interviewed, and another in the custodial ward awaiting serious back surgery, the contents of their bags could now be examined. Unfortunately, the bomb-disposal unit thought that the bag might contain a booby-trapped device and conducted a controlled explosion. This did little more than distribute the contents of the bag all over the scene and completely destroy everything that had been inside.

There was, in fact, quite a bit of military explosive material in the bag, together with detonators and, a first for Hong Kong, some radio-controlled devices for setting off the explosives. There was also a Polish Wz63 9mm Makarov calibre sub-machine gun and a lot of ammunition and pistol magazines. The gun, however, was totally wrecked by the force of the controlled explosion.

There never was a good explanation for these men bringing so much firepower and so many explosives into Hong Kong. One theory was that they were going to hold a well-known bank to ransom with the explosives hidden in the main building, another was that they had been hired to carry out a hit job on one of the rich family members and were going to plant a remotely detonated bomb in his car.

The robber who was shot, YIP Kai-foon, had his spine smashed by the bullet and is now confined to a wheelchair for the rest of his life. Some say that it is retribution for all the people he killed and maimed during his days as a totally ruthless robber. Personally, I am just glad he is off the streets and no longer a threat to law-abiding citizens.

There is a postscript to this story. About 18 months after his arrest, an informer came forward to report that there was a cache of weapons and ammunition buried on a hillside in Aberdeen. It was a terribly difficult place to get to, as the slope was almost vertical but, in the appointed spot, buried nearly five feet deep, was a 50-gallon plastic water barrel containing a huge cache of pistols, AK 47 assault rifles, ammunition, explosives and detonators. A couple of weeks later, another informer told us of another cache of weapons which was buried very close to the first. This time there was an even larger cache of arms, ammunition, explosives and detonators. We later found through microscopic examinations that the guns had been used in virtually all the cases attributed to YIP Kai-foon.

Much later, it was discovered that the information came from two members of YIP's gang who had been arrested in Mainland China. They had been charged with a number of minor crimes on the Mainland and, after trial, had received the death sentence. In an effort to have their sentence commuted to something a little less severe, they offered up the information on the whereabouts of YIP's Hong Kong-based weapon stores. The story goes that the

Chinese said 'thank you very much', took them straight down to the local football stadium and, in front of several thousand who had paid for the privilege, shot the two of them in the back of the head. They don't mess about up there!

According to sources, the informants were two undercover Mainland agents who had been sent down to Hong Kong to offer up the information.

As an aside, I had several offers from my Beijing counterparts to go and witness these executions and, whilst professionally it would have been quite interesting and would have significantly added to my knowledge of terminal ballistics, I could never quite bring myself round to actually going.

CHAPTER 27

UNEXPECTED AND GROTESQUE CONSEQUENCES OF GUNSHOT RESIDUE

Gunshot residues were involved in a quite unexpected way during my investigation into the murder of a young insurance saleswoman. This girl was, as most in the Hong Kong insurance business are, struggling to keep her job and willing to go to virtually any lengths to secure a customer. One day, while cold calling for customers using nothing more sophisticated than the local telephone book, she happened upon a youth in his late twenties who seemed to offer the prospect of some big insurance sales. This youth informed her that he had a friend on Lantau, a large island off Hong Kong, who was extremely rich and needed substantial life insurance. She took the bait, hook, line and sinker and agreed to meet the youth that evening at the Outlying Island Ferry Pier so that he could take her to discuss business with the supposed customer.

283

At the appointed time she was there, and about 10 minutes later, the youth arrived with one of his friends who said that he might need life insurance as well. Together the three of them set off for Lantau. On arriving at the island there was a bit of a bus journey, then a walk down a village path that was, by then, almost pitch black. By this time the girl must have started to realise that something was amiss, but that was the last time anybody saw her alive.

Several days later the girl's sister received a telephone call from the youth to say that her sister had been kidnapped and a HK$300,000 (£24,000) ransom was required for her to be released. He also said that if the money wasn't paid into his bank account, he would cut off her sister's hands and legs and send them to her in the post. Not a bright move, for once we had his bank account number it was easy to identify him, and 10 days later he was picked up on his way back from China.

After some questioning he admitted killing the girl and said that he and his accomplice cut her into pieces, put them in plastic sacks and threw them away on a Lantau hilltop. The next day he took us to the location and there we found four black plastic garbage sacks containing the very decomposed torso, legs, arms and head of a young woman. We then went to his flat where we recovered a starting pistol which had been converted into a double-barrelled .22 pistol, together with a round of live Chinese-made .22 calibre ammunition. We also discovered that the ferry company had a surveillance camera installed and the video tapes showed the deceased together with the arrested person and his accomplice boarding the boat to Lantau. Despite the admission, most of it was circumstantial evidence and the case still required hard facts before it could be brought to court.

The post mortem was without doubt the worst I have ever encountered and the images will haunt me for a long time to come. What remained of this young girl's body was black with putrefication, badly swollen and the skin was peeling off. It was full of maggots and other unidentifiable insects and the smell was unbelievably bad. The head, arms and legs had been hacked off and were in a similar condition. She had obviously been raped, although the decomposition was such that it was impossible to blood group the remains of the semen. She had also been shot twice in the head.

I was only concerned with the bullet holes in the head and my primary objective was to determine the range at which she had been shot. It was obvious that if there was going to be a defence case, and as it turned out there was, it would be based around an accidental discharge of the gun during a struggle. The range of firing was, therefore, crucial. Less than three feet and it could have been an accidental discharge during a struggle, over that range it would have been impossible, as a person's arms are not that long.

Both bullet entry holes were situated on the top left of the head above the ear and were within an inch of each other. One of the holes was a normal entry hole with no gunshot residues or powder flakes present around the wound. This indicated that the distance from gun to skin was over three feet, which is the maximum range at which such residues would be present. The other hole was surrounded by a pappy area of khaki-coloured flesh with an unpleasant shiny, wet appearance. I had never seen anything like that before, but I wondered whether it could have been caused by the gun-smoke residues which are deposited on the skin when a gun is fired at very close range. As the gun-smoke residues from nitrocellulose propellants contain a high concentration of nitrates and nitrites it was possible that they could be accelerating the decomposition process of any skin on which they were deposited. It was, however, only supposition.

I scanned through all the literature I could find on the decomposition of bodies, but there was nothing, not even a passing mention of such a thing as catalysation of the process by gunshot residues or even by nitrates and nitrites. Could I be on the wrong trail? No matter how unpleasant it might seem, I was going to have to carry out some control tests. Using the belly skin from young pigs I shot it at various ranges, then wrapped it in black polythene bags, similar to those in which the body had been wrapped, and left it to fester in the sun on the roof of police headquarters. Every day I opened the bags and examined the various pieces of skin as they turned black and began to smell terrible. I wasn't prepared for the speed at which they started to decompose, and the first opening had me gagging for air as the stench from the bag hit me full in the face.

It was estimated by the pathologists that the bags had been on the hillside for about six days and at about the same time the pigskin started to resemble that of the body. It was interesting to note that the skin which had been shot at close range was decomposing at a rate faster than that shot at greater distances. After eght days the skin which had been blackened by the gunshot residues had exactly the same pappy, khaki texture and colour as that on the head of the deceased. I repeated the test twice more and the results were almost exactly the same, showing beyond reasonable doubt that one of the shots had been at a distance of about three inches and the other well in excess of three feet.

I test fired the gun a number of times and found that, soon after leaving the barrel, the bullets started to tumble due to the lack of rifling in the barrel. As the hole in the skull from the close-range shot was almost perfectly round and the other very elongated, it reinforced my opinion about the range at which they had been fired. Unfortunately, the barrel was oversized and it was not possible to determine with any certainty whether either of the bullets had been fired from it. It was, however, possible to say that they had been fired from two different unrifled and oversized barrels.

In court, as predicted, the other side brought in a defence expert who tried to convince the jury that it had been an accidental discharge, but the evidence was overwhelming and both men were convicted of murder and sentenced to life imprisonment with no parole. A couple of months later they were also convicted of beating to death an old couple, once again on Lantau, before the insurance girl's murder, just to steal a few dollars and some small items of gold.

One of the very last cases I dealt with concerned an armed robbery in a small import/export company that was situated on the second floor of a modest-sized commercial building in Kowloon Tong. It was a Friday lunchtime, the manageress had just collected the staff's monthly salary from the bank and was at her desk busily counting it out, when a masked robber walked in holding a small gun. Without uttering a word he calmly stuck the gun in the back of her neck and pulled the trigger. There was a loud bang, a big cloud of smoke and the next thing she knew she was being rushed to hospital in a blaze of flashing lights and blaring sirens.

At the hospital the doctor made a quick examination of her neck and pronounced that the robber could only have had a blank-firing gun, because all he could see was some powder tattooing round the hairline. Obviously a budding forensic firearms examiner in the making! After swabbing the area with some disinfectant, he stuck a large plaster over the burnt area and declared her fit to go home.

The accompanying police officer wanted to get on with the case and asked whether she was up to giving a quick statement. Wanting the whole matter over as soon as possible she agreed and was whisked back to the local police station in no time at all. Halfway through the statement she started to complain of a headache and stiff neck and said that she felt really dizzy. Then the officer noticed that the whole of the back of her shirt was saturated in blood. Once again she was unconscious and in an ambulance and was soon back at the hospital for a more thorough investigation.

After shaving the back of her head the doctor (a different one this time) found three small puncture wounds at the nape of her neck. X-rays of her neck revealed a number of small missiles embedded deep in the tissues. She was operated on immediately and four 0.20 steel ball bearings were extracted from the upper neck muscle. A 0.22 lead bullet was also found but this was embedded in the spine and had to be removed by a neurosurgeon several days later. She was very lucky to be alive.

Judging by the gun-shot residue particles in her hair, the type of missiles, the complete lack of rifling on the lead bullet and the fact that there were only three entry wounds for five missiles, it was fairly obvious that she had been shot with a Chinese multi-barrelled 'anti-riot' pistol. These are peculiar little weapons, each consisting of a long, six-chambered steel cylinder which fits into a cheap alloy frame. The cylinders are individually fired by an electrical current and after all five chambers have been discharged the cylinder can easily be removed for factory reloading.

Originally, these pistols were intended for use by security guards and the barrels were invariably loaded with small, non-lethal, rubber balls. Recently, however, they have been found loaded with tear gas, steel ball bearings, .22 calibre lead bullets, even 'dust shot' and it seems that the factory will reload them with whatever type of missile is required. Normally all the chambers are loaded with the same type of missile but occasionally they are mixed, e.g. tear gas in the first chamber to dissuade an attacker, rubber balls in the second to show that you mean business and a lead bullet or steel balls in the third if he hasn't got the message by then. In this case the first two chambers fired would have been loaded with a 0.20 ball bearing and the third with a lead bullet.

No weapon or suspect was ever found in this case and it is suspected that the robbery was carried out by an illegal immigrant who sneaked over the border to make some quick cash. The 30,000-odd dollars he netted from the robbery would have bought his family a small country cottage and he would still have had enough money left over to keep them in food for several years.

CHAPTER 28

GWAN TAI, THE POLICE GOD, AND THE FINAL HANDOVER

The Hong Kong Chinese are among the most hard-working and down-to-earth people I have ever encountered. Some of their superstitions, however, I find really strange. No matter how crowded a bus or tram might be, for instance, a seat will remain empty for as long as it remains warm from the last occupant. It is considered that the spirit of the last person will be occupying the seat until it is cold and to sit on a spirit is very bad luck indeed.

It is also believed that bad spirits live in the lungs, and the more you hawk and spit the more of the devil you will expel and the healthier you will be. I am afraid that even after 24 years of exposure, all this hawking, which often sounds as if they are trying to bring something up from their toe nails, and spitting is one thing that I have never been able to come to terms with.

Spitting and, more particularly, hawking have become something of an art form in the Far East. All the rasping and gurgling noises that only phlegm can make are brought from the depths of the lungs with a thespian performance before being spat out of a bus or tram window, with huge gusto, on to the pavement. For many years I rode a motorcycle in Hong Kong and became very astute at dodging these flying fried eggs which came at me, jet propelled, from all directions. I always wondered whether I would be covered by my normal fully comprehensive insurance if I fell off my motorcycle attempting to avoid such an incident. Knowing Hong Kong insurance companies and their reluctance to settle claims it would probably be classified as an 'Act of God'.

Another superstition, and in some ways one which is understandable, is that if a person has died in a seat no one will ever, under any circumstance, go near it. On many occasions I have had to hunt round for a European police officer to sit in the seat of a car where someone has been shot so that I can reconstruct the scene.

At times these superstitions can be most bizarre and cause terrible inconvenience for those concerned. Paul Smith had a local wife who would not allow him to enter their flat if he had been anywhere near a dead body, until he had showered twice and changed all his clothes. The clothes he had been wearing had to be washed outside the house, at least twice, before she would allow him back in.

Personally I am not all that convinced about the afterlife, ghosts and such things, but there have been a number of 'happenings' for which there is no logical explanation. One of these concerns the small altar to Gwan Tai, the police god, which resides in the bureau.

Virtually every major formation in the Hong Kong Police Force has, somewhere in its offices, an altar to Gwan Tai, and every morning an officer is appointed to light joss sticks and make small 'good luck' offerings of tea, cakes and sometimes Chinese wine to the Gwan Tai. If there has been a breakthrough or successful prosecution in a big case, then a Bai Gwan Tai, or party to Gwan Tai, is held to say thanks for his help. Large numbers of joss sticks are lit, suits of paper clothes, boots and fake money are burnt, and offerings of roast pig, ducks, chickens, brandy, beer and Chinese wine are made. After the offerings have been made, everyone who had a hand in the case then eats and drinks what is left after Gwan Tai has 'taken his fill'.

If, on the other hand, the case is not going too well, offerings are made in much the same way seeking his help. Or, if there has been promotion or an unsuccessful attempt to gain promotions a Bai Gwan Tai is held to say thank you, Gwan Tai, for your help or please help me next time. Many of the local officers take Gwan Tai very seriously indeed, but it is also an excuse for a morale-boosting get-together that works extremely well.

The Gwan Tai in the FFEB (Forensic Firearms Bureau, as it became after I took over as its head) is over 100 years old and is a very revered altar. While nobody in the bureau would admit to believing in the power of Gwan Tai, everybody takes a turn at lighting the joss sticks 'just in case'.

It was early 1997 and just before the handover. The bureau was really running well, new equipment was arriving by the truckload and morale was at an all-time high. Then, one day, just before Princess Alexander, the honorary Commandant of the Royal Hong Kong Police Force, was due to make an official inspection of the bureau, my boss came down and ordered me to get rid of 'that old-fashioned altar which wasn't at all in keeping with the modernised bureau'. I pleaded and said that it was a historical part of the office and the force, but he was adamant and so our Gwan Tai was removed to a storeroom. Joss sticks were still presented every morning and the four red-coloured lightbulbs were alight, but it was now a sorry sight, tucked away in a dark corner of the storeroom.

Immediately the altar was removed the bureau seemed to change in character. Where it had been a happy, bright bureau, it suddenly seemed dark and oppressive. The four red lightbulbs in the altar, which had been alight for as long as anyone could remember, suddenly all blew out together. This was really ominous; the Cantonese word for 'four' sounds very much like the word for death, and the Chinese take these word associations, especially the one between four and death, very seriously indeed. What made it even worse was that after replacing the four bulbs they almost immediately burnt out again, and again, and again making four times in all. Double, double death, this was a very bad omen and the gloom deepened. Within days the aunt of one of my staff mysteriously died, my mother became extremely ill, the mother of another of my staff was literally on her deathbed, everyone in the office went down with one illness or another and I, who hadn't had a day off ill in 20 years, caught a severe dose of flu and was in bed for four days. To make things worse every piece of equipment we had delivered arrived broken and virtually every computer in the place broke down.

That was it; morale was suddenly at an all-time low and it just couldn't go on. So, despite what my boss had said, I arranged for a Taoist priest and a Geomancer to come to my office to re-site the altar. Duly they both arrived in flowing red robes, and with much pomp, ceremony, chanting, tinkling of bells and burning of joss sticks they reinstalled the altar in the most favourable Feng Shui position. After they had reinstalled the altar I laid on a party and we made huge offerings of food and drink, then one after another each member of my staff bowed deeply three times and inserted three joss sticks into the major (top) and minor (bottom) altar.

The party, Geomancer and priest cost me a small fortune but it was worth it and, while we couldn't bring back the poor departed aunt, the two mothers recovered, all the computers mysteriously started working and the equipment started arriving in one piece and in working order. Also, in the five years since it was reinstated, not one single bulb has burned out!

It was 1997 and the return of Hong Kong to China was fast

approaching. The doom and gloom merchants were having a field day with stories of the PLA taking over the streets armed with Chinese Type 56 rifles (AK 47 variant), rampant corruption, overseas enterprises shutting up shop and the total collapse of the economy. These were everyday topics of conversation for those with nothing better to do. Any sane evaluation of the situation could see that nothing could be further from the truth and that China did not want to get involved and couldn't care less about such petty affairs as ensuring that the 'Royal' prefix on many clubs and organisations, including the police, were removed and that the red-coloured colonial postboxes were repainted purple.

There were going to be changes, there had to be, but nothing that was going to adversely affect the man in the street or how he did business. One big problem, however, was the way in which expatriates working for the Government had been employed. They had all been taken on as Crown Servants and once the handover was completed their contract of employment was, in effect, no longer valid. As a result every expatriate civil servant was given the option of either being re-employed by the Special Administrative Region (SAR) of Hong Kong or taking early retirement and a compensation package.

In many ways it was a blessing in disguise for the Hong Kong Government as those merchants of gloom and doom, who obviously had a totally negative attitude towards Hong Kong, together with much of the dead wood clogging up the system, were given the chance to leave. Those who had something to offer and could see the future in a positive light had the possibility of continued employment with promotional prospects not hampered by a logjam of people well past their mental and physical prime. Unfortunately, it also meant that some of the gifted younger members of the Government who were worried about the future, not in the next 5 or 10 years, but 15 or 20 years down the track, were also caught up in the exodus.

For my bureau it was pretty dramatic, as 60 per cent of the staff decided to take the money and run. Losing such a large percentage of one's staff in one fell swoop does rather put the pressure on, but, in many ways it was good for the bureau because most of those who left we were better off without and their absence was hardly noticed. The Hong Kong Police were also in the fortunate position of having almost total control of the major crime situation and, consequently, there was hardly any casework.

The hierarchy was, naturally, very concerned with my lack of staff and I was given a completely free hand to employ whoever I wanted. And I did. I upset the general forensic chemists no end by poaching one of their PhDs, I took away one of the best crime fighters in the Organised and Serious Crime Bureau, a data expert from the Criminal Intelligence Bureau and, sometime later, acquired a young woman inspector from the Regional Criminal Investigation Department. All these officers had at least an honours degree in some scientific or science-related subject and were, potentially, a very strong team.

As if losing 60 per cent of my team wasn't bad enough, two months before the handover the bureau was due to move into new premises and everything in my old office, from the desks upwards, had been disposed of because it was felt to be unserviceable. All I had to move into was an empty box. Not only that, but the previous bureau head had not made any budgetary provisions for the move or the purchase of the new equipment. Over the years I had, however, made many friends in the force and lots of people owed me small favours. It was time to call in the chips. Within two years I had spent over HK$30,000,000 (£2.5 million) on the best and most modern equipment available and the bureau was now the best-equipped and most technically advanced facility of its type in the world.

After 30 years of being on almost permanent 24-hour call I could now hand the reins over to my staff and take on an administrative and supervisory role. The relief of being able to go to bed in the certain knowledge (well, almost, my men still occasionally called me for advice) that I would not have to turn out at a minute's notice was like a ton weight off my back. I could go to a party or dinner dance and have too much to drink without worrying about having to attend a crime scene, unload a gun and make rational judgements. A relief, yes, but it was also terrible. I can't explain how much I missed being on the front line with the investigators, helping them to solve a case.

In my six years as bureau director I had, however, turned it around from being an under-equipped, under-staffed, heavily polluted and dangerous environment to what was probably the most modern, best-equipped and safest bureau of its type in the world. To ensure that it conformed to international standards I had the bureau accredited by the world's foremost institution in such matters, the American Society of Crime Laboratory Directors' Laboratory Accreditation Bureau. The international accreditation team not only passed the bureau first time, something which is almost unheard of, but gave us the highest score ever recorded. If further accolades were required, the team also said that the protocols, training programmes and facilities that I had put in place were second to none. I had achieved my ultimate goal of giving the Hong Kong Police Force and, of course, the people of Hong Kong the definitive crime-detection facility. I was ready to retire.

My major concern was, however, a viable succession plan as all but one of my staff were very inexperienced. Despite being adamant that I wanted to leave on my due date, the Commissioner of Police cajoled me into staying for a further year to ensure that a viable succession plan could be implemented.

My succession plan, weak though it was, consisted of drafting in a general forensic chemist who could rapidly be trained in the forensic examination of firearms and, hopefully, eventually take over the running of the bureau. The extension of my service, as proposed by the Commissioner, was designed to give this forensic chemist a little more experience and ease him into the post. Unfortunately it backfired in a way I could never have anticipated.

On the date I should have retired I took a well-earned six weeks' leave and came back refreshed and ready to start the grooming process. From the very beginning it was obvious that all was not well. The normally happy and content atmosphere in the bureau had been replaced by one of gloom and foreboding. And then, out of nowhere, the Commissioner of Police received an anonymous allegation to the effect that I had been giving equipment orders to friends at inflated prices. I was being accused of conspiracy to defraud the Government; a very serious matter. As a result of this blatantly untrue attack on my integrity I never did get to put in a succession plan. Nobody was promoted, the equipment which had cost well in excess of £3.5 million fell into disuse, staff were either not replaced on retirement or moved sideways, and most of the functions of the bureau were handed over to the general forensic chemists. What was, without any question or doubt, the finest, most advanced and best-equipped bureau of its type in the world is now barely operating. The Hong Kong Police now has no confidence in what staff are left and the few functions they perform.

But, that is another story for another time and another place.

GENERAL GLOSSARY OF FORENSIC AND FIREARMS-RELATED TERMS

ACP: Abbreviation for Automatic Colt Pistol. Used to designate calibres designed for use in Colt self-loading pistols.

Action: The mechanism of a firearm.

Air Gun: A weapon using compressed air to propel the missile. Usually this is achieved by a spring-powered piston.

Ammunition: Bulleted ammunition consists of a cartridge case, propellant, priming compound and missile. Blank ammunition is the same but with the omission of the bullet.

Ammunition, Ball: A military term to describe ammunition with a fully-jacketed bullet.

Ammunition, Small Arms: A military term to describe ammunition with a calibre of less than 1 inch.

Angle of Departure: The angle of elevation of the barrel from the horizontal.

Annulus: The space between the primer cup and the primer pocket.

Antimony (Sb): A white metal which, when alloyed with lead, increases its hardness.

Antimony Sulphide: Common additive to modern priming compounds which acts as a fuel to increase the burning time of the mixture.

Anvil: Metallic component of a primer cup against which the priming compound is crushed by the firing pin. In a Boxer primer the anvil constitutes part of the primer cup, in a Berdan primer it is part of the cartridge case.

AP: Abbreviation for armour-piercing bullet. In this type of ammunition there is usually a hard tungsten core to the bullet.

Assault Rifle: Generally a compact military weapon firing a centre-fire cartridge of a power below that of a rifle cartridge but above that used in sub-machine guns.

Atomic Absorption (AA): A method of qualitative and quantitative analysis often used in GSR examinations. Atomic Absorption derives it name from the fact that the atoms of an element will absorb light at a wavelength which is particular to that element. If an element is introduced into a flame through which light of an appropriate wavelength is shone, a portion of the light will be absorbed by the free atoms present. It is the wavelength of the light absorbed which identifies the element present and the quantity of light absorbed which reveals the quantity of the element present.

Auto loading: See **Self-loading**

Automatic: A term often misused to describe semi-automatic or self-loading weapons. When correctly applied to a pistol or rifle, signifies a weapon whereby the action will continue to operate until the finger is removed from the trigger or the magazine is empty.

Axis, Bullet: The centre line through a bullet about which it rotates.

Backlash: The continuing rearward movement of the trigger after the firing pin or hammer has been released to fire the weapon.

Backstrap: The portion of a pistol's frame which forms the rear of the grip.

Ball Burnishing: A method of applying a mirror-like finish to the tops of the lands in a rifled barrel by forcing a hardened steel ball down the bore.

Ball Powder: Spherical propellant introduced by Winchester Western in 1933.

Ballistic Coefficient: The ratio of the sectional density of the bullet to its form factor. This gives a numerical factor showing the rate of deceleration of a missile due to air resistance.

Ballistics: The study of a missile's movement from the time of cartridge ignition until it reaches the target. Often wrongly confused with Forensic Firearms Examination.

Ballistics, Exterior: The study of the flight of a missile from the moment it leaves the barrel until it reaches the target.

Ballistics, Interior: The study of what happens between the moment the firing pin strikes the primer and the missile leaves the barrel.

Ballistics, Terminal: The study of the effect the missile has on the target.

Barium Nitrate: A component of most priming compounds which supplies oxygen to the reaction.

Barrel: The tube in a firearm through which the missile is projected. Can be rifled or smooth bored.

Barrel Pressure: An extremely thick-walled barrel with a pressure measuring device. To measure the pressure produced during the firing of a cartridge.

Barrel Swaging: The process of manufacturing the rifling in a barrel by either squeezing or hammering the barrel onto a negative form of the rifling.

Battery: When the standing breech of a weapon is in correct alignment with the rear of the barrel ready for firing.

Battery Cup: A flanged metal cup used in shotgun cartridge primers.

BB: Designation for shotgun pellets having a diameter of 0.16 inch. Also used for steel balls used in air guns of 0.175 inch diameter.

BB Cap: A very short .22 inch rim fire cartridge with a round ball. Very popular at the turn of the century for use in indoor gallery shooting.

Bearing Surface: The portion of a bullet which comes into contact with the rifling.

Bent: A step in the hammer into which the sear is held engaged under spring tension, until withdrawn by pulling the trigger. In American terminology often referred to as the Sear Notch.

Berdan Primer: See **Primer, Berdan**

Black Powder: A mechanical mixture of Potassium Nitrate, Sulphur and Charcoal.

Blank: See **Cartridge, Blank**.

Blish Action: A blowback system using a phosphor bronze Hshaped block sliding in angled slots. Originally designed for the Thompson sub-machine gun but is of dubious value.

Blowback Action: In self-loading or fully automatic weapons which use the rearwards force of the cartridge case on the standing breech to cycle the weapon.

Blowback, Delayed: Also referred to as 'Retarded Action'. A firearms action incorporating some form of mechanism to delay the opening of the action until the internal pressures have fallen to a safe level.

Boattail Bullet: See **Bullet, Boattail**

Bolt Action: The type of breech closure which is accomplished by the longitudinal movement of a bolt. The actual locking movement can be 'Turn Bolt', 'Straight Pull' or 'Camming Bolt'.

Bolt Face: See **Breech Face**

Bolt Handle: The extension from the bolt by which it is operated.

Bolt Head: The forward part of the bolt including the Breech (or Bolt) Face

Bore: English term describing the size of a shotgun bore. Based on the number of round lead balls of the same diameter as the barrel which weigh 1lb. Thus a 12-bore barrel has the same diameter as a ball of lead weighing one twelfth of a pound.

Bore: The inside of the barrel.

Bore Diameter: The inside diameter of the barrel measured across the tops of the barrel **lands** or, across a circle formed by the lands if there an uneven number.

Bottleneck Cartridge: See **Cartridge, Bottleneck**

Boxer Primer: See **Primer, Boxer**

Breech: The rear of the barrel where the cartridge is inserted.

Breech Block: The moveable part of a firearm which seals the breech.

Breech Face: The part of the breech block or breech bolt which is in contact with the head of the cartridge during firing.

Breech Face Markings: A negative impression of the marks on the breech face which are impressed onto the head of a cartridge case during firing.

Breech Plug: The metal plug which seals the breech end of a muzzle loading weapon.

Breech Pressure: Incorrect terminology for Chamber Pressure. Chamber Pressure is the pressure produced in the chamber during firing.

Breech, Standing: That part of a revolver's frame which supports the cartridge head during firing.

Buckshot: An American term describing shotgun pellets ranging in size from 0.2 to 0.36 inches in diameter.

Buffer: A granular substance, nowadays generally polyethylene, used in shotgun cartridges to protect the shot from distortion during firing.

Bullet: A non-spherical missile for use in rifled barrels.

Bullet, Armour-Piercing (AP): A bullet designed to penetrate metal. Generally with a core of Tungsten but can be any hardened metal.

Bullet, Boattail: Bullet with a tapered base to reduce drag.

Bullet, Cast: Plain lead bullet formed by pouring molten lead into a mould.

Bullet, Coated: Lead bullet with a surface coating of a harder metal to reduce metal fouling in the bore. Generally either copper or brass.

Bullet, Copper Washed: Generally steel jacketed bullets bullet which have received a coat of copper to reduce corrosion.

Bullet Core: The inner portion of a jacketed bullet, usually plain lead.

Bullet Drop: The fall of a bullet during its flight due to gravity.

Bullet, Dum-Dum: Soft-nosed .303 inch bullets produced in 1894 by the Indian Dum-Dum Armoury. A term often wrongly applied to hollow-point bullets.

Bullet Engraving: The impressed rifling on a bullet.

Bullet, Frangible: A bullet designed to break up on impact with a hard surface to minimise ricochet. Can be made from brass or tungsten dust in epoxy resin or compressed iron dust.

Bullet, Full Metal Jacket (FMJ): A bullet which has a lead core covered with a hard metal jacket leaving only the base exposed. The jacket can be of almost any material, although brass and steel are the most common. Also referred to as Full Metal Case, Fully Jacketed and Ball Ammunition.

Bullet, Gallery: Frangible .22 inch bullet made from compressed iron filings.

Bullet, Gas Check: Small brass cup which fits onto the base of plain lead bullets to reduce metal fouling in the bore.

Bullet Groove: The portion of the bullet engraved by the raised part of the barrels rifling. When viewing a cross-section of a fired bullet, the bullet grooves will be the parts on the bearing surface of the bullet which are depressed.

Bullet, Hollow Point: A bullet with a cavity in the nose to assist in expansion when striking tissue.

Bullet, Incendiary: A military bullet with a chemical compound in the nose which ignites on impact.

Bullet Jacket: The metal covering to a jacketed bullet.

Bullet Jump: The distance a bullet must travel from the cartridge case until it reaches the rifling. In self-loading pistols and rifles this is generally very small, but in revolvers the distance from the cylinder to the rifling in the barrel can be appreciable.

Bullet, Land: The portion of the bullet not engraved by the raised part of the rifling in the bore of the weapon. When viewing a cross section of a fired bullet, the bullet lands will be the parts on the bearing surface of the bullet which are standing proud of the rest.

Bullet Ogive: The curved forward part of a bullets nose.

Bullet Recovery System: A system for the undamaged recovery of test-fired bullets for examination under a microscope. High-grade cotton wool and water are the most commonly used mediums.

Bullet, Semi-Jacketed Hollow Point: Bullet with a partial jacket which exposes a hollow pointed nose.

Bullet, Semi-wad Cutter: A bullet primarily for target use which has a truncated cone nose shape.

Bullet, Soft Point: Jacketed bullet with the lead core at the nose exposed.

Bullet Spin: The rotation motion of a bullet imparted by the rifling.

Bullet, Swaged: A bullet which has been made by compressing a plug of plain lead into a die.

Bullet, Tracer: Bullet, usually military, with a small pellet of brightly-burning compound in the base which permits its trajectory to be viewed. Can be day or night tracer.

Bullet Trap: A means of stopping a bullet when recovery is not the object. Can be an angled steel plate, sand, telephone books etc.

Bullet, Truncated Cone: Conical shaped nose rather than the conventional ogival shape.

Bullet, Wad Cutter: A bullet with a flat nose intended to cleanly cut a hole in the paper target when target shooting.

Bullet Wipe: The discoloured area surrounding a bullet hole caused by bullet lubricant and discharge residues wiped off the bullet surface. Can be useful in determining the bullet entry/exit hole.

Butt: The bottom part of a handgun grip or the rear of the stock in a long arm.

Button Rifling: See **Rifling, Button**

Calcium Silicide: A common component of priming compounds which acts as a fuel.

Calibre: In weapons the approximate diameter of the inside of the bore across the tops of the rifling lands. In ammunition the approximate diameter of the missile.

Cannelure: A groove round the bearing surface of a bullet for either crimping the mouth of the cartridge case or to hold bullet lubricant.

Carbine: A short-barrelled rifle, originally intended for mounted troops.

Cartridge: An imprecise term usually referring to a single, live, unfired round of ammunition comprising of missile, cartridge case, propellant and primer. The correct term is, however, a Round of ammunition.

Cartridge, Blank: A round of ammunition, without a missile, which is intended to make a large report on firing.

Cartridge, Bottleneck: A cartridge case with main diameter steeply stepping down to a case mouth of a smaller diameter.

Cartridge Case: Refers to the ammunition case and primer and does not include the bullet. Can be either a 'fired cartridge case' or a 'live cartridge case'. A 'live cartridge case' has a live, unfired, primer but there is no propellant or bullet present.

Cartridge Case, Belted: A cartridge case which has an extra band of metal ahead of the extractor groove. Intended to give extra support to the base of the cartridge in high-power Magnums.

Cartridge Case, Centre Fire: A cartridge case that has the primer contained in a small, metal cup placed in a receptacle in the centre of the head of the cartridge case.

Cartridge Case Mouth: The open end of a cartridge into which the bullet would be seated.

Cartridge Case, Rebated: This is a cartridge case which has a rim diameter which is less than the diameter of the cartridge case. The designation used in the metric system is 'RB'. This type of cartridge case configuration tends to be reserved for high-powered cannon ammunition.

Cartridge Case, Rimless: This is a cartridge case in which the case head diameter is the same as the case body and there is, for extraction purposes, a groove around the case body just in front of the flange. There is generally no letter system to designate this cartridge base type. Self-loading pistols are almost invariably designed for use with semi-rimmed or rimless ammunition.

Cartridge Case, Rimmed: A cartridge case with a flanged head that is larger in diameter than the body of the cartridge case.

Cartridge Case, Semi-Rimmed: A cartridge case with a case head flange only slightly larger than the case body.

Cartridge, Cook-Off: The ignition of a cartridge due to overheating. This generally happens above $350^{\circ}C$ and it is the priming compound which ignites first, not the propellant.

Cartridge, Drill/Dummy: A cartridge which cannot be fired, usually used for demonstration purposes.

Cartridge NATO: Military ammunition conforming to NATO standards. Usually 9mm Parabellum and 7.62x51mm.

Cartridge Proof: Special high-pressure cartridges used for proofing commercial weapons.

Cartridge, Rimfire: A flanged cartridge with the priming compound in the hollow rim.

Caseless Ammunition: Ammunition which has the propellant and primer moulded round the bullet and thus requires no cartridge case.

CB Cap: A very short, low-powered cartridge, generally .22 calibre, with a conical shaped bullet.

Chamber: The portion of the rear end of the barrel which receives and supports the cartridge. In a revolver the chambers are not part of the barrel, but are bored in the revolving cylinder behind the barrel.

Chamber, fluted: A chamber which has longitudinal grooves cut in the wall to assist in extraction.

Chamber Marks: Individual microscopic marks present on the chamber walls as a result of manufacturing.

Chamber Throat: The area in a chamber immediately in front of the case mouth, which leads the bullet into the rifling. Also called Leade or Forcing Cone.

Charger: A clip containing rounds of ammunition as a means of rapidly reloading a magazine. Also called Clip or Stripper Clip.

Choke: A constriction near the muzzle of a shotgun to reduce the spread of shot. A fully choked barrel, whatever its bore, will have a restriction of 0.04.

Chronograph: A device to measure the velocity of missiles, consisting of two photoelectric detectors connected to a microsecond clock. As the missile passes over the first detector it starts the clock and when it passes over the second it stops the clock. By knowing the separation of the detectors and the time taken, the velocity can be calculated.

Cock: To place a firing mechanism under spring tension. In flintlock weapons this was the spring-loaded vice used to hold the flint.

Coefficient of Form: A numerical term indicating the profile of a missile.

Comparison Microscope: Basically the bottom half of two normal microscopes connect by an optical bridge to one set of eye-pieces. This allows the comparison of two objects simultaneously.

Compensator: A device attached or integral to the muzzle of a weapon to divert some of the combustion gases in an upward direction to counter recoil.

Copper Units of Pressure (C.U.P): A means of comparing the degree of compression of copper cylinders to pounds pressure produced. See **Crusher Gauge**

Crane: The part of a solid frame revolver on which the cylinder is swung out to load and unload. Also called a Yoke.

Crimp: The bevelling of the top of a cartridge case to hold the projectile in place. In shotgun cartridges a portion of the top of the cartridge case will be folded over to achieve the same purpose.

Crusher Gauge: A means of measuring the pressure produced in a barrel. Achieved by venting some of the gases off and allowing them to act on a piston to crush a cylinder of metal of known hardness. The degree of crushing will give an indication of the pressure produced.

Cup, Percussion: Small metallic cup containing a priming compound. Used with percussion muzzle loading weapons as an ignition system for the propellant.

Cylinder: The rotating part of a revolver, which contains the chambers.

Cylinder Gap: The gap between the end of the barrel and the front of the cylinder.

Cylinder Stop: A metal peg which locates with cut-outs in the exterior of the cylinder. This stops the cylinder rotation in the correct position to align the chamber and bore.

Cylinder Stop Cut Out: Grooves cut into the external surface of the cylinder into which the cylinder stop engages to ensure correct alignment of chamber and barrel. Also called Bolt Notch or Cylinder Stop Notch.

Damascus: An obsolete barrel-making process involving the hot welding together of steel and iron wires which is then wound round a mandril and hot welded into a tube.

Dermal Nitrate Test: The treatment of paraffin wax casts of the hands with a solution of diphenylamine in concentrated sulphuric acid. This reagent visualises propellant particles, i.e. oxidizing agents, as deep purple-coloured spots. Also gives positive reactions to urine, face powder, fertiliser, weed killer etc. Unreliable and no longer used. Also known as Paraffin Wax Test.

Detonate: Term used with explosives meaning 'to explode with sudden violence'. Propellants do not detonate under normal circumstances, but merely rapidly burn.

Discharge: The firing of a weapon.

Double Action: A method of operating a revolver whereby a single long and relatively heavy pull on the trigger rotates the cylinder, cocks the hammer then drops it, all in one action. Some self-loading pistols also have a double-action trigger mechanism where a long pull on the trigger cocks the hammer then drops it to fire the weapon.

Double Base Powder: A propellant containing both nitrocellulose and nitro-glycerine.

Drilling: A three-barrelled long arm containing a combination of smooth and rifled barrels.

Driving Edge: The driving edge of the rifling on a fired bullet with a right twist is the left edge of the rifling groove. Also called the Leading Edge.

Dum-Dum Bullet: Soft point .303 calibre rifle bullets made by the Dum-Dum armoury in India. Hollow point bullets are often wrongly called dum-dum bullets.

Ejection: The act of expelling a fired cartridge case from a weapon.

Ejection Port: The opening in the receiver or slide of a self-loading or automatic weapon through which the fired cartridge case is ejected.

Ejector: Generally a small pin which the cartridge case strikes when it has been pulled out of the chamber by the extractor.

Ejector Marks: Marks left on the base of a fired or sometimes unfired cartridge case by the ejector.

Energy: The capacity of an object to do work. Generally expressed in Joules or foot pounds.

Energy, Muzzle: The energy of the projectile at the muzzle. Normally measured over a short distance from a few feet in front of the muzzle.

Escutcheon: Small metal plate on a weapon displaying the company name.

Express Cartridge: A rifle calibre cartridge of higher than normal velocity.

Exterior Ballistics: The study of a missile from the muzzle to the target.

Extractor: A spring-loaded claw attached to the bolt or breechblock which engages in the extractor groove as the breech is closed. When the breech is opened the extractor claw extracts the cartridge from the chamber.

Extractor Groove: The groove in a cartridge just forward of the cartridge head into which the extractor engages.

Extractor Mark: The mark left in the extractor groove of a cartridge.

Feed Ramp: A sloping surface at the breech end of the chamber of magazine-fed weapons which guides the cartridge from the magazine into the chamber.

Firearms Identification: A discipline of Forensic Science concerned with the forensic examination of arms and ammunition. Often wrongly referred to as Ballistics Examination.

Firing Pin: The part of the mechanism which strikes the primer to fire the cartridge.

Firing Pin Drag Marks: Marks caused by the firing pin dragging across the primer during the extraction process.

Firing Pin Impression: The mark left on the primer of a fired cartridge case by the firing pin.

Flash Hole: The hole connecting the primer pocket to the main body of the cartridge case which allows the flash from the primer to reach the propellant charge.

Flash Suppressor: A muzzle attachment designed to reduce the muzzle flash produced on firing. Generally only on military weapons.

Flechette: Small dart like nail generally loaded as multiple projectiles in shotgun and rifle cartridges.

Frangible Bullet: A missile designed to disintegrate on impact with a hard surface to minimise ricochet. Usually constructed from compressed lead or iron dust. Bullets of this type are usually encountered in fair ground shooting galleries, but have also been used in anti-hijack ammunition for use in planes.

Full Auto: A designation for fully automatic fire.

Full Cock: The position of the hammer when the weapon is in the position ready to fire.

Fulminate of Mercury: High explosive compound used in primers.

Gas Operated: An automatic or semi-automatic weapon in which the propellant gases are used to operate the mechanism.

Gauge: An American term for the bore of a shotgun. Based on the number of round lead balls of the same diameter as the barrel which weigh 1lb. Thus a 12-bore barrel has the same diameter as a ball of lead weighing one-twelfth of a pound.

Gilding Metal: Copper/zinc alloys used for bullet jackets. Generally in the region 90-95 per cent copper and 5–10 per cent zinc.

Grain: Avoirdupois measurement of weight with 7,000 grains equalling 1 pound. Generally used in American and English measurements relating to ammunition components.

Grease Groove: Cannelure used to hold bullet lubricant.

Greiss test: Chemical spot test for nitrites.

Grip: In handguns the part of the weapon held by the hand and in long arms the piece of stock to the rear of the trigger.

Grip Safety: A safety mechanism on some weapons which prevents the weapon being fired unless the weapon is tightly held.

Groove: See **Rifling**

Gun Cotton: Another name for Nitrocellulose.

Gunpowder: The generic name for Black Powder.

Gunshot Residues (GSR): The residues emanating from a fired weapon. These include Primer Residues and Propellant Residues.

Half Cock: The hammer position when it is held in an

intermediate, and deep bent, and cannot be released by pulling the trigger.

Hammer: The component of a firearm which provides the force on the firing pin to discharge the primer.

Hammer Block: A safety mechanism which blocks the hammer from reaching the firing pin.

Hand: The lever which engages in the Ratchet at the rear of the cylinder which rotates it to bring a fresh cartridge in line with the firing pin. Also called Cylinder Pawl.

Handgun: Weapon designed to be fired in the hand.

Hand loading: The process of assembling ammunition from cartridge case, propellant and primer.

Hang fire: When a cartridge fails to fire immediately after the firing pin strikes the primer.

Headspace: The distance from the face of the closed breech to the surface in the chamber on which the cartridge rests. It is basically the distance the cartridge case is allowed to stretch during firing.

Ignition Time: The time from firing pin contact with the primer until the bullet begins to move out of the cartridge.

In Battery: When the breech mechanism is in the closed position ready to fire.

Incendiary Bullet: Bullet containing a chemical compound in the nose which ignites on striking a hard object.

Individual Characteristics: Those marks produced during manufacture or subsequently due to corrosion, mistreatment etc. which are individual to that weapon and none other.

Inside Lubricated Bullet: One in which the bullet lubricant is held within a cannelure which is situated inside the cartridge case.

Interior Ballistics: The study of what happens between the moment the firing pin strikes the primer and the missile leaves the barrel.

Land, Bullet: The portion of the bullet not engraved by the raised part of the rifling in the bore of the weapon. When viewing a cross section of a fired bullet, the bullet lands will be the parts on the bearing surface of the bullet which are standing proud of the rest.

Land, Rifling: The raised portion between the grooves in a rifled bore.

Lead Azide: A highly explosive chemical used in priming compounds.

Leading: The accumulation of lead in the bore of a weapon, generally through insufficient bullet lubricant or a very rough bore.

Lead Styphenate: A highly explosive chemical used in priming compounds.

Load, Duplex : A round of ammunition containing two projectiles.or a round of ammunition containing two different types of propellant powder.

Loading Density: The ratio of case volume to propellant volume.

Long Recoil: A mechanism, designed to reduce recoil, in which the barrel and bolt recoil to the rear, locked together. At the fullest extent of the recoil the barrel unlocks from the breech and moves forward. When fully forward the breech moves forward feeding the next cartridge into the chamber.

Long Rifle: Designation for one type of 0.22 calibre rim fire cartridges.

Lubaloy: Winchester Western trade name for a very thin coating of copper applied to plain lead bullets. Now only seen on .22 calibre rim fire ammunition.

Magazine: Spring-loaded container for cartridges, can be box, drum, rotary or tubular.

Magazine Safety: A safety device found on some semi-automatic pistols which prevents the weapon being fired unless a magazine has been inserted.

Magnum: Designation for a cartridge which is larger, contains a heavier missile or produces a larger velocity than the standard round.

Mainspring: The spring in the lockwork which produces the power for the hammer or striker.

Marshall's Reagent: Reagent used in the Greiss test as a spot test for nitrites in GSR.

Maximum Range: The maximum range obtainable when firing a weapon at the optimum angle. This angle is generally between $30°$ and $45°$.

Metal Fouling: Lead or jacket material stripped from the bullet and deposited in the bore of the weapon leading to inaccuracy and in extreme cases bullets stuck in the bore. Generally caused by either lack of lubrication or a very rough bore.

Metal Patched Bullet: Another name for a fully-jacketed bullet.

Microphotograph: Misnomer for photomicrograph i.e. a photograph taken through a microscope.

Microscopic Comparison: The comparison of two items under a comparison microscope.

Minute of Angle: One sixtieth of 1 degree. A minute of angle at 100 yards equals 1.047 inch at 100 yards. Thus, if the sights of a rifle are set 1 minute off-centre then at a range of 100 yards the bullet will strike the target 1.047 inch off centre.

Misfire: The failure of the primer to ignite or the primer to ignite the propellant.

Muzzle: The end of the barrel from which the bullet emerges.

Muzzle Brake: A device fitted to the muzzle end of the barrel which vents the high-pressure gases produced on firing in an upward direction to reduce recoil.

Muzzle Crown: A slight counter boring at the muzzle end of the bore primarily to protect the rifling.

Muzzle Energy: The kinetic energy of the missile as it leaves the muzzle.

Muzzle Flash: The flash caused by incandescent gases as they emerge from the muzzle of a fired weapon.

Muzzle Loader: A weapon in which the propellant and missile are loaded from the muzzle end of the barrel.

Nipple: A hollow cone-shaped tube inserted into the breech end of a muzzle loader onto which is placed a percussion cap. When the cap is struck by the hammer the flame so produced travels down the hollow nipple and into the propellant, igniting it.

Nitrocellulose: Nitrated cellulose of any form but generally cotton wool. The primary ingredient of modern propellants.

Nitro-glycerine: Nitrated glycerine. By itself a high explosive, but when dissolved in nitrocellulose becomes stable and produces an extremely efficient propellant.

Obturation: The sealing of the chamber due to the expansion of the cartridge case as a result of the high pressures produced. Also, the sealing of the bore of a weapon due to the expansion (upset) of the bullet due to the high pressures produced.

Outside Lubricated Bullet: A bullet in which the bullet lubricant is in a cannelure situated outside of the cartridge case. Generally only .22-inch rim fire ammunition has this type of lubrication system.

Over Powder Wad: A thin card-like disk placed over the propellant to seal the bore.

Over Shot Wad: A thin card-like disk placed over the shot to retain it in place.

Pantascopic Camera: A camera designed to photograph the circumference of a bullet. Also called a Peripheral Camera or a Balliscan Camera.

Parabellum: Latin, meaning 'For War'. Designation for military pistol cartridges in particular 7.65mm Parabellum and 9mm Parabellum.

Paraffin Test: See **Dermal Nitrate Test**

Pellet: General name for air gun ammunition.

Pen Gun: A weapon disguised to look like a pen. Usually .22 calibre.

Percussion Cap: Small metal cap containing a priming compound for use with muzzle loaning percussion weapons.

Piezoelectric Pressure Measurement: Method of measuring

breech pressures using a quartz crystal which when compressed gives out a small electric charge. As the charge is proportional to the pressure applied, accurate breech pressure measurements may be obtained.

Pistol: A handgun. When using English terminology a weapon can be a self-loading pistol, a revolving pistol or single-shot pistol. Using American terminology a pistol is generally either a self-loading pistol or a single shot pistol.

Polygonal Rifling: Rifling grooves which have a rounded rather than a sharp-edged profile.

Potassium Nitrate: Component of black powder which supplies oxygen for the burning.

Powder: Common term for propellant.

Powder, Ball: Propellant in spherical balls. Introduced by Winchester Western in 1933.

Powder, Black: Mechanical mixture of potassium nitrate, sulphur and charcoal.

Powder, Blank: A very fast-burning powder designed for use in blank cartridges.

Powder, Double Based: Propellant consisting of nitro-glycerine dissolved in nitrocellulose.

Powder, Semi-Smokeless: An obsolete propellant consisting of a mixture of nitrocellulose and black powder.

Powder, Single Based: Propellant consisting only of nitrocellulose.

Powder, Smokeless: A modern propellant, either single or double based, which produces far less smoke than black powder.

Pressure Barrel: A very heavy barrel fitted with a pressure measuring device to measure the pressure during firing.

Primer: The ignition system for the propellant.

Primer, Battery Cup: Type of primer container used in shotgun ammunition which serves as a holder for the primer components.

Primer, Berdan: A plain cup containing only the priming compound and a foil covering. In this system the anvil is integral to the cartridge case. An American design used mainly in military ammunition.

Primer, Boxer: A self-contained priming system consisting of priming compound, anvil and foil cover in a primer cup. British design and used almost exclusively in commercial ammunition.

Primer, Corrosive: A priming mixture the residues of which tend to corrode the bore.

Primer Pocket: Cavity in the centre of the head of a cartridge case into which the primer cap fits.

Primer Residues: The residues from the discharge of a primer, usually referred to as GSR.

Primer, Rimfire: A priming system where the priming compound is held in the hollow rim of flanged ammunition. Generally only .22 calibre rimfire ammunition is available nowadays.

Primer Setback: When the primer cap moves partially out of its pocket during firing.

Proof Mark: A stamp applied to a weapon to show that it has passed a test showing that it is capable of firing cartridges of commercial pressure.

Propellant: In firearms, the chemical compound or mixture of chemical compounds which when ignited produce a high volume of gases. These gases are used to propel a missile from the barrel of a weapon.

Pump Action: A type of breech closure which is accomplished through an operating rod attached to a moveable fore-end. This fore-end is moved back and forward to open and close the action. Also called Slide Action.

Pyrodex: Modern substitute for black powder.

Range: An area for the firing of weapons. The distance between firearm and target.

Range, Effective: The maximum range from which a projectile could be expected to produce a lethal wound. A very subjective measurement.

Range, Maximum: The maximum distance a missile will reach when fired at its optimum angle of elevation. This angle is usually between 35° and 45°.

Ratchet: A notched area at the rear of the cylinder of a revolver which causes the cylinder to rotate when moved by the hand.

Rate of Twist: The distance over which the rifling completes one turn.

Receiver: The basic part of the firearm which houses the action and breech and to which the barrel and butt stock are assembled.

Recoil: The rearward motion of the weapon as a result of firing.

Recoil Shield: The plate at the rear of the cylinder of a revolver which supports the cartridge during firing.

Recoil Spring: The large spring which controls the rearward movement of the slide during the firing stage and returns the slide to battery .

Reload: A cartridge which has been assembled, often non-commercially, from cartridge case, primer, propellant and bullet. Usually the cartridge case has already been fired and is not new.

Revolver: A handgun having a series of chambers in a cylinder mounted in line with the barrel. A mechanism revolves the cylinder so that the chambers are successively aligned with the bore. Only the chamber which is, at any one time, in line with the bore is fired.

Ricochet: A bullet which has struck an object and glanced off.

Rifling: The spiral cut into the bore to impart a spinning motion to the bullet. Normally the rifling is composed of 'Lands' and 'Grooves'. The lands are the parts of the bore left standing after the grooves have been cut away.

Sabot: A lightweight carrier for a small calibre projectile allowing it to be fired in a larger calibre bore.

Safety: A mechanism designed to prevent accidental discharge of a firearm.

Scanning Electron Microscope (SEM): A very sophisticated microscope using electrons to visualise the object rather than light. It is capable of magnifications in excess of 1,000,000, times. With an Energy Dispersive X-ray Analyser (EDX) attachment is also capable of non-destructively analysing the object under view.

Sear: A part of the mechanism which connects with the bent to keep the action in the cocked position until released by the trigger.

Sectional Density: The ratio of the bullet weight to its cross-sectional area.

Self Loader/Semi-automatic: A repeating firearm requiring a separate pull of the trigger for each shot fired. After manually loading the first round from the magazine the weapon will use the energy of discharge to eject the fired cartridge and load a new cartridge from the magazine into the barrel ready for firing.

Shot: Spherical pellets, generally of lead, loaded into shotgun cartridges.

Shot, Steel: A replacement for lead shot in shotgun cartridges.

Silencer: A device attached to the muzzle of a weapon to reduce the report of firing. Due to the gases escaping from the gap between the cylinder and barrel, this type of device is of little use in revolvers. Likewise, if the bullet is travelling faster than the speed of sound, the supersonic crack will not be reduced.

Skid Marks: As a bullet travels from the cylinder of a revolver to the rifling in the barrel it has considerable forward velocity but no rotational velocity. As it hits the rifling it takes a short period of time for it to catch up, giving rise to a widening of the land impression marks. These are called skid marks.

Sodium Rhodizonate: A chemical used as a spot test for lead.

Spalling: Material dislodged from the face opposite the strike face by the impact of a missile.

Striations (Stria): Longitudinal marks caused by imperfections in the tool making them. These are by their nature individual to that tool and none other.

Swaging: The process of manufacturing the rifling in a barrel by either squeezing or hammering the barrel onto a negative form of the rifling.

Tattooing: Marks on the skin caused by the close-range impact of propellant particles.

Terminal Ballistics: The effect a missile has on the target.

Terminal Velocity: The maximum velocity obtainable by a falling object in free air.

Trace Metal Detection: A chemical spray test to reveal traces of metal which may have been transferred to a hand through the holding of a metallic object.

Tracer Bullet: Bullet, usually military, with a small pellet of brightly burning compound in the base which permits its trajectory to be viewed. Can be day or night tracer.

Trajectory: The curved path of a bullet from muzzle to target due to the gravitational effects on the bullet.

Transfer Bar: A bar which, when the trigger is pulled, interposes itself between the hammer and firing pin thus allowing the weapon to be fired.

Trigger: That part of the mechanism which, when manually pulled, causes the firearm to fire.

Trigger Guard: A curved piece of metal protecting the trigger from being accidentally pulled.

Trigger Pull: The pressure required on the trigger to fire the weapon.

Twist, Direction Of: The direction in which the rifling spirals.

Ultraviolet Light (UV): That part of the spectrum of light beyond violet and before X-rays.

Velocity: The speed of a missile.

Velocity, Terminal: The maximum velocity attainable by a free-falling object in air.

Wad: A card, felt or plastic sealing device in a shotgun cartridge. Generally Over Powder, Cushion Wad, Under Shot and Over Shot.

Wad Cutter Bullet: A bullet with a flat nose to neatly cut the paper in target shooting.

Walker Test: A spot test for nitrites in GSR.

Yaw, Bullet: The spiral movement of the bullet about its axis before it settles down to stable gyroscopically stable flight.